Fairfax County Stories

1607–2007

**Compiled by the Fairfax County 2007 Community Citizen
Planning Committee**

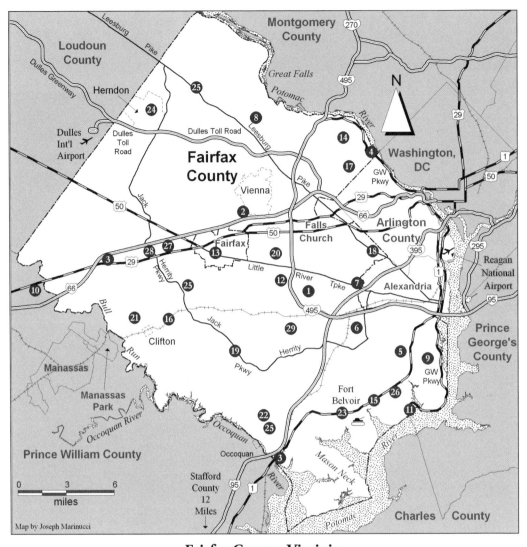

Map by Joseph Marinucci

Fairfax County, Virginia
Locations of Places, Events, and People from the Text

Funding for the publication of *Fairfax County Stories: 1607–2007* was provided by

Fairfax County Board of Supervisors
Gerald E. Connolly, Chairman, At Large

District Supervisors
Sharon Bulova (Vice Chairman), Braddock District
Joan M. DuBois, Dranesville District
Cathy M. Hudgins, Hunter Mill District
Dana Kauffman, Lee District
Penelope A. Gross, Mason District
Gerald W. Hyland, Mount Vernon District
Linda Q. Smyth, Providence District
Elaine McConnell, Springfield District
Michael R. Frey, Sully District

Fairfax County Stories
1607–2007

Compiled by the Fairfax County 2007 Community Citizen
Planning Committee

The County of Fairfax
Established 1742

Fairfax, Virginia
2007

Fairfax County Stories: 1607–2007

Compiled by the Fairfax County 2007 Community Citizen Planning Committee

Book Design and Editing by Kathy W. Marinucci, Springfield, Virginia
Map by Joseph L. Marinucci, Springfield, Virginia
Index by History4All, Inc., Fairfax, Virginia
Book Layout and Pre-press by Allen Wayne Ltd., Chantilly, Virginia
Manufactured by Goetz Printing Company Inc., Springfield, Virginia

 To request this information in an alternate format, call the County of Fairfax's Office of Public Affairs at 703-324-3187 or TTY 711.
www.fairfaxcounty.gov/opa/

Disclaimer
The stories within this anthology are the writers' original products, as they have attested to on their submission forms on file at the Office of Public Affairs. The writers bear the sole responsibility for the accuracy of the material contained within their stories. The County of Fairfax cannot be held responsible for omissions or errors, and therefore disclaims all liability in connection with the stories as written herein.

Cataloging-in-Publication Data available from the Library of Congress
ISBN 978-0-9623905-8-6

Table of Contents

Preface

Few states in our nation have a history as rich as that of Virginia, and few localities in Virginia have a deeper, more meaningful historic background than that of Fairfax County. We can proudly proclaim that the first president of the United States (George Washington) and the framer of the United States Bill of Rights and author of the Virginia Declaration of Rights (George Mason) called our county home.

There are several well-known historic sites in southern Fairfax County, including Mount Vernon, Gunston Hall, Pohick Church, and Woodlawn Plantation. The northern part of the county has numerous historic sites, too, such as the Dranesville Tavern, Colvin Run Mill, Ox Hill Battlefield, and Sully Plantation, which was the 1794 home of Northern Virginia's first congressman, Richard Bland Lee.

Gerald E. Connolly

Fairfax County was established in 1742. Back then, an estimated 4,125 inhabitants resided in the county, which at that time included what is now Loudoun County (separated in 1757) as well as the City of Alexandria and Alexandria County. The major commercial sites in 1742 were tobacco warehouses along the Occoquan River at Colchester, at the Little Falls on the Potomac River, and at the mouth of the Great Hunting Creek, where the City of Alexandria is today.

What a dramatic transformation Fairfax County has experienced since its formal establishment in 1742. The population is now approximately 1.1 million and growing. The fiscal year 2007 county budget is $3.21 billion. More than half of that money goes to educate the more than 164,000 students in Fairfax County Public Schools, which can proudly claim that all of its high schools rank among the best in the nation.

Governing magazine rated Fairfax County one of the best-managed local governments in the nation in 2002. Let us count our blessings that we have so many amenities in this county: outstanding public schools, superior public safety and human services programs, and nearly 10 percent of our land area in parks and open space. In addition, Fairfax County is among the wealthiest counties in the nation, thanks in large part to the number of top international and national companies located here, so conveniently close to the nation's capital and Dulles International Airport.

As we travel today on six- or eight-lane highways, let us reflect on how difficult it must have been for our Fairfax County ancestors of two and three centuries ago to travel any distance by boat or on rutted, muddy roads. Rather than shop for food at a supermarket or "get take-out" for dinner, they generally ate the food they grew themselves. Talking with a friend or neighbor meant traveling to speak in person, rather than telephoning or sending an electronic message on the Internet. How far we have progressed.

We, the Fairfax County Board of Supervisors, express our deep appreciation to the Fairfax County 2007 Community Citizen Planning Committee for undertaking publication of this anthology of history articles as its legacy project in commemoration of the 400th anniversary of the founding of Jamestown, the first permanent English settlement in the New World.

Gerald E. Connolly, Chairman
Fairfax County Board of Supervisors

Introduction

During this year of 2007, Virginia is commemorating the 400th anniversary of the founding of Jamestown, the oldest permanent English settlement in America. In 2005, Governor Mark Warner encouraged every jurisdiction in Virginia to participate in this year-long observance by holding special events and sponsoring projects, programs, and observances.

The Fairfax County Board of Supervisors appointed the Fairfax County 2007 Community Citizen Planning Committee, comprising more than 25 representatives of the various segments of the countywide community, to plan and implement such a program during this special year. The Virginia Jamestown 2007 Committee charged each participating jurisdiction with undertaking a legacy project. The Fairfax County committee established a Legacy Book Subcommittee, which recommended publication of a historical anthology as its legacy project and the full committee approved this venture. Thus, this book was born.

The public was invited to submit original writings of historic interest that reflected stories or events that took place at any time during the past 400 years—between 1607 and 2007. A panel of judges selected the entries to be included. While the plan was to publish 16 essays, the final number was more than twice that many. The stories, written by amateurs with a special interest in the county's history, are in chronological order and include stories about Indians, spies, rich and poor, historic preservation, everyday life, immigration, a ghost, politics, and people—lots of people.

The committee thanks the Fairfax County Board of Supervisors for lending its moral and financial support for publication of this book.

Irma A. Clifton, Chair
Legacy Book Subcommittee

Appreciating Our Historical Legacy
A Tribute to Fairfax County
By Jacob P. Asma, *Burke, Virginia*

In school we learned Columbus sailed the ocean blue in 1492.
But many have since forgot: A Fairfax County born in 1742!
And, lest our historical learning about Fairfax be somewhat lax,
It was named after its original owner, Lord Thomas Fairfax.

After that birth, came colonist cries of liberty across Virginia's virgin land:
"By rights divine, let us be free from bondage to Mother England."
The American Revolution spawned various Fairfax County VIPs,
Among these, two super patriots provided liberty's timely keys:
George Washington, who, as general, had the British in his sights
And George Mason, who helped shape the Constitution's Bill of Rights.

Let's journey onward through the corridor of time and dates,
To yet another conflict over "rights"—the War Between the States.
Both Union and Confederate troops were encamped throughout the county,
Few suspected how terrible the struggle and hardships would be.
After the war, farmers tilled the soil again for yet another century
Till planned communities and industry invaded the terrain of tranquility.

As we enter the 21st century, Fairfax's population is more than one million!
That is quite a "County on a Hill" as to "people power" in my opinion.
As a culturally diverse population learns to appreciate its rich history,
We can truly be assured of a grand and glorious Fairfax destiny.
A final lesson from Fairfax's history we can and must readily distill,
God in His providence directs the acts of man after His own will.

Fairfax County at the Very Beginning
Colonial Stafford County and the Northern Neck of Virginia
By Carolyn Werle, *Woodbridge, Virginia*

From the minute Europeans first set foot on North America, they have been dependent upon one another. We cannot say we began at one point and ignore how we got there. Communities, by their very nature, are constantly changing. The development of counties within the English lands of the New World endured the same growing pains as their ancestral homelands. It is important to understand that places and words used hundreds of years ago have changed meaning over time. As an example, how would you define Virginia? The frame of reference for an individual in the 1600s was very different from what we expect today. The Woodland Indians of the East Coast farmed and hunted, moving wherever the land and game were plentiful, without really considering ownership of land in the same sense as the Europeans. The Spanish claimed Cacique de Ajacan (also spelled Axacan) as part of Spanish Florida through the Treaty of Tordesillas signed solely between Portugal and Spain.[1] England later becomes a powerful nation that didn't recognize the Tordesillas Treaty. Two groups of merchants petitioned the English Crown in 1605 for a patent for Virginia. Virginia was defined in the first charter as all the territory extending from north of present-day South Carolina to Maine and from "sea to sea." Jamestown was established on the Atlantic coast in 1607, but were they the first Europeans in colonial Stafford County?

Known Visitors
Giovanni de Verrazano sailed past Virginia in 1524 without stopping. Naval records show an English ship was forced to ride out a storm in 1546 in a large bay given as 37 degrees, most likely the Chesapeake Bay. Between 1570 and 1572, Accomac fishermen saw Spanish ships come into the lower Chesapeake Bay to bring Jesuit missionaries. (France and Spain both supported Jesuit missions during this period.) Spanish records in 1588 indicate a ship seized two children whom they hoped to educate and return to the area as guides to the local Indians. The child taken from the Potomac soon died of grief, and the child from the Eastern Shore managed to go to Santo Domingo, only to die of smallpox.[2] The Indians could not have known what happened to their children. The Spanish also reported two Jesuit priests, three scholastics, three lay brothers, and a serving boy named Alonzo landed near Aquia and worked in the area until February of 1570. The adults were massacred and Alonzo went to live with the Indians. A rescue party from Florida arrived the next year and was met by the child, who reported the events to the ship's captain.[3]

One of the lay brothers was an Indian the Spanish had named Don Luis.[4] Letters of Juan Rogal to Francis Borgia dated August 18, 1572, reported the renegade Indian named Luiz deserted the mission and rejoined his tribe. The Indians deliberately chose February 15th (on the Julian Calendar, February 2 on the Gregorian Calendar) to return to the mission to massacre the adults. The date was then known as Candlemas, or the Feast of the Presentation of the Lord, or the Feast of the Purification of Mary on the Catholic calendar, when Mary went to the temple in Jerusalem 40 days after the birth and presented Jesus to God.[5]

The Spanish Governor Menendez de Aviles of Florida made two attempts to establish colonies near the Chesapeake Bay, which they called "The Bay of the Mother of God."[6] The first attempt in 1566 was a complete failure, but in 1570 a Jesuit mission returned. They sailed up the James River to what is now known as College Creek, near present-day Williamsburg, and reached the York River. The fathers built a chapel and hut. Eight of the nine missionaries were killed by the Indians; Alonzo was allowed to escape.[7] Two Spanish missions, undertaken around the same time and in very different places, met the same fate. The Indians were very aware of the European habit of stealing their children, and it is very possible the fate of these missions was intended as a message to all newcomers.

An English ship under Captain Bartolomew Gilbert entered the Chesapeake Bay in 1603, only to be shot at by the locals. Again, a few years before the founding of Jamestown, another English ship, captained by Samuel Mace, managed to record a meeting with Powhatan before proceeding north where they killed the Rappahannock chief and took prisoners.[8] The Indians had several similar stories of European encounters and had good reason to be fearful of the Europeans. Powhatan was the most powerful chief of the Virginias. In the winter of 1607, he had John Smith brought before him and went through all the motions of an execution when Pocahontas saved Smith from the unfolding fate. Later, Captain Samuel Argoll offered the Potawomeke Chief and his wife a copper kettle if they would induce Pocahontas to come aboard his ship. The deception allowed the English to kidnap her. It was during this year with the colonists that she met John Rolfe. (Pocahontas' real name was Matoaka, meaning "playful one.")[9]

Upon Powhatan's death in 1618, Opechancanough (who had captured Smith in 1607), the younger brother of Otiotan (formerly called Opitchapan) became chief of the Powhatan's Chiefdom. Chief of the Occohannock and Accomac was Esmy Chichans, also known as the "Laughing King."[10] Both the Occohannock and Accomac befriended the English and protected them through the early settlement years. By the mid-1600s, there were several petitions made by settlers to the courts in order to acquire "fatherless children" from the local Indian tribes. "Some of these children, if not all, were slaves rather than servants.[11] There are records of Indians freely working for settlers in spite of, or because of, the decimation of their own tribes or food sources.

Swiss Baron Christoph von Graffenried's in his papers, which were translated into English in 1997, provides a story of being similarly captured by Indians, then released in the area of New Bern, North Carolina (then a part of Virginia). The baron petitioned Queen Anne and was granted the right to bring two groups of German settlers to "Virginia" in 1711 and 1714.

First Settlements

The Potawomecks lived on Marlborough Point and the hostile Manahoacs, who later joined the Siouans, lived on the west. Along the Occoquan River lived three distinct Indian groups: the Mayanones, who later joined the Piscataways; the Anacostans; and the Doegs, also linguistically aligned to the Algonquins, who roamed the Potomac Bay area.[12]

The Doeg (also spelled "Doge" and "Dogue") Indians along the Occoquan River probably did not have the same relationship with the Powhatan tribes and were less wary of contact with the Europeans. They lived in longhouses near the land they farmed. The men plowed the fields and went hunting, while the women took care of the crops. The chief's house—the town of Tauxenent—was on a hill near the Occoquan River, probably where the Lazy Susan Dinner Theatre is today. The majority of the settlement was within present-day Fairfax County. Pohick Bay was sometimes known as Doeg Island Creek or Miompses Creek as late as 1737. Doge Island was once an Indian settlement that has since eroded, near present-day Mason Neck State Park.[13]

Several Doeg Indians of Maryland felt cheated in a 1675 trade with Thomas Mathew, a wealthy planter who lived on the Potomac River. In the process of stealing some pigs to satisfy their claim, Mathew's men killed the raiders. The Doeg then revenged their kinsmen by killing the attackers. The Virginia militia, under George Brent and George Mason, found a tribe of Doeg and killed the chief, 10 Indians, and 14 Susquehannocks before one of the Indians managed to place his hands on Mason's and tell him they were friends. These events were the beginnings of Bacon's Rebellion. The British government sent inspectors to investigate the shameful affair and Governor Berkeley was sent back to England.[14] Berkeley served as governor of Virginia for 22 years. By 1654, the Doeg moved toward the Rappahannock and united with the Susquehannocks.

John Smith's travels were recorded by a member of his party, Dr. Walter Russell. His diary is reprinted in *The Capital and the Bay: Narratives of Washington and the Chesapeake Bay Region, ca 1600–1925,* found in the Library of Congress' rare book collection. Page 128 tells of an Indian that came out and met John Smith on the Potomac River. Because he had a "thicke blacke bush beard," they assume he had French ancestors. The colonials of this period were still spelling phonetically, with numerous inconsistencies appearing throughout documents of the period. Dr. Russell spelled this Indian's name "Mosco." Smith had found a native who was not afraid of the Englishmen and volunteered to act as their guide. He did not appear to be part of any particular tribe, but had a keen knowledge of the local tribes and the geography of the area. On more than one occasion Mosco saved the explorers' lives.

John Smith encouraged Mosco to marry the daughter of the chief of the Rappahannock tribe.

Colonial Stafford County

Charles II granted the entire Northern Neck to his loyal supporters while in exile in France. The proprietors of colonial Virginia were Edward, Earl of Clarendon; William, Lord Craven; George, Duke of Albemarle; John, Lord Berkeley; Anthony, Lord Ashley; Sir George Carteret; Sir William Berkley; and Sir John Colleton.

The northern bank of the Rappahannock was laid out as a county in 1648, one year prior to the five-million-acre land grant given to Lord Fairfax by Charles II 11 years before he actually had the authority to do so as king of England.[15] Westmoreland County encompassed the majority of the Northern Neck's mother county, Northumberland, in July of 1653.[16] Land from Westmoreland County (present-day King George County) and the Northern Neck were combined in 1664 to form the colonial county of Stafford, named after Staffordshire, England.[17] Colonial Stafford County included the current counties of Fairfax, Alexandria, Arlington, Loudoun, Prince William, Fauquier, and Stafford. Confusion abounded between government land patents and grants. The first land patent in Prince William was granted to Thomas Burbage in 1633 for 3,000 acres between Occoquan and Neabsco Creek.[18]

Lord Fairfax and the Northern Neck

The English Civil War ended on January 30, 1649, when the Puritans decapitated Charles I. His son, Charles II, fled to France and the Puritans under Cromwell took control of England. In September of 1649, Charles II granted the Northern Neck of Virginia to Lord Culpeper and six other supporters, even though he did not regain the throne until 1660. (Lord Culpeper's grandson, the sixth Lord Fairfax, obtained clear legal title to the claim 100 years after it was awarded to his grandfather.)

This granted Fairfax proprietary control over all the land between the Rappahannock and Potomac rivers, and on the west, defined in documents as the "first heads or springs" of the Rappahannock and Potomac rivers. The Virginia government claimed the grant was limited to the confluence of the Shenandoah and the Potomac at Harpers Ferry, including the Rappahannock falls of Fredericksburg, Virginia. In order to settle disputes on the claim, both Virginia Governor Gooch and Lord Fairfax appointed three commissioners each to survey the entire grant in 1736. The 1688 grant by King James II confirmed that Culpeper owned five-sixths of the grant. The remaining sixth was granted to his cousin, Alexander Fairfax. It wasn't until Katherine Culpeper married Thomas, Fifth Lord Fairfax, in 1719 that the lands were again reunited.[19]

Lord Fairfax returned to England in 1737 and again in 1747 to defend his claim.

The "back line" of Lord Fairfax's claim was approved by English officials in 1746 and granted his claim to more than 5 million acres of Virginia. Lord Fairfax lived with his cousin, William Fairfax (his estate was located within what is now Fort Belvoir), before building a hunting lodge he called "Greenway Court" west of the Blue Ridge.[20]

Brent Town

The first chartered towns were Colchester and Marborough (1691), neither of which was ever developed. The first town to come into existence in the newly formed Stafford County was Brent Town (or Brenton) in 1647. Nicholas Hayward, a London lawyer, created a company with merchants Robert Bristow, Robert Brent, and Richard Foote (Hayward's brother-in-law). They purchased 30,000 acres from Lord Culpeper and began development in 1685.[21] King James granted them religious freedom through the Religious Freedom Act of 1785, allowing the company to recruit from a larger pool of settlers. George Brent, a lawyer and surveyor, was put in charge of the settlement. The declaration of religious freedom allowed the agents to recruit settlers beyond English borders. Originally they proposed soliciting immigrants from among the persecuted Huguenots of France.

Catholic Giles Brent (40 years old) married the Indian daughter of the Piscataway King, Kittamaquod ("Big Beaver"), when she was 12 years old. The Piscataway were being threatened by the Susquehannas from the northern end of the Chesapeake and probably viewed an alliance with the English as a valuable asset. She was baptized July 5, 1640, by Father White, a Jesuit priest. They were married in a public ceremony immediately following the baptism. Her name was recorded as Mary Brent in county records. Giles asserted his claim to the Indian lands of Maryland based on English hereditary laws. The king of England had granted the same lands to his cousin, Lord Baltimore, and refused all arguments from Brent. In 1647 Giles Brent became the first settler in Brent Town where his nephew, George Brent, was in charge of the settlement.[22] It is quite possible that he believed this area on Aquia Creek was part of Lord Baltimore's Maryland, since Baltimore's first map includes this area. The Brents named their home "Peace." The community was designed to have one acre in town and 100 wooded acres allocated to each settler. Unfortunately, recruiting the French Huguenots met stiff competition from the Carolinas. Even with King Carter as their land agent of the community, the town dissolved in 1695.

New Bern and Germanna

The next two towns to be established were named by the German immigrants that settled in colonial Virginia. Baron von Greffenried received a contract during the time of Queen Anne to create two settlements in colonial Virginia. The first German and Swiss settlers were to be located on the Neuse River (what is known today as New Bern, North Carolina). Queen Anne had "suggested" that the second settlers (Germans) be placed along the Potomac. The communities were named Germanna and German Town.[23]

The German and Swiss settlers arrived in 1710. When Baron Graffenried arrived in 1711, he discovered surveyor general John Lawson had placed the colonists on property he owned on the Trent River, instead of the lands they had been granted to the north. More than a year after their arrival, the settlers are finally situated on the property provided for them on the Neuse River.

John Just Albrect acted as a recruiting agent for Baron Christof von Graffenreid, landgrave of the two German settlements. Albrect was specifically instructed to contract with Germans who had mining skills for the second Virginia colony. Greffenreid returned to England in 1713 to find 14 German men and their families from Germany's Reinland already there. His patron, the Duke of Beaufort, and Queen Anne died before the end of the year and before he was able to make supplication for the coming settlement. The 7,200 pounds sterling he anticipated in the original business contract was not forthcoming. The Germans paid their way to London, where they awaited transportation to the colony. Nathaniel Blakiston, agent for the Virginia Colony, formed a company to mine ore and acquired Queen Anne's approbation for the venture under the name of the Georg Ritter Company. The company had approval of the English Board of Trade and Plantations to mine for silver.[24] In a desperate attempt to complete the journey, the Germans agreed to indentured service of four years. Blakiston formed the company with Governor Spotswood as the principle, then sent the Germans on to Virginia, obligating Spotswood to pay 150 pounds for their passage.[25] The second group arrived in colonial Stafford in 1714.

Germans Finally Get Their Own Property Rights

Queen Anne's letter to the governor specifically required him to furnish the Germans with their own land upon their arrival. Instead, the settlers arrived in Virginia in the spring of 1714, and they were transported up the Rappahannock River to Tappahanock. They made their way overland to the site of Spotswood's estate, almost 30 miles west of present-day Fredericksburg. They found they were required to pay indentured service to Spotswood.[26] It took 10 years of service and an appeal to the Virginia courts before they were granted their own property rights. The colony of Germanna was moved on paper from Stafford to Spotsylvania County and finally Fauquier County. Today the site is known as Crockett Park, with a lake covering much of the original settlement.

In 1717, Spotswood decided to add to the settlement. Captain Andrew Tarbett landed in Virginia with a group of Lutheran settlers bound for Pennsylvania. Despite the fact that the settlers had paid for their passage, the captain demanded additional monies and refused to complete the trip northward. Spotswood used this extortion to secure their indentured service and additional land headrights for himself.[27] Thus, they joined the earlier settlers at Germanna, on Spotswood's property.

On February 20, 1719, a 15,000-acre mine site was patented to Robert Beverly, Spotswood's friend. In December 1719, an additional 3,065 acres adjoining Germanna was transferred to Spotswood by Richard Hickam. On April 22, 1720, 1,920 acres across from Germanna were conveyed to Spotswood by Robert Beverly. The patents on these lands were delayed until new rules providing for settlement of Spotsylvania were passed in 1719.[28] In 1720, Lieutenant Governor Spotswood built on his estate the first seat of government for Spotsylvania. During his 12 years as governor, Spotswood acquired 180,000 acres of land and established a county seat on the property he named after himself. Spotswood was removed from his government position after 12 years as governor in 1722, and he retired to his estate. In 1724, most of his original German settlers moved onto Licking Run River (now in Fauquier County) where they were given their headrights as free men. They named their new settlement German Town. The 1717 settlers were eventually given land in what is now Madison County, and they also moved from Germanna.

Colonel George Mason purchased 534 acres bordering the Occoquan River of the 3,000 acres Thomas Babage owned in the area.[29] He created a ferry site in front of the entrance to Occoquan. Political and geographic dissention created a need to divide the Northern Neck in 1720. The Indian uprising of 1676 motivated the colonial government to create a law enacted in 1684 that required Colonel Mason to provide an "able boat for transporting souldiers [sic] and horses" across the Occoquan River.[30] The Indian path known as the Potomac Path, or King's Highway, was the primary road north at the time and was located west of the current location of Route 1. Mason's great grandson, George Mason IV, willed the rights to both sides of the river to his son, Thomas, in 1774. In 1795, Thomas built a wooden toll bridge across the Occoquan River, replacing his ferry service, and renamed his estate "Woodbridge."

Later Towns Before the First Divisions of Stafford County

Robert Carter thought he had found copper on Frying Pan Road in 1728 but was denied trespass by the Lee family. He created his own road, now known as Ox Road, from Occoquan. The mine was green sandstone instead of copper, but the road proved to be of greater value to the development of the interior community than the mine itself.[31]

Colonel John Tayloe found iron near Neabsco Creek. The discovery led Presley Thorton, John Ballendine, and Tayloe to establish an iron furnace and forge on the Occoquan River.[32] Changes were in the air; the Virginia Assembly took the busy trading port and established their first town, Falmouth, in 1728. Disagreements over governance led to the division of the Province of Carolina in 1729 into North Carolina and South Carolina. The first town established was Fauquier in Warrenton County in 1760 and dissolved in 1790. Dumfries, another port town, became the first chartered town in colonial Stafford that is still in existence. Graham Park came from Scotland around 1733 and groups of Huguenots (French Protestants) followed between 1685 and 1720.[33] By 1749, the busy port town was created from 60 acres of land donated by Graham Park.

Dividing Stafford County

Prince William County was formed in January 1731, then delayed three months to March 25, 1731.[34] The General Assembly extended the date to allow the new public officials time to get organized. Prince William County and the other Hamilton Parish celebrated their birthdates on March 25, 1731. The date was set for the beginning of spring, also considered the beginning of the New Year in colonial times.

Local traffic was drawn from the King's Highway to the east when George Mason provided land for Prince William County's first courthouse in 1742, complete with stocks, jail, and pillory.[35] Thomas Fairfax, the 6th Lord Fairfax of Cameron, went to London to petition the king to separate the upper territory from the rest of Prince William County. He was successful in his plea and Fairfax County was formed in 1742.

Hans Jacob Richter's family is listed on the ship's manifest as arriving in Virginia in 1714 as one of the 12 German families that were placed on Governor Spotswood's newly acquired plantation. Richter's name in colonial records is listed as John Jacob Rector. Governor Spotswood had official documents created listing these individuals as the colonies' first marines or rangers providing protection in Virginia's westernmost wilderness for the tidewater communities. They built a fort and were issued a cannon, without any further provisions or support for their labor. It is from their community and exploration that the gentlemen Knights of the Golden Horseshoe departed and officially opened the Blue Ridge Mountains.

John Jacob was granted lands in Fauquier County on Licking Run Creek (also listed as Rectortown). One of his descendants (son or grandson) moved to Fairfax after the American Revolution to open a store. Later descendants included James Lawson Kemper, governor of Virginia from 1874 to 1878, and William Meade Fishbach, governor of Arkansas from 1893 to 1895.

Endnotes

1. *Morteo Illustres,* 1657 tit Segura, Spain.

2. Helen Rountree and Thomas Davidson, *Eastern Shore Indians of Virginia and Maryland* (Charlottesville, Virginia: University Press of Virginia, 1997), 48.

3. John Taquette Goolrick, *The Story of Stafford: A Narrative History of Stafford County, Virginia* (Fredericksburg, Virginia: Fredericksburg Press, 1976), 12 and 27.

4. Frederic W. Gleach, *Powhatan's World and Colonial Virginia: A Conflict of Cultures* (Lincoln, Nebraska: University of Nebraska Press, 1997), 96.

5. Ibid., 90–1.

6. Emily J. Salmon, *The Hornbook of Virginia History: A Ready-Reference Guide to the Old Dominion's People, Places, and Past* (Richmond, Virginia: Library of Virginia, 1994), 7.

7. Virginius Dabney, *Virginia: The New Dominion* (Charlottesville, Virginia: University Press of Virginia, 1971), 6.

8. Rountree and Davidson, 49.

9. www.dumfries.com.

10. Rountree and Davidson, 44.

11. Rountree and Davidson, 78.

12. Pamela Gould, "First Inhabitants Often Forgotten," *Potomac News,* January 28, 1999.

13. www/belvoir.army.mil/history.asp?id-Native.

14. Helen Rountree, *The Powhatan Indians of Virginia: Their Traditional Culture* (Norman, Oklahoma: University of Oklahoma Press, 1989), 195.

15. "Heritage of Prince William and the Fairfax Grant," Prince William County historic file, May 90.

16. "Cradle of Patriots," www.historypoint.org.

17. en.wikipedia.org/wiki/Stafford_County%2C_Virginia.

18. Fairfax Harrison, *Landmarks of Old Prince William: A Study of Origins in Virginia* (Baltimore, Maryland: Gateway Press, 1987).

19. www.yale.edu/lawweb/avalon/avalon.htm.

20. www.virginiaplaces.org/settleland/Fairfaxgrant.html.

21. Fairfax Harrison, *Landmarks of Old Prince William*, 178-9.

22. Annye Beatrix Clark and Catherine Smith, *History of Prince William County* (Manassas, Virginia: Prince William County School Board, 1933), 26.

23. www.ah.dcr.state.nc.us/sections/hp/colonial/bookshelf/graff/treaty.htm.

24. "Germanna, First Colony of 1714," www.germanna.org/history.html.

25. Ibid.

26. Ibid.

27. Ibid.

28. "Germanna, Second Colony of 1717," www.germanna.org/history.html.

29. "In the Beginning," *Prince William Handbook,* Prince William County historic file, 1991, 7.

30. "A Bridge Made of Wood Gave Woodbridge a Name," *Potomac News,* November 25, 1991, A2.

31. "The Heritage of Prince William County," *Prince William County History,* May, 1990.

32. "Prince William Offered 'Revolutionary' Ideas," Prince William County historic files, Chinn Center, 6.

33. "Echoes of Our Past," *Potomac News,* January 1, 1999, 8.

34. Fairfax Harrison, *Landmarks of Old Prince William*, 311.

35. "Prince William—A Past to Preserve," Prince William County historic files, Chinn Center.

In the Shadow of Ravensworth
William Fitzhugh in Fairfax County
By Charles P. Fitzhugh, *Alexandria, Virginia*

England in the 17th century was a tumultuous place to live and work: Civil and religious wars had run their course for decades, and in the 1660s and 1670s the country saw the death of Oliver Cromwell and the restoration of the Stuart monarchy and King Charles II. From the small town of Bedford, outside London, a youngest son born into a comfortable middle-class family may have come to the heart-wrenching realization that the future looked brighter in parts of the world that were still unknown and that lay beyond familiar shores.

William Fitzhugh was the youngest son of Henry Fitzhugh, a prominent English woolen draper who later became mayor of the town of Bedford. When Henry tried to start a new business venture of canal building and retail merchandising across England, he was dealt a devastating financial blow through court actions brought about by his partners. Narrowly escaping debtor's prison by fleeing to Ireland, Henry, before he left, said goodbye forever to his youngest son, William, and arranged for him to be placed on a ship to the Americas. In his early 20s, William Fitzhugh took leave of his family and all that he had known and traveled to America with the hopes and dreams of a better life. It was 1670.

William Fitzhugh probably first stepped onto land at Jamestown, Virginia Colony, or on the nearby wooded coast in the summer of the year, although the name of the ship and the exact place, date, and time of arrival are lost to posterity and not recorded. His existing portrait, later painted by Hesselius, a colonial portrait painter, prove him to be a proud and fashionable man and, as his own actions and writings demonstrate, of definite interests and strong opinions. To begin his new life in the Americas he probably wore his finest clothes upon his first day of arrival in Virginia and undoubtedly cut a fine, new figure among the existing English colonists.

Trained to practice as an attorney, Fitzhugh gained notoriety in this field and in the Jamestown Assembly (House of Burgesses). He experimented with a variety of businesses and entrepreneurial exploits including, but not limited to, tobacco farming. Over the years he owned more than 50,000 acres in the Virginia's Northern Neck, with more than half of his holdings at his death being his Ravensworth Plantation (named after an ancestral family estate in England) in present-day Fairfax County. Today, a major part of Fairfax County can be traced back to Fitzhugh's holdings.

Historians have written much about his marriage to an 11-year-old Westmoreland County, Virginia, heiress named Sarah Tucker. In the marriage settlement, the couple received two slaves, three cows, six ewes and a ram, a number of hogs, a bay gelding, a pearl necklace, and enough dishes, furniture, and household furnishings to set up housekeeping at once. Sarah's father, who had recently died, also left her more than

5,000 pounds of tobacco—a gigantic fortune at the time. Many of his later American descendants contend that Fitzhugh refused to begin married life until the young girl was sent to England for two years of "personal improvement and education," but there is no evidence that this trip ever happened for the young girl, based upon the relative difficulties of transoceanic travel of the day. Nevertheless, this story is a popular family legend.

Eagle's Nest and Other Farms

For the majority of his life in America, William Fitzhugh established his family at Eagle's Nest, a prosperous tobacco plantation he built on the south banks of the Potomac River in King George County, Virginia. Eagle's Nest had more than 1,000 acres and a commanding view of the Potomac River. The property consisted of a house with 13 rooms, a dairy, dovecote, stables, barns, kitchen, and an apple orchard of more than 2,000 trees. A mile from Eagle's Nest was a large grist mill owned by the family. Other farm properties were named using past family names, places, and connections: Bedford, Boscobel, Marmion, and Ravensworth. William and Sarah had several children, and upon his death he proved himself a more forward-thinking man of his time by not following the old rules of primogeniture when he divided his holdings among his five sons.

One of the rarest and most interesting firsthand depictions of William Fitzhugh's personal life was written in a travel journal by a French traveler after a visit to remote Northern Virginia at Christmas, 1686. Monsieur Durand, a Huguenot gentleman traveling with his valet, was partially motivated by a desire to find land in which his religious compatriots in Europe might come to settle. William Fitzhugh, sometimes called "the Colonel" for his involvement with the Stafford County militia, had, at about this time, offered up some of the landholdings at Ravensworth Plantation (in the vicinity of present-day Annandale) for sale or lease to various Huguenot immigrants. Durand wrote of his visit to Eagle's Nest on Christmas Eve:

> We rode twenty strong to Colonel Fichous', but he has such a large establishment that he did not mind. We were all of us provided with beds, one for two men. He treated us royally, there was good wine, and all kinds of beverages and imported foods, so there was a great deal of carousing. The Colonel had sent for three fiddlers, a jester, a tight rope dancer, and an acrobat that tumbled around, and they gave us all the entertainment that one could wish for. It was very cold, yet no one ever thought of going near the fire, for they never put less than a whole cartload of wood in the fireplaces and the whole room is kept warm. . . . The next day, we decided to cross the great river [Potomac]. The Colonel had a quantity of wine and one of his best punch bowls brought down to the shore to help send us off, he also lent us his boat for the crossing.[1]

The Fitzhughs seemed to have defied frontier conditions and worked hard to bring civilization and culture to their lives in the Virginia colony. With his payments on shipments of tobacco to England, Colonel Fitzhugh bought his own ships and often ordered great quantities of English goods to include silver, household embellishments and furnishings, and farm equipment for his own use or that were later resold in the Virginia colony. Fitzhugh enumerated large quantities of household silver in his will, and his purchasing of goods fashioned in this metal—candlesticks, salt cellars, dishes and other utensils—was conducted for show as well as investment, since it could easily be transformed into currency or sold for cash. Because of the lack of ready currency, the family depended quite heavily on the barter system, as most early Virginians did, to conduct business and pay for their affairs and daily purchases.

Life at Home and Travels

William Fitzhugh had many personal interests, including commercial farming, world affairs, shipbuilding and commerce, mining, architecture, writing, and art. His was one of the earliest of the colonial Virginia families to have portraits painted of family members to decorate their plantation homes. Records show that he was an avid reader, and that he brought to Virginia an extensive library, and is said to have written and published several books on Virginia law and the history of the Virginia Colony. Although his sons were said to have been sent to England for their education, over the years he campaigned heavily for the establishment of the College of William and Mary, now the oldest institution of higher education in America.[2]

In the Library of Congress there exists today a letter book that holds copies of the extensive written correspondence of William Fitzhugh, and that gives important insight into life in the 17th century and the early years of Northern Virginia. "The Fitzhugh Letters," as they became known, preserve more than 200 letters from William Fitzhugh to his family in England, legal clients, business associates, and friends. In one letter in which he sends money for his sister, Dorothy, to join him in America, he is careful of outward appearances and warns her about the importance of being well dressed in Virginia and to travel with a "ladies maid."

No doubt William traveled often throughout Virginia's Northern Neck, in a time when travel was slow and laborious, with few of the comforts of home to be found. Virginia at this time was mostly an unknown frontier, and danger could await around any curve in the trail. As early as 1686 Fitzhugh in his writings mentions the cultivation of his Ravensworth Plantation property in present-day Fairfax County. Fitzhugh hired overseers to manage his slaves and live on his plantation properties.

In the early days, living conditions at Ravensworth were probably very primitive, with shelter being little more than wooden huts, and there was always the possibility of attack by Indians, wild buffalo, wolves, and other animals. Tenants frequently gave up and left the plantation to live in more heavily populated areas, usually near the Potomac River.

Tobacco was the main crop at Ravensworth in those early days, and to transport it to the Potomac, Fitzhugh packed the harvested crop in wooden casks that could be rolled to the ship-loading docks and waterways several miles away. In fact, several Virginia writers claim the present-day alignment of Rolling Road in south Fairfax County was once actually known as "Colonel Fitzhugh's Rolling Road."

The passage of time seems to blur the individual contributions of the Fitzhugh family throughout Northern Virginia. In 1701, at the age of 50, William Fitzhugh died of a "bloody flux" in King George County, Virginia, after possibly returning to England for a last visit in 1700. He left his Ravensworth holdings to his two eldest sons, William and Henry, and the Marmion Plantation in King George County to his youngest son, John. The Fitzhughs owned many of these properties for the next 150 years.

Three homes were later built by the Fitzhughs at Ravensworth in the 18th century: Oak Hill, Ossian Hall, and Ravensworth. The Ravensworth Plantation later became the property of Mary Randolph Custis Lee, wife of Confederate Gen. Robert E. Lee and niece of William Fitzhugh III of Chatham Manor in Fredericksburg. When Mrs. Lee fled Arlington House during the Civil War, she stayed at Ravensworth briefly, but, fearing that Union troops might damage the mansion, she moved further south. As late as 1915, Col. Bob Lee still lived in the mansion known as Ravensworth, which was located near the present-day intersection of Braddock Road and the Capital Beltway. The mansion burned to the ground in 1925.

In September 1959, the Annandale Fire Department used the Ossian Hall mansion for practice fires, eventually burning it to the ground. The Bristow subdivision now occupies the area. Oak Hill, the oldest of the three homes, is privately owned and stands on four acres, just off Wakefield Chapel Road.[3]

In retrospect, William Fitzhugh's greatest success seems to have been in the ability to start a new and prosperous life and build a family in America that has proven to be strong and enduring. In 1903 the same Fitzhugh family in England became virtually extinct, but today William's many descendants in America number in the hundreds and are contributing residents of every state in the country.

The Fitzhugh descendants still meet every few years to celebrate the life of William and Sarah Fitzhugh, their first English ancestors in America, at a reunion held on the grounds of Eagle's Nest, which still stands, in King George County, Virginia.

Endnotes

1. Richard Beale Davis, *William Fitzhugh and His Chesapeake World* (Chapel Hill, North Carolina: Published for the Virginia Historical Society, 1963).

2. Terrick V.H. and Henry Fitzhugh, *The History of the Fitzhugh Family in Two Volumes: Fitzhugh, the Story of a Family through Six Centuries* and *The History of Our Fitzhugh Family*, 2004.

3. Robert M. Moxham, *Annandale, Virginia, A Brief History* (Annandale, Virginia: Fairfax County History Commission, 1992).

William Fitzhugh, c. 1697, by an unknown artist. Fitzhugh, born in Britain, was one of the first Virginia colonists to establish a dynasty in America; he owned about 54,000 acres. A self-made man, he made his money mostly in tobacco, and was also a lawyer. He was not given to overindulgence—pursuing women, drinking, and overeating—but occasionally entertained guests with lavish parties that included good wine and food, and performers such as jesters, fiddlers, tightrope walkers, and acrobats. Fitzhugh's large Ravensworth mansion was handsomely decorated, with lush tapestries and 122 pieces of engraved English silver, which Fitzhugh thought of as a sound financial investment, since it could be melted down, as well as a statement about his social standing.

Jeremiah Moore's Lasting Legacy
Freedom of Religion
By Betty Lishman Holman, *Vienna, Virginia*

One ordinary man can make a difference. Even 260 years after his birth, Jeremiah Moore is still remembered as an important part of Fairfax County and Virginia history.

This is extraordinary when one considers that Fairfax's history also includes many prominent and famous historical citizens such as George Washington, the first president of the United States, and George Mason of Gunston Hall. Both lived in the same time period as Moore, but unlike them, he was not born into the gentry. Where they owned thousands of acres of land, he owned hundreds. Yet as a middle-class farmer, mill owner, Revolutionary War soldier, minister, husband, and father of 11 children, Jeremiah Moore left a lasting mark on our history.

Born June 7, 1746, near Dumfries, Virginia, Jeremiah came into the world as a British subject, as were all children born in the colony of Virginia at that time. As a young boy, he learned to ride a horse; hunt and fish; farm the soil; and raise chickens, hogs, cattle, and horses. These were the ordinary skills that a young man needed to know. However, unlike many children in those days, Jeremiah also learned to read and write proficiently. That proficiency would have a profound effect on his life and contributed to why he is still remembered today.

Like the Washingtons, the Masons, and most Virginia families, Jeremiah and his family were members of the Church of England. This was the established official state church. Laws governed church attendance and support of the church. Taxes were collected to pay the clergymen and to build and repair the churches.

At Quantico Church, Jeremiah was appointed as a lay reader with an annual salary of 2,400 pounds of tobacco. No doubt this was a help financially to a young farmer working to support a growing family. At 19, he married Lydia Renno of Prince William County. It was the beginning of a lifetime of love and respect for her as evidenced in his own words in his last will and testament.

In 1772, at the age of 26, Jeremiah had a religious conversion and united with other believers into the Baptist faith. This was the most defining moment of his life. He was not only leaving the church of his family, neighbors, and friends, but his certain yearly income as a lay reader. But it also had other repercussions, as the Church of England was *the* state church, and other religious groups were not treated kindly by government officials.

The Virginia Assembly in 1643 enacted this law: "All members shall be conformable to the orders and constitution of the Church of England and the laws therein established and not otherwise to be permitted to teach or preach publicly or privately." There were no laws regarding freedom of religion and no protection under the law for other religious groups.

In 1773, Jeremiah and Lydia moved their family to Fairfax County. He had a farm on Difficult Run and was also a Baptist pastor, traveling to various churches to preach. During the American Revolution, he put his patriotism into action, leaving his home, wife, and children to fight for independence from England as a corporal in the Virginia infantry. Jeremiah highly valued personal freedom because he had experienced being arrested as a Baptist pastor, suffering physical harm, and even being jailed, some say as many as three times, in Alexandria because of his religious beliefs. His church services had been disrupted and he had witnessed other church members and pastors being harassed and physically harmed. Yet he endured the violence and deprivation of war so that others could one day be free to worship as they believed.

First Amendment of the Bill of Rights

After the United States won its independence and established its own constitution and laws, Jeremiah worked tirelessly to ensure there would be freedom of religion in this country. He corresponded with Thomas Jefferson, James Madison, and other leaders in the government. He was a part of the delegation that presented to Thomas Jefferson a petition of 10,000 signatures demanding religious freedom be written into the laws of the United States.

The long hours of work and sacrifice by Moore and men like him resulted in the First Amendment of the Bill of Rights. "Congress shall make no law respecting an establishment of religion, or prohibiting the free exercise thereof. . . ."

But his legacy doesn't end there. He was pastor of several churches, including Frying Pan Spring Meeting House from 1797 to 1815. He was founder of the First Baptist Church of Washington, DC, in 1802; First Baptist Church of Alexandria in 1803; and the Second Baptist Church of Washington, DC, in 1810. Traveling by horseback, he preached in other areas of Virginia, Maryland, North Carolina, South Carolina, Tennessee, Kentucky, Pennsylvania, Delaware, New Jersey, and New York. Jeremiah was 68 when he died on February 23, 1815, at Moorefield, his home in present-day Vienna, Virginia.

The shadow he cast two centuries ago can still be seen in his letters and writings, the churches that he founded and his descendants, three of whom made their own mark on Virginia history: Thomas Moore, the first superintendent of Fairfax County schools; R. Walton Moore, a City of Fairfax resident who served in the Virginia legislature and helped rewrite a modern Virginia constitution; and E. Blackburn Moore, the longtime speaker of the Virginia House of Delegates.

Robert B. Semple, an author who knew Jeremiah personally and had heard him preach, wrote, "In points of talents Mr. Moore certainly stands in the front row of Virginia preachers. His person and voice are extremely advantageous; his style is strong and energetic, and indeed elegant . . . his ideas are brilliant. He is well versed in the Scriptures. . . . It is doubtful if any preacher in Virginia has run a more honorable course than Mr. Moore: honorable to his God, honorable to himself, and honorable to his people."

One ordinary man can make a difference. Jeremiah Moore did.

Sources

Thomas V. DiBacco, *Moorefield* (Fairfax: Fairfax County Office of Comprehensive Planning, 1971).

William A. Simpson, Jr., *Virginia Baptist Ministers 1760–1790,* Vol. 1, (Richmond, Virginia: 1990).

Lewis Peyton Little, *Imprisoned Preachers and Religious Liberty in Virginia,* (Lynchburg: Virginia, J.P. Bell Co., 1938).

William Cabell Moore, *Jeremiah Moore, 1746–1815, William and Mary College Quarterly,* January, 1933.

Connie Pendleton Stuntz and Mayo Sturdevant Stuntz, *This Was Vienna* (Vienna, Virginia: 1987).

Jeremiah Moore served as pastor at the Frying Pan Spring Meeting House from 1797 to 1815. This historical highway marker, placed in 1994 by the Virginia Department of Historic Resources, reads: "The Frying Pan Meeting House, constructed by 1791 on land donated by the Carter family in 1783, was used for Baptist services until 1968. Named for nearby Frying Pan Branch, the church is a rare example of 18th-century architecture in western Fairfax County. By 1840 the congregation consisted of 33 whites and 29 blacks; both black and white members are buried in the church cemetery. During the Civil War, Union and Confederate forces each used the meetinghouse several times as a picket post. The last surviving church trustee conveyed the property to the Fairfax County Park Authority in 1984."

Jeremiah Moore died in Vienna in 1815 at the age of 68. This is his headstone, next to a Sons of the American Revolution marker, in a Vienna cemetery.

Fairfax County's First Two Post Offices
Colchester and Centreville
By Robert L. Lisbeth, *Falls Church, Virginia*

Colchester and Centreville were the first two post offices in the area of present-day Fairfax County. They were the only two post offices in Fairfax County during the 18th century. Both provided critical communications between individuals and businesses before the telephone, telegraph, and e-mail. These two post offices took root in the county and allowed the county to grow. Colchester dissolved while Centreville survived, even under Confederate control during the Civil War. Both mirrored the events and early development of Fairfax County.

Colchester
The first Virginian appointed to administer the colonial post offices in America was Head Lynch of Caroline County. This deputy postmaster general of the colonies served from 1740 to 1743. During his tenure, Fairfax County was established in 1742.

Colchester, the first post office established in present-day Fairfax County, like most colonial post offices, was near a major, navigable waterway—the Potomac River—and a poorly maintained stagecoach road of the King's Highway. This tobacco port and ferry crossing town was laid out in 1753 on the north side of the Occoquan River, just east of present-day Route 95 and the Richmond, Fredericksburg & Potomac Railroad tracks.

The enterprising, influential, and wealthy merchant Alexander Henderson of Scotland (1738–1815) was appointed its first postmaster on November 24, 1774, and was the first postmaster in present-day Fairfax County. One of his four "chain stores" and stable probably served as the Colchester post office while he was postmaster. It was located on Fairfax Street, three buildings from the Occoquan River, one block east of present-day Old Colchester Road. Patrols went to their post office to pick up their mail as well as neighbors' mail until large cities began delivering mail in 1863. In 18th-century Virginia, post offices usually operated out of residences, coffee houses, taverns, and stores. Henderson took in only one-sixth of the postal revenues compared to the thriving post offices in Alexandria, Dumfries, and Fredericksburg in the two years after 1776. His postmaster salary was about $1.40 during the fourth quarter of 1790. It possibly served as the post office for George Mason at the nearby 1759 Gunston Hall Plantation. Only two manuscript postmarks from Colchester are known to exist, both to merchants—June 30, 1774 (before it was established as a post office) to Dumfries, and June 24, 1794, to Alexandria.

By 1789, Colchester was one of 75 post offices in America and one of 14 in Virginia, and the only one not operating today. But, by then, Colchester businesses were in decline. During the service of the five succeeding postmasters and until it closed on October 7, 1815, the post office took in less and less revenue each year compared to the Alexandria, Dumfries, and Fredericksburg post offices. Nonetheless, it was the only post office in present-day Fairfax County to see radical postal changes from a British colonial postal system under King George III with postage in shillings, through the American Continental Congress and confederation period, through Virginia statehood in 1788, through the establishment of the Post Office Department in 1789, and into postage expressed in cents in 1792.

Colchester's final demise may have been due to the growing population of Occoquan in Prince William County, where streets and lots were laid out in 1804 or 1805 and a post office was established in 1808. More importantly, the next year a new stagecoach line and road were established by Nathaniel Ellicott of Occoquan to travel between Alexandria and Dumfries, thus bypassing nearby Colchester. The Occoquan Turnpike was chartered in 1811 to replace the antiquated King's Highway and a bridge across the Occoquan River eventually replaced the ferry at Colchester. In addition, the population declined due to pleurisy; the tobacco business declined; and the flood of 1807 prevented ships from using the port of Colchester. All contributed to its gradual decline to the point where a post office was no longer viable. It is ironic that its first postmaster died the same year as the discontinuance of the post office.

The Colchester postmasters and their appointment dates are as follows:

Alexander Henderson, appointed November 24, 1774
Eleon Moore, appointed July 5, 1782
William Thompson, appointed July 5, 1784
George W. Lindsay, appointed April 24, 1793
Zachariah Ware, appointed December 4, 1799
Samuel Bailey (Bayly), appointed January 27, 1802
Thomas Morgan, appointed March 5, 1813
Discontinued October 7, 1815

Centreville

The roads from Alexandria and Colchester converged at a village called Newgate. About 1792 this prospering village on Braddock Road was founded and its name changed from Newgate to Centerville (the original spelling). The only other Fairfax County town to acquire a post office in the 18th century was Centreville, which also was, like Colchester, near Prince William County, but in the western reaches of the county. It was laid out much like Alexandria and Colchester in a simple grid pattern.

Anthony Thornton was appointed its first postmaster on November 27, 1797, and by then the spelling was changed to Centreville. Also about this time, the Newgate Tavern became known as the Eagle Tavern, whose new owner was Anthony Thornton. This busy establishment on the roads from Colchester and Alexandria was well known to local travelers headed to or from Winchester, or Warrenton on, and it was natural that a post office would operate at the ordinary. However, a year later Thornton sold it to George Newman, although Thornton remained postmaster until mid-1799.

The second postmaster was Charles Tyler, Jr. Tyler was prosperous, based on the description of his house, built about 1790. His store/post office was operated from his dining room two blocks from the Eagle Tavern. In 1933 it underwent major renovations. Today it is known as the Havener House at 13940 Braddock Road (Route 620).

John Hening became the next postmaster during the second quarter of 1809. By 1815 he owned the Havener House, which he called Willow Spring. The house was made into a hotel and continued as a post office. In an 1820 ad for the hotel, John Hening said "He keeps the post office. . . ."

In late 1815, the Centreville post office was firmly established and the Colchester post office was discontinued. The Centreville post office served as a busy Confederate States of America post office to numerous occupying Confederate soldiers stationed in Centreville in 1861 and 1862. All known Centreville postmarks were made with handstamps. The Centreville post office is the oldest operating post office in Fairfax County and has operated continuously since its establishment in 1797.

Sources

"History of the Henderson Clan," www.clanhendersonusa.org/historyshendersons_us.htm.

Robert Lisbeth, *Virginia Postal History: 1607–1790* (Springfield, Virginia: 1988).

Robert Lisbeth, *Virginia Postal Markings and Postmasters: Colonial–1865* (Richmond, Virginia: Second Edition, 1992).

Register of Appointments of Postmasters (microfilm). National Archives, Washington, DC.

Eugenia Smith, *Centreville, Virginia: Its History and Architecture* (Fairfax, Virginia: Fairfax County Office of Comprehensive Planning, 1973).

Edith Moore Sprouse, *Colchester: Colonial Port on the Potomac* (Fairfax, Virginia: Fairfax County of Comprehensive Planning, 1975), 88–90.

Mayo S. Stuntz and Robert Lisbeth. "Development of Postal Service in Fairfax County, Virginia: 1750–1890." *Way Markings* 7 (August 1976): 9–19.

U.S. Post Office Department, *Post Roads Established by Law 1810–1825* (1825).

U.S. Post Office Department, *The Ledger of Doctor Benjamin Franklin: Postmaster General, 1776, A Fac-simile of the Original Manuscript* (Washington, DC: 1865).

Fairfax County's Most Famous Duel
Henry Clay and John Randolph Face Off
By Katherine Cooch Rau, *Warwick, Rhode Island*

Can you imagine the secretary of state and a powerful, longtime senator arguing at a Senate hearing? Definitely, right? Now imagine that confrontation escalating when one of the two claims the other has hurt his reputation and that the disagreement must be dealt with through a duel. While this scenario might seem ridiculous, arguments were resolved in this manner in the United States for hundreds of years. The practice of dueling occurred throughout the U.S., including in Virginia, and more specifically, in Fairfax County. This particular scenario, of the secretary of state and a senator fighting to the death over politics, took place in Fairfax County's most famous duel—the one between Secretary of State Henry Clay and Sen. John Randolph.

The origins of dueling are hard to precisely pinpoint. Its precursor, judicial combat, appears as far back as 501 AD when Gundebald, King of the Burgundian "legally established trial by combat, or judicial duel."[1] Judicial combat was "a legal process for adjudicating questions of difference between the parties. According to this idea the encounter no longer decided who was *able* to prevail, but who *ought* to prevail on principles of justice; a view that rested upon the belief that God would interfere directly in the combat to protect the innocent and punish the guilty."[2]

Judicial combat evolved into the modern duel during the Middle Ages. As described by Clara S. McCarty in her book *Duels in Virginia and Nearby Bladensburg,* "strip these [judicial combat] of legal and religious sanction and the modern duel is found."[3] It grew out of the idea of chivalry, under which questions of honor became paramount. The modern duel came to the fore in France. It spread to England, Ireland, the rest of Europe, and eventually, to the new world.

The Code Explained
Although practices varied from place to place, a "Code Duello" (rules of dueling) was finally written down in Ireland in 1777. Until that time the rules were passed and changed verbally. The Code Duello contained specific rules for the governing of a duel, covering everything from the "rules of procedure for the sending of a challenge, the naming of seconds, the choice of dueling ground, and the selection of weapons."[4] These rules were used throughout Europe and in America.

With some variation, a typical duel was started after a perceived insult or offense. The insulted person issued a challenge. "Seconds," usually persons of equal societal rank to the "principals" (those who had the disagreement that prompted a duel challenge), worked out the details of where the duel should take place, the time, the weapons to be used, etc. The other duty of seconds was to try to work out the disagreement so a duel did not take place. Even during the duel, between shots, the

Portrait of John Randolph by artist Gilbert Stuart. Randolph, a descendant of Pocahontas, was the son of a rich tobacco farmer. An odd affliction when he was young left Randolph beardless and with a high voice, yet later he was considered a great orator. He suffered from ill health, made worse by heavy drinking and occasional opium use. Randolph made provisions in his will for freeing his slaves and provided funds to transport those slaves to Ohio. He died of tuberculosis in Philadelphia. Before his death, he left instructions to be buried facing west, so he could keep an eye on Henry Clay. (Courtesy Museum of Charlotte County, Virginia)

Henry Clay, by Frederick and William Langenheim, 1850. "The Great Compromiser," Clay became a great orator by practicing as a young man in the forest, in the field and even the barn, speaking to whatever audience was handy, human or beast. He learned to state his position clearly, using facts, patriotism, and occasional sarcasm. Clay died in 1852, in Washington, DC, and was the first person to lie in state in the U.S. Capitol. Buried in Lexington, Kentucky, his headstone reads: "I know no North—no South—no East—no West."

seconds tried to resolve the argument. A duel could be stopped at any time by an apology or after honor was satisfied. The satisfaction of honor could mean anything from several shots being fired, even if they were misses, to severe injury or death.

Famous Duels in Virginia

Even though the most famous duel in America occurred in New Jersey—the 1804 duel between Alexander Hamilton and Aaron Burr—the majority of duels took place in the South. The practice also persisted longer in the South.

Many duels took place in Virginia. Some of the more famous ones include Thurston versus Harrison, Conway versus Thornton, and Poe versus Daniel. These more famous duels give a flavor of what constituted an offense worth dueling over, and how duels could end.

John Thurston, son of a revolutionary war hero, and John Harrison, a revolutionary war soldier and member of the Harrison family that later produced two presidents of the United States, almost fought a duel over 12½¢. Both were justices of the peace in Virginia. In 1792, after Thurston sent a case over to Harrison to settle, he demanded the 12½¢ that it cost him to issue the original warrant. Harrison replied that he had settled the case and had not collected any fees. From this disagreement a duel challenge was issued and accepted. At the very last minute, the seconds were able to broker a peace and the duel did not take place.[5]

In 1803, Francis Fitzhugh Conway and William Thornton fought a duel as a result of their competition for President James Madison's niece, Nellie Madison. The duel took place in Fredericksburg, Virginia, and resulted in the deaths of both men.[6]

Edgar Allen Poe was involved in an "almost duel" in Richmond, Virginia, in 1848 with newspaper editor John M. Daniel. Daniel had local notoriety for his work on the newspaper and for his dueling. It is unclear exactly what prompted Poe to challenge Daniel—a debt or a literary disagreement are possibilities. Nevertheless, the challenge was issued. It appears that Poe either sobered up or wised up and the argument was resolved between the two men without a duel.[7]

Fairfax County's Most Famous Duel

The most famous duel that took place in Fairfax County was between Henry Clay and John Randolph. At the time, Henry Clay was secretary of state for John Quincy Adam's administration and John Randolph was a senator from Virginia.[8] Both men had distinguished careers in public office before and after their duel. John Randolph was a lawyer who served several terms in Congress until his appointment in 1825 to the Senate. After the duel in 1826, he was elected to the Senate and went on to serve as a member of the Virginia Constitutional Convention, was a United States minister to Russia, and finished his career back in Congress.

Henry Clay had an equally impressive resume. He was an attorney who practiced law in his home state of Kentucky before becoming a member of the state House of

Representatives. He was elected to the United States Senate to fill a resignation vacancy. He went on to serve, over the course of his career, in both the House and the Senate. He served several times as speaker of the House. He was appointed secretary of state by John Quincy Adams in 1825. After the duel he finished his term as secretary of state and was elected to the Senate. He served there and in the House for the rest of his career. He was also a candidate for president three times, once before the duel and twice afterwards.[9]

In addition to extensive career achievements, Randolph and Clay also had in common a history of dueling. Secretary Clay had engaged in a duel with Humphrey Marshal when they were both members of the Kentucky legislature. Both received minor wounds in the duel.[10] When Senator Randolph was 18, he fought a duel with Robert Taylor when they were both students at the College of William and Mary. Both survived and were expelled, although there were widespread protests at the school over their expulsion and the ordinance that led to their expulsion was largely ignored for duels that followed.[11] In 1807, James Wilkerson challenged Randolph to a duel, which he ignored because he felt Wilkerson was unworthy, having been implicated in the Aaron Burr treason affair. In 1815 Randolph was again challenged to a duel, this time by Bolling Robertson, a fellow member of the House of Representatives, after Randolph excoriated him on the floor of the House.[12]

The 1826 conflict between the senator and the secretary appears to have arisen as a result of political differences over foreign policy. Senator Randolph seems to have not liked the foreign policy of John Quincy Adams; specifically he was against the United States sending a delegation to the Panamanian Congress of Latin American Republics. As detailed in the *Alexandria Gazette* account of the affair, the duel occurred, "in consequence of certain expressions used by the latter [Randolph] in a recent debate in the Senate, which Mr. Clay considered offensive, and applied *personally* to him."[13]

The details of the floor speech were decidedly juicier than the *Gazette* account stated. On the floor of the Senate, Randolph railed against the president and Secretary Clay, whom he felt had influenced the president on this matter. He said, among other things, the mission was "a Kentucky cuckoo's egg, laid in a Spanish American nest" and that he "was defeated, horse, foot, and dragoons—cut up, and clean broke down by the coalition of Blifil and Black George [scoundrels from Fielding's *Tom Jones*]—the combination, unheard of until then, of the puritan and the blackleg."[14] The puritan he was referring to was President Adams, and the blackleg (someone who cheats at cards, a scoundrel) was Secretary Clay.

The result of this speech was that Secretary Clay challenged Senator Randolph to a duel, which Randolph accepted.[15] The seconds for John Randolph were Maj. James Hamilton and Col. Tattnall. The seconds for Henry Clay were Senator Johnson of Louisiana and General Jessup. Only the seconds, a surgeon for each man, and Sen.

Thomas Benton of Missouri, who was a relation of Clay and a friend of Randolph, were allowed to be present for the duel.

There is some disparity among accounts of what occurred on the day of the duel. Most evidence suggests what was originally written about the event in the *Alexandria Gazette* is accurate, since they talked to all parties immediately afterwards. Its report was also "authorized by the friends of the parties."[16]

The duel took place at 4:30 p.m. on Saturday, April 8th. It occurred "at Little Falls, just beyond the Chain Bridge, at the time a thick forest, and thirty-five years later a spot described as being at the base of Fort Marcey."[17] This area was selected "in deference to Randolph, who declared that if it were his fate to fall, he wanted to be on the sacred soil of the Old Dominion."[18] Randolph showed up to the duel in a long white bathrobe and gave no explanation as to why.[19]

The two took their positions at 10 paces and prepared to fire smoothbore pistols.[20] Before they could officially start, Senator Randolph's pistol accidentally went off. Apparently, while he was an excellent marksman, he was not used to a "hair trigger," which was being used for the duel. Secretary Clay accepted his explanation and after the senator got a new gun and seconds fruitlessly tried to end the affair, the duelists again got into position. When the duel started anew, Secretary Clay shot Senator Randolph through his coat. Senator Randolph fired his pistol straight up and declared "I do not fire at you, Mr. Clay; it was not my intention to have fired at you at all; the unfortunate circumstance of my pistol going off accidentally changed my determination."[21] Henry Clay responded, "I trust in God, my dear sir, you are untouched. After what has occurred I would not have harmed you for a thousand worlds."[22] At this the two men shook hands and John Randolph added, "You owe me a coat, Mr. Clay."[23] Henry Clay replied, "I am glad the debt is no greater" and the matter was considered settled.[24]

Some accounts disagree with this one a bit in terms of the exact language used and how many shots were exchanged. These differing accounts have Clay and Randolph exchanging a round of shots before the round where Clay shot Randolph's coat.[25] However, the majority of the research and the accounts written at the time match the first narrative.

The End of Dueling

Fairfax County's most famous duel was not condemned at the time and, while it was reported in the papers, no legal action was taken against either man involved. The *Alexandria Gazette* gave an account of the duel with no mention of legalities and ended its article noting that, at the completion of the event, Secretary Clay and Senator Randolph shook hands "and the affair then honorable and happily closed."[26] In fact, the reputations of both men were enhanced and the duel was considered quite honorable. Senator Benton said of the duel, "It was about the last high-toned duel that I have witnessed and so happily conducted to a fortunate issue, a result due to the noble character of the seconds as well as to the generous and heroic spirit of the principles."[27]

Interestingly, at the time of the Clay-Randolph duel, dueling was outlawed in every state of the union, including Virginia. These laws had existed since the turn of the century. In 1806, legislation was passed at the federal level to regulate dueling in the army. After congressmen Jonathan Cilley and William J. Graves engaged in a duel in 1838, Congress passed a law that made it illegal to duel and/or propose or accept a duel challenge in the District of Columbia. When the legislation was passed in 1839, Henry Clay was in the Senate and voted for the measure. John Randolph died in 1833.[28] Some of the floor debate over the bill indicates the issue with creating a law that wouldn't be enforced due to public opinion. Senator Linn of Missouri said of the bill, "What community can be found that would pronounce a man either a murderer or a felon, who may have chanced to kill another in a fair and equal combat?"[29]

While public opinion did not favor harsh punishment for dueling and therefore made the enforcement of anti-dueling measures impossible, it is interesting to note that many religious and political leaders had always spoken out against the practice. For example, the Roman Catholic Church at the Council of Trent "decreed that the custom was detestable and that principles as well as seconds would be excommunicated."[30] Thomas Paine called dueling "gothic and absurd."[31] Thomas Jefferson wrote in 1806 of dueling, "It is not inclination in anyone but a fear of the opinion of the world which leads one to the absurd and immoral decision of differences by duel."[32]

Public opinion slowly shifted and the practice was gradually seen as barbaric and eventually silly. Deaths of well-known Americans, such as the war hero Stephen Decatur, also helped turn the tide of popular opinion. Cartoons and satirical articles appeared in newspapers across the country. For example, in 1858, *Harper's New Monthly Magazine* stated, "The process of reasoning behind a duel 'assumed that an argument made by a rhetorician might be intelligible or inconclusive, but that a syllogism propelled by powder, if properly aimed, could hardly fail to carry conviction to the dullest intellect.'"[33] In fact, by 1860 the same *Alexandria Gazette* that did not condemn the Clay-Randolph duel published an editorial against dueling, stating in part, "The practice of Duelling is now justly recognized by the civil and religious authorities of our country, as not only inhuman, but barbarous."[34] Dueling gradually died out and the practice was largely unheard of in Virginia and, more specifically, in Fairfax County, by the turn of the next century.

Endnotes

1. Robert Baldick, *The Duel: A History* (New York: Barnes & Noble Books, 1996), 12.

2. A.W. Patterson, *The Code Duello: with special reference to the State of Virginia* (Richmond, Virginia: Richmond Press, Inc., 1927), 7.

3. Clara S. McCarty, *Duels in Virginia and Nearby Bladensburg* (Richmond, Virginia: The Dietz Press, Inc., 1976), 1.

4. Jeannette Hussey, *The Code Duello in America* (Washington, DC: Smithsonian Institution, 1980), 7.

5. A.W. Patterson, *The Code Duello,* 25.

6. Ibid., 26.

7. Ibid., 44.

8. Clara S. McCarty, *Duels in Virginia,* 46.

9. Biographical Directory of the United States Congress, bioguide.congress.gov/biosearch/biosearch.asp.

10. Hamilton Cochran, *Noted American Duels and Hostile Encounters* (New York: Chilton Books, 1963), 136.

11. William Oliver Stevens, *The Story of the Code of Honor in America* (Boston, Massachusetts: The Riverside Press Cambridge, 1940), 41.

12. A.W. Paterson, *The Code Duello,* 32.

13. *Alexandria Gazette,* April 11, 1826.

14. Jeannette Hussey, *The Code Duello in America,* 28.

15. Clara S. McCarty, *Duels in Virginia,* 46–47.

16. *Alexandria Gazette,* April 11, 1926.

17. Clara S. McCarty, *Duels in Virginia,* 47.

18. William Oliver Stevens, *The Story of the Code of Honor,* 216.

19. Barbara Holland, *Gentlemen's Blood* (New York: Bloomsbury, 2003), 125.

20. William Oliver Stevens, *The Story of the Code of Honor,* 216.

21. *Alexandria Gazette,* April 11, 1826.

22. Clara S. McCarty, *Duels in Virginia,* 47.

23. Ibid.

24. Ibid.

25. Barbara Holland, *Gentlemen's Blood,* 126.

26. *Alexandria Gazette,* April 11, 1826.

27. William Oliver Stevens, *The Story of the Code of Honor,* 219.

28. Jeannette Hussey, *The Code Duello in America,* 29.

29. A.W. Patterson, *The Code Duello,* 74.

30. Hamilton Cochran, *Noted American Duels and Hostile Encounters,* 7.

31. Jeannette Hussey, *The Code Duello in America,* 6.

32. A.W. Patterson, *The Code Duello,* 69.

33. Jeannette Hussey, *The Code Duello in America,* 6.

34. *Alexandria Gazette,* April 11, 1826.

The History of Mount Zephyr
From George Washington to Suburban Development
By Dan Burrier and Sharon Bertschi, *Alexandria, Virginia*

The neighborhood of Mount Zephyr is uniquely connected to the extraordinary beginnings of our nation. In 1674, Lord Culpeper granted 5,000 acres along the Potomac River, including Mount Zephyr, to Nicholas Spencer and John Washington, who was the great, great-grandfather of George Washington. The 2,500 acres belonging to the Washington family were passed from father to son until George took possession in 1752. Mount Zephyr Farm existed at that time and when Washington resurveyed the land, he included portions of Mount Zephyr Farm in the Muddy Hole Farm lands and a portion in Union Farm. The Mount Zephyr Farm became a segment between these two creations of Washington but always remained autonomous. Mount Zephyr Farm contained 648 acres with boundaries from Old Mill Road to the south, to Buckman Road to the west, east to Mt. Vernon Highway and north to Gum Springs.

George Washington began his farming career on land that was in poor condition, thanks to years of nutrient-depleting tobacco crops. He revived the soil by rotating plantings and fencing off areas for cattle and their beneficial manure. His land was meticulously cared for with manicured hedgerows, healthy livestock, and well-built barns. Mount Zephyr was sectioned into various plots that included fields for wheat and corn, an orchard, pastureland, and timberland for building and firewood.

After Washington's death in 1799, his holdings passed to his wife, Martha. After her death in 1802, Washington's nephew, Bushrod Washington, Sr., inherited much of his uncle's land, including the mansion and Union Farm, including Mount Zephyr. Bushrod was an intellectual with little interest or time for farming. He had been appointed to the Supreme Court by Thomas Jefferson in 1798 and spent most of his time in Philadelphia. Bushrod also suffered from conflicting sympathies about the necessity of slave labor to maintain his farms. During his ownership of Mount Vernon, he emancipated a number of slaves. Unrest and jealousy among the remaining slaves made it virtually impossible to manage a productive and successful farm.

The time that Bushrod spent at Mount Vernon was quiet—interrupted just once during the War of 1812. The mansion stood completely exposed to a fleet of passing warships when it was shaken by the firing of ammunition. No damage was done and the home's occupants soon learned the guns had not been pointed in their direction. The ship's captain had ordered a volley of cannon fire as a salutation to George Washington when passing Mount Vernon. The impromptu ceremony concluded and the fleet continued its journey to wreak havoc on Fort Washington and later, the City of Alexandria.

George Washington inherited the Mount Vernon estate in 1761 and ran it as five separate farms, using a scientific approach. He kept careful records of the agricultural activities and labor operations. Washington built a distillery next to his gristmill near his Mount Zephyr farm and was, for a time, perhaps the largest whiskey distiller in the country. The distillery was excavated, rebuilt, and opened to the public in 2007. (Courtesy Library of Congress)

Bushrod Washington couldn't escape being compared to his uncle, George Washington, even though he served a non-distinguished term as 11th justice of the Supreme Court. He was short and disheveled, enjoyed snuff, and suffered from ill health. He inherited Mount Vernon from his uncle, who had instructed that his slaves be freed. Bushrod did that, but brought in his own slaves and later had to sell them to raise funds. Bushrod died in Philadelphia and three days later, his wife also died, while transporting his body for burial. (Courtesy Library of Congress)

In 1829, Bushrod and his wife died within days of each other. The couple had no children, so the Mount Vernon estate was passed down to his adult nephews and a niece. Union Farm was divided between the Washington brothers George C. and Bushrod, Jr. By this time, the lands that were once the pride of America's first president had fallen into a sorry state. Fields were overgrown and saplings were quickly making new forests of the original owner's pastures and fields. Older brother George C. enjoyed a comfortable life in Georgetown as an agriculturist and politician. Bushrod, Jr., and his large family lived on Mount Zephyr Farm in a house that was located in the area of Washington Avenue and Woodley Drive near Little Dogue Creek. Court records show that Bushrod, Jr., was often in debt and had to be bailed out by his uncle on different occasions. His financial woes may be the reason his more responsible brother, George C., was appointed trustee for the Mount Zephyr tract that Bushrod, Jr., had inherited. Bushrod, Jr.'s debt might have been the result of poor growing conditions or simply poor judgment and lack of skill. The soil of Mount Vernon and its surrounding area is marine clay, created eons ago when the area was completely submerged under a body of water. Soil improvement was a major concern for George Washington and it remains so today.

Whiteall Wins the Final Bid

George C. apparently was not sentimental about owning a piece of the first president's land because he unloaded his portion of Union Farm within two years to a Georgetown neighbor named Samuel Whiteall for $3,000. Bushrod, Jr., continued farming Mount Zephyr until 1840, when a lawsuit forced him to sell his portion. Samuel Whiteall won the final bid at $3 per acre when the second auction took place on the courthouse steps.

Samuel Whiteall's family consisted of 14 family members and three servants. He rented a luxurious mansion in Georgetown with land for farming and gardening but needed more to support his large household. He sent his oldest daughter, her husband, and their five young children to live at Union Farm and start a dairy business. They occupied the "overlooker's house," once owned by George Washington's overseer, and a brick barn located to the south of Mount Zephyr Farm. The two family units were never able to make ends meet and accrued an impressive list of debts owed to food merchants, lumber and hardware dealers, and loans at two banks. Eight creditors filed a joint lawsuit against Whiteall in 1848. A portion of Union Farm was placed on the auction block. The *Alexandria Gazette* advertised the sale to be held August 21, 1848, at the Fairfax Courthouse, and described the property "of good quality and well located."

Aaron Leggett, a Quaker from New York City, bought the 603-acre tract for $2 an acre. The sale brought only temporary relief to the financially strapped Whiteall. A second lawsuit resulted in 1852 in a court order to sell the remainder of Union Farm that now included the rest of Mount Zephyr. Aaron Leggett once again snapped up the property, but this time paid considerably more, at $16.56 per acre for the remaining 107-acre tract. Leggett was a New York City businessman who longed to escape the rat race and retreat to the peace and quiet of country living. He was acquainted with the area through the network of Quakers who were already in the area west of Union Farm.

Northern Quakers saw rural Virginia as a profitable site for harvesting second-growth timbers for the shipbuilding boom. Accotink Creek was the site of a number of Quaker businesses, including a saw mill, gristmill, and a shipbuilding yard. The Friends Meetinghouse was the center of their community and still stands today at Fort Belvoir. Leggett, a die-hard bachelor, came from a successful family that owned businesses ranging from dry goods stores to a company that brought gas lighting to New York City. He had solid Quaker values and, like his fellow Friends, abhorred slavery. Among the chattel included in Leggett's purchase of Union Farm and Mount Zephyr was a slave woman named Daphne Kelley. She was from Prince William County and had a husband, children, and grandchildren living in the area. She remained at Mount Zephyr as a member of the household until Leggett's death in 1860. Leggett's will ordered the emancipation of Daphne and designated funds to buy the rest of her family to win their freedom.

Leggett set up housekeeping in the Mount Zephyr house and then turned to the business of farming. If there was ever a barn near the house, it was no longer useful. He envisioned a new Pennsylvania-style bank barn made of stone and wood, large enough to hold the bounty he hoped his land would produce. He paid his nephew, John Griffin, $550 to build the structure and include a stable. The dimensions were 107 x 43 feet at its base, with a seven-foot overhang on the second floor. In 1853, the landscape of Mount Zephyr was marked by a high ridge that ran along the eastern side of Washington Avenue. Leggett nestled the stone foundation of his barn into the ridge's earthen bank. It was located at the northern corner of Washington Avenue and Woodley Drive, where the foundation footstones still exist today.

Leggett Gives up Farming

Leggett enjoyed his time at Mount Zephyr and was a successful and happy farmer. By his 63rd birthday, his enthusiasm still bubbled over. In a letter he wrote to a friend in September of 1855, he gushed, "Here I am and I think on a first-rate farm, wanting only a good and first-rate manager to make it a princely place and happy, healthy residence as well as very profitable." He went on to tell his friend about his barn and his plans to buy steers, oxen, and sheep. An ad in the July 19, 1858, edition of the *Alexandria Gazette* advertised "400 Fine Wool Merino Sheep for Sale." Eventually, Leggett quit the farming life and moved back to New York, where he died at age 70 in 1860. Leggett had remained a bachelor all his life and had no suitable heirs to continue the farm. Mount Zephyr and Union Farm were divided into parcels and sold as farmettes to various buyers for $10 per acre.

The Civil War found Mount Zephyr in a state of uneasy quiet. The area was a no-man's land between Federal troops that occupied Alexandria and Confederate armies gathered near Mount Zephyr. The Quaker families living in this buffer zone became targets of hostility from their neighbors, who had loyalties to the slaveholding South. Soldiers from both sides often swooped in to ransack the farms and homes for food and supplies. After Leggett's death, the Mount Zephyr land was sold to Hugh Whitton, a Delaware resident who never lived on the land, but mysteriously disappeared behind Confederate lines during the war. The land passed to his daughter, Elizabeth Briscoe of Philadelphia. After the Briscoes moved to Mount Zephyr, they petitioned to restore an old road that had been closed by George Washington. That road is known today as the Mount Vernon Highway. The Briscoes farmed their land and prospered until 1875, when Briscoe sold the farm and moved back to Philadelphia.

The 11 years that followed saw a whirlwind of various owners until the farm was finally bought in 1886 by Circuit Court Judge Park Agnew. He and his wife, Matilda, lived in the Mount Zephyr house with their three children. Unfortunately, only one son survived childhood. He inherited the land from his father and sold it to developer George Beach in 1938.

As a Washingtonian, Beach had a front-row seat to observe the area's tremendous growth during the time between World Wars I and II. Rural areas like Mount Zephyr were perfect for the kind of development he envisioned. He pictured a development of sturdy, modest, Cape Cod structures that would be economically viable to returning World War II veterans. A few modern homes already existed in the area of Halfe Street and Agnew Avenue in a gated community called Mount Zephyr Park. The current childcare center at the northern tip of Washington Avenue was the office of Houston and Associates, an architectural and surveying firm. Beach contracted the firm to lay out a subdivision plan of half-acre lots and filed it with Fairfax County in December 1940.

Houston's original concept was that all the Mount Zephyr homes would look like the brick or stone cottages on Washington Avenue. Tennessee Crab Orchard stone was brought in truckloads from a quarry in Tennessee to Mount Zephyr, where local stonemasons cut and assembled the exterior walls. The earliest stone homes have neatly stacked, square-cut stones, a practice that soon proved too costly and time consuming. Beach abandoned this technique for the easier method of puzzle-fitting rocks into place. This accounts for the two types of stone construction on these nearly identical Cape Cod homes. The first Cape Cod construction phase took place between 1941 and 1942 and started with the house at the northern tip of Washington Avenue. The Martin family lived there and operated a hardware store.

Beach continued his construction, but few of his homes were actually finished and made habitable. World War II complicated the construction business by depleting the labor pool. Supplies were increasingly difficult to obtain and, for a time, not even plaster could be found to finish walls. Beach reluctantly filed bankruptcy and sold the Mount Zephyr tract to a team of four investors in 1946.

The Neighborhood Develops

The investment team formed the Veteran's Development Corporation (VDC). Their sales practices were unique and perhaps intended to instill a sense of community in their homebuyers. Instead of providing their clients with deeds, the team issued stock shares, with each plot equaling 100 shares.

The VDC finished what Beach had been unable to complete; 20 foundations had been poured while other homes had only exterior walls before Beach stopped construction. Mount Zephyr once again awoke to the sound of hammers and construction and by 1949, all the homes George Beach had started were now complete. The four members of the VDC eventually agreed to quit the business and divided up their remaining interests equally. As Mount Zephyr residents themselves, they endeavored to maintain a sense of community. Some of the VDC members continued to build houses in the neighborhood. While the Cape Cod cottages were nearly identical, the partners produced unique, custom-built homes. This accounts for the diversity of architectural styles, such as the brick ramblers with bay windows, split-levels, and individual facades. The personal tastes of the different families helped Mount Zephyr avoid the cookie-cutter appearance that comes from having only one or two architectural themes.

Up until the early 21st century, Mount Zephyr retained much of its historic appearance. Streets were narrow and lined with giant trees. One longtime resident remembers that driving Mount Zephyr streets, with the trees arching over the shaded roadways, was like riding through a tunnel. The area had its own water company near the corner of Jackson Place and Radford Avenue with a second pumping station on Mohawk Lane and Richmond Avenue. The plant was in business as late as 1970 and supplied the entire neighborhood with what some remember as the "best artesian water you ever tasted." Even the bridge across Little Dogue Creek on Woodley Drive wasn't built until the 1970s. Mount Zephyr today comprises 125 acres of the original 648-acre farm and is a modern neighborhood with paved roads, sidewalks, and city water. The Mount Zephyr Ladies Association was formed in 1947. Its members intended to build a clubhouse for the community in Section 1 north of the business park but the plans were never finalized. The Mount Zephyr Citizens Association was established in 1953 and was active until 1960. The next generation association was begun in 1965, reorganized in 1985 and a new association was incorporated in 2005.

Traces of the past still connect the community to its historic beginnings. The close proximity to Mount Vernon is an obvious reminder of its roots. Closer to home, residents still unearth an occasional relic when digging in their gardens. The waters of Little Dogue Creek still meander quietly through Mount Zephyr and down past George Washington's Grist Mill before spilling into the Potomac. The Mount Zephyr of today is a neighborhood that keeps pace with the times while remembering and honoring its past.

Sources

Barbara J. Carlby, Spann, 1976.
Library of Congress.
The Papers of George Washington, University of Virginia, 1996–2005.
Oral history by Mount Zephyr residents.
Special thanks to Barbara McMillan, librarian, Mount Vernon.

A History of Franconia
From Farms to Suburbia
By Sue L. Patterson, *Alexandria, Virginia*

Before the beginning of the housing boom in Fairfax County in the 1960s, people from all over the area came to Franconia for church social activities, dances at the Franconia School, and the volunteer fire department parades. Franconia has evolved from a farming community into a suburban community with a mix of residential/commercial uses and a transportation system that allows convenient access to/from anywhere in the Washington, DC, area via highway, train, bus, and three Metro stations. The future of Franconia is to become more of an urban community as the scarcity and high value of land and the convenient access drive redevelopment of commercial areas such as Springfield Mall into a high-density development of mixed use and redevelopment of infill areas into top-of-the-line homes. In 2005, Beulah Street already had so-called "McMansions" replacing or going up next to small, single-story houses built in the 1940s and 1950s.

The Franconia area has changed rapidly in the last 50 years with the landmarks of former days razed and no longer visible. The history of Franconia has not had as much recognition as some of the more famous areas of Fairfax County. Due to its location, 10 miles from Washington and practically next door to Mount Vernon, the founding fathers and their relatives traversed Franconia's original farms and roads. Remnants of the occupation by Union troops during the Civil War are still visible in the area if you know where to look. As with many communities, Franconia had its start with the coming of the railroad after the Civil War in the 1870s. The derivation of the name "Franconia" has caused almost as much speculation as defining the boundaries of Franconia.

In 1859, the wealthy Alexandria businessman William Fowle, of English descent, purchased 191 acres from Joseph Broders of Oak Grove Farm. This property was located generally between where Fleet Drive and Beulah Street are today. William Fowle died in 1860. His son, Robert Rollins Fowle, received the 191 acres as his share of his father's estate. Rollins died in 1873 and his wife stayed on the property until at least 1906.

After the Civil War, Fowle's farm was known as the Frankhonia Farm. Rollins Fowle sold 18 acres to the Alexandria and Frederick Railroad Company in 1871 for a railroad station, which was named after the farm. Initially, the Franconia Station was situated south of Franconia Road near present-day Fleet Drive. After a fire in 1903, the station was relocated to the north side of Franconia Road. It was an important stop between Washington and Quantico. Regular service was discontinued around 1953.

Prior to the Civil War, former slaves settled in the Franconia area, laying the foundation for a small but thriving African American community in the late 19th century

The chapel of the Olivet Episcopal Church dates from 1853 and is still in use today. (Courtesy Franconia Museum Collections)

and the first part of the 20th century. The small black settlement known as Carrolltown, located in today's Kingstowne and Manchester Lakes area, was named after George Washington Carroll, an original trustee of Laurel Grove Baptist Church. His mother, Jane Carroll, was a former slave belonging to Dennis Johnston of West Grove. She and her children received 10 acres of land by 1856 from Johnston's estate, located at the corner of Old Telegraph Road and Hayfield Road. George Carroll brought an adjacent 121 acres in 1899 and 1903 from Dennis Johnston's heirs. George ran a hog farm and a small general store on present day Kingstowne Village Parkway until his death in 1917. His sons sold the land and the store after his death.

In November 1846, William Jasper, a slave, was emancipated by the will of William Hayward Foote of Hayfield Farms. Foote was the foster son and nephew of Elizabeth Foote Washington, wife of Lund Washington. William brought 13 acres on Beulah Street from Thompson Javins in November 1860. He grew tired of walking to Alfred Street Baptist Church in Alexandria and he did not want his children to walk to school. In 1881, he and his second wife, Georginna, gave half an acre to Fairfax County for a schoolhouse. In 1884, the Jaspers deeded another half acre for the building of the Laurel Grove Baptist Church.

William died in 1896 in Franconia. His descendants sold the land to the Fried Properties for redevelopment into an office park. Today, the school is a museum. The church burned in December 2004.

A Succession of Schools

The Franconia School was built in 1872. It was located on Old Franconia Road across from Potters Lane. When the present Franconia Elementary school was built in the early 1930s, the old building was sold in 1935 for $75. It was used as a residence until it was torn down in 1986. The Potters Hill School was successively located on three corners of the intersection of Telegraph Road at old Beulah Road. The land was acquired in November 1877 from Charles Potter. The last school building, dedicated in March 1917, burned in 1939.

Sharon Chapel was built in 1849 on land donated by John J. Frobel of Wilton Hill. Burned in 1864 by Union soldiers, the church was rebuilt using lumber from Fort Lyon and stood until 1903, when it was replaced by a third building. That chapel was demolished in 1971 after the present church was built. Olivet Church is the third of four structures to house its Episcopal congregation. The first, a log structure, was built on land given by Virginia Gunnell Scott of Bush Hill in 1853. A larger, Gothic-style chapel was dedicated in 1861. Both buildings were destroyed in the Civil War. In 1872, a new church was built at the corner of Bush Hill Drive and Franconia Road, and may have been moved in 1892 to its present site at Beulah Street and Franconia Road. The brick sanctuary was constructed in 1957.

During the Civil War, various Union soldiers units were encamped in the Franconia area. The 3rd and 4th Maine and the 38th and 40th New York regiments camped at Camp Knox in the winter of 1861. Gen. John Sedgwick established his headquarters on Lawson's Hill, which took its name from a former landowner. Cameron Methodist Church was built on part of the site at Franconia and Telegraph roads in 1963. The exact location of Camp Michigan is unknown, but relics found near Lee District Park and the Stoneybrooke subdivision suggest that the 3rd and 5th Michigan Infantry, as well as the 37th New York, may have been in this vicinity. Fort Lyon, built in 1861, was the second largest fort in the defenses of Washington. Its position on the plateau now occupied by the Huntington Metro station afforded protection for the railroad, the Little River Turnpike, and the city of Alexandria. In June 1863, the powder magazine exploded. The damage was so great that President Lincoln came to inspect the aftermath. Until 1931 the fort was one of the best preserved around the capitol, but suburban growth has left few traces.

Noted Citizens and Homes

Franconia was home to a number of well-known citizens and private homes that were examples of the architecture of the 18th and 19th century. Unfortunately, only a few of those buildings are still standing. Round Hill was the home of the Triplett family since the 1740s. The original house burned in 1806. The land passed out of the family by 1915 and was made part of Fort Belvoir during World War II. William Triplett, a lieutenant in the Revolution, is buried in the family cemetery, located near Telegraph Road.

Dennis McCarty, a member of the Virginia Assembly, built Mount Air in the 1730s. The majority of the house was damaged by fire around 1859. Maine troops occupied the farm during the Civil War, and engineer battalions camped there in World War I while they built a railroad spur into Camp Humphreys (now Fort Belvoir). Part of the tract was confiscated in World War II to build Davison Airfield. The house burned in 1992. The ruins, one of Fairfax County's historic overlay districts, are owned by the Fairfax County Park Authority.

George D. Fowle, brother of Rollins, built Evergreen, part of the Burgundy Plantation, about 1850 in the Italianate villa style. From 1884 to 1885, Gen. Fitzhugh Lee and his family occupied it during his campaign for governor of Virginia. He was the only governor of Virginia born in Fairfax County (at Clermont in Franconia). When a subdivision was built on the tract in 1969, the house was relocated from 4050 Franconia Road to its present site at 5719 Cannon Lane.

Alexandria merchant James Irwin established a ropewalk on the Mount Erin tract by 1803. In 1815, Dr. Thomas Tracy, a native of Ireland and a Revolutionary War veteran, acquired the property. His heirs sold a portion of the farm in 1841, for the Old Mount Vernon Race Course. The Pulman family lived there during the Civil War. Two of their children were killed and a third wounded when a stray shell exploded on the front lawn. Today, it is a private residence.

Where the Sunrise Assisted Living facility now stands at Franconia Road and Frontier Drive was the site of a 19th-century brick house, occupied by the Broders family. Oak Grove was built around 1825 by John H. Broders and a wing was added around 1877 for a post office. The house was demolished in 1996 but the family cemetery still exists off nearby Elder Avenue.

Ashland was the home of William W. Triplett, brother of the owner of nearby Flagg Hill. The oldest, log portion of the house was built around 1820. The 195-acre farm was sold after the Civil War to former Rep. W.W. Boyce of South Carolina. Today, it is a private residence.

The Retirement Plantation was given its name by Commodore Walter Brooke of the Virginia naval forces after he resigned in 1781. The 400-acre farm retained this name until the mid-1940s, when new owners enlarged the dwelling and encased it in stone. The Cohens then named it for themselves: Ben-Mae Manor. Today, the house is owned by the Fairfax County Park Authority, and used as a community center for the Stoneybrooke subdivision.

Hayfield was the home of Lund Washington, cousin of George Washington and manager of his estate during the Revolution. A late 19th-century feature of the farm was its 16-sided barn, a copy of one previously at Mount Vernon. The original house burned in 1916, but the barn and outbuildings remained until the Hayfield Farm subdivision was built. The barn burned in 1967.

Alexandrian Josiah Watson constructed Bush Hill before 1795. Richard Marshall Scott, a member of the House of Delegates, next acquired Bush Hill. During the Civil War, Gen. O.O. Howard, who later founded Howard University, had his headquarters on the grounds. In World War II the house was used for two years as a detention center for Hitler's advisor Ernst "Putzi" Hanfstaengl. The brick house remained in the hands of descendants until it burned in 1977.

The French and Dulany families owned Clermont in the 18th century. Gen. John Mason, youngest son of George Mason of Gunston, later owned Clermont. After his death, the plantation was purchased by Capt. French Forrest, USN, who became a commodore in the Confederate Navy. The farm was confiscated as enemy property in the Civil War, and the dwelling used as a smallpox hospital. It burned in 1865 while Union troops were decontaminating the structure.

Rose Hill Farm was the home until his death in 1771 of Daniel French, Jr., builder of Pohick Church. In 1846, Maynadier Mason, grandson of George Mason, owned the plantation. The original house burned in 1895.

James H. Hooe, an Alexandria merchant, acquired the Burgundy Plantation in 1806. In 1854 his grandson, George D. Fowle, purchased the farm and redesigned the house in the style of baronial mansions he had seen on a European trip. During the Civil War, the 3rd and 4th Maine established Camp Howard on his farm. Thomas Walsh lived there from 1869 until 1915. The house burned a year later.

The Franconia Railroad Station was owned and operated by the Alexandria & Fredericksburg Railway Company. Serving twice as the Garfield Post Office, it was originally south of Franconia Road, near Fleet Drive, and after a fire, was relocated in 1903 to the north side of Franconia Road. Regular train service ended around 1952. (Courtesy Franconia Museum Collections)

This photo of Ward's Corner, the heart of the Franconia community, shows the Sylvia Theater on the far left and a grocery store on the right, with two gas pumps in front. (Notice the woman entering the store just left of center.) Over the years it also offered a dance hall and a bar. The building burned down in 1959. (Courtesy Franconia Museum Collections)

John A. Fairfax owned the Sisters' House during the Civil War, known as Fairview Farm. More recently the land took its name from a Catholic order, which used the house as a retreat and a camp for city children.

John J. Frobel owned Wilton Hill. He was a native of Holland, became a protégé of the Washington family, and moved up from Richmond when Judge Bushrod Washington came to Mount Vernon. He taught music and was both vestryman and organist at Christ Church in Alexandria. Anne, his daughter, kept a diary during the Civil War that vividly illustrated the trials of area life during that period.

Benoni Wheat, whose daughter married Francis Triplett, acquired Flagg Hill in 1853. The farmhouse remained in the family until the 1960s, when the tract became a gravel pit. Triplett Lane, which led to the house, is now known as South Van Dorn Street.

William Sims Reid was farming 145 acres on Franconia Road when the Civil War broke out. He spent six months in the Old Capitol Prison after his young son had been caught flying a Confederate flag from a window of their home. Reid died in 1864. The following year part of General Sherman's army camped on the farm, then known as Green Ridge. Today, the Reid House is a private residence on Franconia Road.

Into the 20th Century

A 20th-century hang-out was Wards Corner on Franconia Road. This complex was once the heart of the Franconia neighborhood. Over a period of 25 years the center grew from a two-pump gas station to include a grocery store, a bar, movie theatre, and dance hall. A fire in May 1959 destroyed this center of the community. Franconia Fire Station No. 5 was chartered in 1935. It was the sixth volunteer fire department in Fairfax County, and served the area from Burke to the Occoquan River. Volunteers built the original station on Franconia Road in 1949 (now the site of Franconia Governmental Center). In 1966, land was purchased for the present station on Beulah Street.

From the 1870s to the 1950s, the boundaries of Franconia extended beyond the original Frankhonia Farm to become a thriving farming community, centered on the local Franconia Elementary School, volunteer fire department, and numerous churches found along Franconia Road and Beulah Road (now Beulah Street). However, in the 1960s, the landscape began to change with the addition of many new housing developments bringing an influx of new residents overwhelming the older community with traffic, new buildings, increased land values, and new ways of doing things. Today, not many of the old farms are left in the area, but descendants still live in or retain connections to the area. The Franconia School is still in existence and the volunteer fire department is still a viable organization. A new Franconia community has been shaped based on the foundation of the old one.

Sources

Fairfax County Deed Book B-4, deed between Joseph Broders and William Fowle, dated March 3, 1859, 141.

Fairfax County Will Book 7, William Fowle's will, 505.

Alexandria Gazette, R. Rollins Fowle died at his residence Frankhonia on Saturday morning, March 8, 1873.

Fairfax County Deed Book N-4, deed between R.R. Fowle and wife Barbara and Alexandria and Fredericksburg Railway Company, dated October 18, 1871, 387.

William Schurtz, native of Franconia, 1929–2002, personal knowledge of the termination of Franconia Station service.

"Death of a Worth Colored Woman" (obituary of Milly Ann Carroll), *Fairfax Herald,* January 21, 1910.

Dennis Johnston, dec., et al. *vs.* Annie M. Johnston, et al., Fairfax County, Virginia, Chancery Causes, 1879–022. CFF 53D.

Fairfax County Deed Book K-9, 588–93.

Fairfax County Deed Book A-5, 202–3.

Fairfax County Deed Book E-5, 383–4.

Fairfax County Deed Book H-8, 297–8.

Death Records (loose papers), George Washington Carroll's death certificate, Fairfax County Circuit Court Archives, Fairfax, Virginia.

Fairfax County Will Book V, 75–83.

Fairfax County Will Book W, 299–302.

Fairfax County Deed Book S-3, 64–65.

Remaining information extracted from "Your Guide to Our Home—Historic Franconia," a map, prepared by the Franconia Museum, Inc., Board of Directors in 2003. Permission for publication received.

A History of Lincolnia
Starting with a Single House
By Mary Margaret Lewis Pence, *Alexandria, Virginia*

Prior to the Civil War, as early as 1853, Lincolnia was called Mount Pierce. Later it was called Lebanon. In 1870, the name Lincoln was proposed by Levi Deming to honor President Abraham Lincoln. Finally the name Lincolnia stuck.

In 1740, John Summers and George Harrison obtained a grant from Lord Fairfax for land located in this area, then in Prince William County. In 1750, John Summers built a house there, later called the Cottage Farm, which is west of the Lincolnia Post Office between Barnum Lane and Deming Avenue. All that remains there today is the Summers Cemetery. Elisha Cullen Dick, George Washington's doctor, bought this property in 1814. It has been said that while Dr. Dick lived there, Lafayette visited Cottage Farm. Gen. Winfield Scott Hancock had headquarters at Cottage Farm with General Merritt.

After several owners, Levi Deming bought Cottage Farm—about 152 acres—in 1852 for less than $4,000. This land extended past the old Lincolnia Methodist Church, east of the Lincolnia Post Office, and on the western end of Lincolnia Road near the Peace Lutheran Church. Deming was later joined by other members of the Deming and Barnum families. In 1874, Deming sold a half acre of land for $50 as a building site for the little Methodist church. He also gave the entire road along his property to Fairfax County. This road, used since about 1740, was the first road through the area. Little River Turnpike (Route 236), built in 1785, was America's first toll road and was not paved until 1923. Electric lights were installed in 1922.

Green Spring Farm was originally owned by the John Moss family and later by Capt. Fountain Beattie (one of Mosby's Rangers), who had a large home built there about 1760. Michael and Belinda Straight bought the house and 33 acres of the farm in 1942 and deeded it in 1970 to Fairfax County as a historical site.

Land around Holmes Intermediate School on Montross Street was owned by Albert Minor. I have been told the Minors were some of the original settlers here, and that Ab Minor as well as Captain Beattie rode with Mosby's men.

There were several taverns in the area. Dowell's Tavern was located at the end of the Fitzhugh place, east of Shirley Highway. Mary and John Urquhart ran a tavern at the site of the parking lot of the Plaza at Landmark. They ran the Mount Pierce Post Office from January 24, 1853, until it was discontinued August 22, 1866. In 1870, the first store was located on this property and operated by Albert Mead Lewis, with the post office here.

The first known church in this area was Lebanon Union Church, built about 1855 north of the Lebanon burying ground near Shirley Highway (Route 395) and Route 236. A recent archaeological dig uncovered the foundation. Buried in the cemetery there are some slaves, one of which was 15-year-old Henry Bell, who was

Lincolnia Elementary School, built about 1910, was closed as a school in 1929 and razed in the early 1940s. At the rear is the Lebanon School. (Courtesy Mary Margaret Pence)

Rev. Harry Marsh, minister at Lincolnia Methodist Church from 1917 to 1921, standing next to Bertha Crumbaugh, a Sunday school teacher. (Courtesy Mary Margaret Pence)

buried in 1871. Miss Eunice Barnum, Deming's niece, taught the first pay school in Lebanon in this church. The church was burned in 1862 by the Northern Army in its retreat after the Second Battle of Bull Run. Lebanon sent about five men to the Civil War. The Northern cavalry camped near here and Mosby and his men were around quite often. A story told in my family is that during the Battle of Bull Run soldiers and horses were seen going past very slowly, and as they returned, it was very fast because they were being chased.

Cemeteries, Churches, Farms, and Stores

Terrett Cemetery is a little-known burial ground located at the west end of Lincolnia Road. It is believed to be at the location of Woodville Cottage (owned by the John Hunter Terrett family) on Oakland Plantation. It is thought it was burned when General Sheridan and his Northern soldiers burned almost everything in the area at the end of the Civil War.

In 1872, Henry Manchester purchased five acres of land across from the Lincolnia Methodist Church for $50. He built a house there and later sold part of this tract to the Maynord Orndorff family, who ran a store there in the 1930s.

In 1875, bricks were gathered from the old church and a barn at Cottage Farm, and a one-room school was built east of the cemetery. Later, two frame stories were added and it was used as an elementary school until it closed in 1929, after which the students were bused to Annandale. In 1942, an elementary school was built on Beauregard Street and used until 1978. In 1988, it became low-income housing for the elderly.

During the Civil War, there was an army camp near Bren Mar. Mount Hebron was used as a hospital. Later, Shirley Keyes and her husband, America Johnson, moved to Mount Hebron, where their son, George, was born in 1875. Daisy Keyes McClintock, also born at Mount Hebron, ran a general store around the turn of the century where Key Towers now stands at Route 395 and Duke Street. Members of the Keyes family still reside in Lincolnia. Mount Royal, previously located on Pickett Street, also is thought to have been used as a hospital.

A Methodist church was chartered in Lincolnia in 1864. A church was built on Lincolnia Road in 1876 (east of the Lincolnia Post Office) of hand-hewn logs with help from men in the community. The minister, who sometimes served seven churches, lived in the parsonage built on Lincolnia Road in 1905. Three pulpit chairs were purchased for $15. The pastor's salary was often in arrears and a note found in the minutes asked that each family sell a hen to help with the deficit. Minutes also note that money was spent for cleaning the church, making wood fires and sending flowers to the sick for one dollar! After 79 years on Lincolnia Road, the church was outgrown and land was purchased from a part of the original Oasis Farm. A church was built, its cornerstone laid in December 1964.

Cora Amanda Barnum of Cottage Farm married William H. Lewis. (Cora and William were my grandparents.) In 1880, they bought Oasis Farm, where the Plaza at Landmark is now. Five generations of the Lewis family lived there before it was sold in 1968. Seven generations of the Lewis family have lived in Lincolnia.

Earl Lewis and his wife, Margaret, inherited Oasis Farm in 1921. Earl was a farmer and was often seen going down Route 236 with his horse and wagon to plow someone's garden, or perhaps mow their fields as late as the 1940s.

In 1894, John B. Carter opened a store west of what is now Landmark Mall and took over the post office until Lincolnia got rural delivery. Carter's son, Wesley, later drove the mail route. I have been told men from here worked as telegraphers at Edsall Station at the turn of century. When the train came through someone was waiting as the train slowed to either grab the bag of outgoing mail hung within arm's reach of the train, or to hang a bag of incoming mail it was delivering.

John Carter married Ella Crump. Both families are longtime Lincolnia residents. I have been told that Carter was the first in the area to buy a car. Years later, Wesley Carter had the area's largest commercial chicken hatchery. (It was moved to Charlottesville in 1957.) The hatchery stood next to the Lebanon School where the Plaza at Landmark now stands. The Crump family lived where a part of Lincolnia Hills is now. Ella Crump Carter's parents, Edward and Mary Crump, are buried in the Summers Cemetery. In 1894, students from the Episcopal Theological Seminary came on horseback and held Sunday school and church in the old school. Later a chapel and community hall were built on Lincolnia Road and used until the late 1930s. Adjoining this is St. Paul's Cemetery, which is still used today.

From Farms to Blacksmith Shops to Army Camps

Dove's Little Farm on Edsall Road was a working farm until early in the 21st century. Dove's father, George Munch, bought the property in 1896. The Munch family and, later, the Mark Dove family farmed there and took produce to the Alexandria Market for years.

Vernon M. Lynch and his parents came to the area in 1897 and bought Elmdale Farm, which was a working farm until World War II. They opened a golf course next to Route 236 in 1957. Later Lynch and his sons worked in real estate. In 1979 they gave 20 acres at the south end of Lincoln Avenue for Strawbridge Square, built in 1979 as low-income housing. Most of the Lynch Farm was sold and many townhouses have been built there.

James Howdershell came to the area in 1899 and purchased 450 acres of land on the west end of Lincolnia Road. An authentic deed shows the land was partitioned in 1855 and 64 acres were sold for $1,000. It is said that a house here was the main quarters for a big farm with many slaves. Winding stairs led to two small rooms used as slave quarters. Several years later, James' son, John Howdershell (who had married Josephine Nelson), came into this property. Josephine was principal of both the old

Lincolnia School and Annandale Elementary School for many years. This house was burned in 1959 to make room for the Peace Evangelical Lutheran Church, which was built about 1960. John's sister, Minnie Howdershell, married Willie Lee Clark. The Clarks built a house on Braddock Road past the Parklawn School in 1902 and ran a dairy farm there for more than 50 years. The Clark House was deeded to the Fairfax County Park Authority as a historical site in 1989. A dedication ceremony was held in May 1994 to mark its restoration.

Waldo Foster opened a blacksmith shop on Lincolnia Road in 1913. He remained there for 58 years and retired with a modern auto repair shop in 1971. Now there are townhouses on the property previously known as the Atkinson Farm and later owned by Foster's parents, who bought it in 1904. Berta Cassedy, daughter of another longtime Lincolnia family, married Waldo Foster. Her brother, Bill, was born at Cottage Farm in 1885. Before Berta was married, she and her sister Lenna traveled door to door in their horse and buggy, selling Larkin products. Members of the Cassedy family still live in Lincolnia.

In World Wars I and II there were Army camps in Lincolnia. In World War I horses were trained for the cavalry and in World War II men were trained. Both camps were located on a hill behind Oasis Farm.

Rachael Keyes and her daughters ran a weekend restaurant called Happiness Hill Tea House across from the Methodist Church from 1927 to 1932. They served southern fried chicken as their specialty and could also accommodate a few overnight guests. In 1952 two Keyes sons opened the Key Motel near Landmark. I believe these were the first restaurant and hotels in Lincolnia.

Churches, Post Offices, Townhouses, and a High School

Early in the 1930s, the Clyde Veach family opened a store and lunch room on Route 236 where the Brighton Mall is now. In the 1940s, the big attraction of their business was when they got one of the first televisions in the area. The Veaches ran their store until about 1965, when the property was sold, and in 1967, a gas station opened there. The Shoppers Food Warehouse that was in Brighton Mall moved to the Plaza at Landmark in 2000. A Grand Mart that sells international food had that space on the original Oasis Farm as of 2007.

William Durrer, a former area resident, served as the Fairfax County police chief from 1957 to 1975. His father, Haywood Durrer, had served as chief of the Alexandria City Police Department in the 1920s.

Among the several churches in the area is the Mount Pleasant Baptist Church on Lincolnia Road. It was founded by former slaves in 1867 for black parishioners. At first it was a one-room pine-log building and also was used as a school. A frame addition was built on in 1881, followed by a brick addition in 1931. Other additions followed in later years. There is also a cemetery on this property.

Taken near the present-day Lincolnia Methodist Church, this photo shows the widening of Route 236 through Lincolnia in 1948. In the background is the Orndorff family's barn and home. (Courtesy Mary Margaret Pence)

Josephine Lewis standing next to the Department of Highways Lincolnia sign in the 1940s. In the background is the home of Wesley and Ethel Carter. (Courtesy Mary Margaret Pence)

The Oasis Farm home, built in 1880. Five generations of the William and Susanna Lewis family have lived on this farm, located on Route 236 and Oasis Drive. (Courtesy Mary Margaret Pence)

We also have a Pentecostal church on Lincolnia Road, built in 1952; a Baptist church; the Queen of Apostles Church on Sano Street; and a Korean church on the corner of Braddock Road and Lincolnia Road.

Several changes were made in the 1960s. Virginia Plaza, Brighton Square, and Landmark Center opened in 1965. Virginia Village and Orleans Village opened in 1966. Oasis Farm was sold in 1967 and Brighton Mall opened in 1968.

Atlantic Research, which came into the neighborhood in the late 1950s, remained on Cherokee Avenue until it relocated in the 1990s. Many townhouses now stand on this space. Nearby is Cherokee Business Center, which opened in 1984.

The Lincolnia Post Office opened in Virginia Plaza in 1969 and was later moved to Lincolnia Road. Starting in 1969, mail was delivered to each residence.

Lincolnia has seen many changes and has made much progress. The first part of Shirley Highway opened in 1944 and another section in 1951, giving us faster access to our nation's capital. In the 1920s, high school students had to ride the train into Washington to attend school. Today we have the Thomas Jefferson High School for Science and Technology, formerly Thomas Jefferson High School. It opened in 1964.

Lincolnia is on the verge of revitalization, thanks to the efforts of concerned residents, so we look forward to even better things in Lincolnia's future.

The Olivers of Fairfax County
Leaving Their Mark in McLean and Great Falls
By Willard M. Oliver,[1] *Huntsville, Texas*

In 1761, at the height of the French and Indian War, a young man who was seeking adventure, fame, and glory enlisted in a company of Virginia troops.[2] His name was James Oliver, one of the first Olivers to settle in Fairfax County. Where he came from is largely unknown. One family recording says the Olivers came into St. Mary's County, Maryland, in 1632 and later migrated up the Potomac River and into Virginia.[3] Other research shows Olivers ranging from Boston, Massachusetts, to Virginia throughout the early colonial era.[4] The one thing that is clear from the historical record is that the Olivers came from England, seeking new opportunities like so many others during that time.[5] James Oliver found it by serving under Capt. William Edmonds and his county lieutenant, Thomas Harrison, in a newly formed Virginia company of soldiers. If James Oliver saw fighting, it was most likely on the western side of the Blue Ridge Mountains, for once General Braddock was defeated near what is now Pittsburgh, Pennsylvania, settlers to the west of the mountains were attacked by several hostile Indian tribes and required protection.

After the war ended, James Oliver returned to Fairfax County and settled in the Great Falls area. He settled on land owned by the Offutts. The land consisted of 633 acres on both the Maryland and Virginia sides of the Potomac River. The Offutts lived on the Maryland side and leased the land on the Virginia side.[6] In the 1770s or early 1780s, James Oliver built a log cabin, which still exists today on Towlston Road in Great Falls. Whom he married and how many children he had is also unknown. But he did have at least one son to whom he bequeathed his name.

This James Oliver was born in 1787, in that little log cabin in Great Falls.[7] The Great Falls area, known then as Kenmore, was largely a farming area, in which farmers sold their produce primarily to the local populace. Once the first wooden bridge was built across the Potomac in 1797, Virginia farmers could sell more of their produce in Washington, DC. This was further promulgated by the 1802 opening of the Center Market in Washington. Eventually the wooden bridge decayed and a second one was built in 1803. Six months later it was washed away. This cleared the way for the building of a suspension bridge across the river using a system of iron chains. Despite the fact the bridge is long gone, it is still known as Chain Bridge. This bridge brought more stability to the farmers by helping them get their produce to the District of Columbia.[8]

James Oliver married Mary Nalley around 1815. She was also born in Fairfax County, around 1790. According to the 1820 census, when James was 33, he had two "free white females under the age of 10," and four "white males under the age of 10." They were Angelina, Mary Ashley, Harrison, James, Aaron, and Eli. They had five more children in the coming years: Martha, Octavia, William Stanton, Sarah, and Cornelius. The census also listed them as employing two farmhands and owning one "female Slave under the age of 14." On September 29, 1836, after saving his money from farming the land, James purchased 457¾ acres from Eli and Margaret Offutt.[9] By the time James Oliver was 62 years old, his property was valued at $3,000. He died in 1878 at the age of 90, leaving a will dated January 9, 1878, which, in part, read:

> Know all men by these present that James Oliver being in my right mind and wishing to distribute my property as follows . . . all the household and kitchen furniture, I give and bequeath to my daughter Octavia Oliver. . . . I also give her my two horse wagon and double set of harnesses, for the present year. I also give her one cow with privilege of taking her choice and all the pork share. I also give her fifty two and one half acres of land, exclusive of one half acre which is reserved with the right of way this being for a family burying ground . . . and the balance of my land is to be equally divided between my nine children.[10]

It was in this "burying ground" that James Oliver found his final resting place.

More Burials than Markers

James Oliver willed that the Olivers and their descendants be buried in this cemetery. With many of the Oliver women marrying Thompsons, starting with the oldest daughter Angelina, the Thompsons inherited the right of burial in the cemetery. Although James Oliver was buried in the cemetery, there is no marker remaining to designate his gravesite. In 1918, J. Harry Shannon (better known as "The Rambler"), who wrote for the *Washington Star,* visited the Oliver home and cemetery.[11] He interviewed Octavia Swink, who told him she remembered as a little girl going to the funeral of a two-year-old sibling who was buried in a "little red box" around 1838. She also remembered attending the funeral of her brother, Harrison, who died in his early 20s. Other accounts from various descendants also recall attending funerals of relatives for which there are no gravestones. It is estimated there are as many as a dozen Olivers buried in the cemetery with no markers. When Octavia Swink died, her last will and testament added another half-acre to the cemetery. The shaded, one-acre Oliver/Thompson cemetery is still used and still maintained by the Thompsons.[12]

A number of the children of James Oliver raised large families of their own, each having their own impact on Fairfax County. Mary Ashley married Dr. Alfred Leigh, a prominent physician in the community, whose son of the same name also became a well-respected physician in the community. James Oliver, Jr., fought for the Union Army in the Civil War and, surviving the war, died in 1886.[13] He is also buried in the Oliver cemetery. Aaron Oliver did not join the military, but resisted Confederate conscription by selling fowl and produce to the secessionists.[14] At one point, when the Confederates came to take him, he kept out of sight until the men left and later took to the woods, where he hid for three days. His wife, whose principles Oliver said were as strong as his, brought him food. Despite not joining the Union Army, Aaron did assist generals Ord, Reynolds, and Meade as they needed information regarding Fairfax County roads, many of which were not on the maps or details of their obstructions were not known.

One other child of James Oliver, Lewis Edmund Oliver, married Lucretia Alice Tansill, who gave birth to five children, one of whom was Walter Tansill Oliver.[15] Walter Tansill was born in Kenmore on May 10, 1873, and, after attending local public schools and the Potomac Academy, found himself studying law at the University of Virginia in the fall of 1889. He left law school for several principal positions before returning to the University of Virginia to complete his law degree in 1897. He established a law firm in the City of Fairfax with Richard Cassius Leigh Moncure under the firm name of Oliver & Moncure. Walter Tansill purchased a home across from the Fairfax County Courthouse to serve as his residence and office. This building was known throughout most of the 20th century as the Oliver House.[16] Today, it is the Bailiwick Inn, a bed and breakfast of quite elegant prestige.

Walter Tansill Oliver also entered a life of politics, as many lawyers do. He first served as a member of the Fairfax Town Council and then as the town's mayor for five years. In 1908, he represented Fairfax County in the Virginia House of Delegates, a position he held until 1915. In 1919, he was elected state senator, representing the 14th District, which included not only Fairfax County, but Prince William and Arlington counties and the cities of Fairfax and Alexandria. He also served as a member of the board of visitors to the University of Virginia. He and his wife had four children, two of whom became well-known lawyers in their own right: Walter T. Oliver, Jr., and Robert Windsor Oliver. Walter Tansill died on November 22, 1932, after an apparent family dispute in which he suffered a fatal blow to his head.[17] The large obelisk in the Oliver cemetery bears his name.

Perhaps one of the more interesting anecdotes in the history of the sons of James Oliver is that of the three brothers who married three sisters. Aaron Oliver married Sarah Cornwell, Cornelius Oliver married Elizabeth Cornwell, and William Stanton Oliver married Maria Cornwell. William Stanton Oliver was 53 years old when his father, James, passed away. He received one of the four tracts of land from his father in 1862 and by 1870 he had land valued at $8,000 and personal property valued at $1,500.[18] There is the possibility that some of the personal property was also a drover's rest, or inn, located between Bellview Road and Towlston Road on the Georgetown Pike. A license to run this establishment was obtained by William S. Oliver on September 17, 1866, in order to serve the farmers coming from the west to deliver their goods to the Washington, DC, Central Market.[19]

The Oliver Store

William Stanton Oliver and his wife, Maria, had nine children—six girls and three boys: Mary; Eugenia (Ginny); Josephine; Ann; Victoria (Victory); Margaret (Maggie); William (Will) S., Jr.; Jesse; and Benjamin. Little is known about most of these children, but Jesse and Benjamin exerted an influence on Fairfax County. Jesse Oliver was born in December of 1857, growing up a farmer like his father. He married Cora V. Swink in 1889, and they had three children—Harry Lester, Jennings Brian, and Vernon Jesse (who lived only one year). In 1895, Jesse became the Great Falls postmaster in a country store located at the northwest corner of Georgetown Pike and Walker Road. Around this time, Jesse purchased the country store, which was called the Oliver Store for the rest of its history. The Oliver Store, "under Mr. Jesse Oliver's proprietorship, was said to be well stocked, including dry goods in its inventory."[20] In addition, "the presence of a warehouse (behind the store) indicates a capability to maintain a variety of goods in quantity, on site."[21] They also owned a substantial amount of land and a barn, as well as the house that was connected to the store. In 1905, Cora Swink Oliver took over as the Great Falls postmistress.

A series of unfortunate events soon caused the store, house, and farmland (141 acres) to change hands. On July 20, 1913, Jesse Oliver died, leaving everything to his wife. Harry Lester took over as postmaster from his mother following his father's death. However, a little more than a year later, Cora died intestate. Her two surviving sons took over the operation of the store. The ownership issue went to the courts. While it appeared the land would be divided between the two surviving sons, another tragic turn occurred. Jennings Brian and Mary Virginia Downey were married and had a child, Walton Downey Oliver. Jennings Brian and Mary took over running the Oliver Store. But three months after the baby was born, Jennings Brian died from a ruptured appendix. Mary was left to run the store by herself. However, ownership of the property became even more complicated. Harry Lester secured the assistance of Walter Tansill Oliver to bring a lawsuit to resolve the issue.

The judge in the case, Samuel G. Bryant, ordered a survey of the property.[22] The surveyors determined that the farmland, 137 acres, was worth approximately $10,000, while the farmhouse was worth $2,000, and the Oliver Store/house was worth $4,500. The judge determined that since Mary Oliver with a small infant could not feasibly run a farm, the land and farmhouse would go to Harry Lester and the Oliver Store/house would go to the infant Walton Downey Oliver. Because of the inequity in dollar amounts, Harry Lester was then ordered to pay Walton Downey Oliver $3,905 to equalize the portioning of the property. The court finally issued its decree in 1920, but the case remained open until 1951, when it was determined that Harry Lester had in 1937 paid the additional sum of money. The Oliver Store was eventually rented to Sidney M. Follin, Jr., who ran the store until 1931, when Harry Lester took over the store and operated it until 1950, when it was rented to the Ball family. The Balls rented a portion of the house and ran the store. Mary Downey

Oliver, who had married Willard Moore Oliver, a cousin of Jennings Brian Oliver, lived there until Willard's death in 1960. The house was then sold to Ed Schlegel, who ran a television repair shop out of the house until it was condemned and torn down in 1966.

Benjamin Oliver, the other son of William Stanton Oliver, about which much is known, also contributed to life in the Great Falls area. Although he had grown up as a farmer and worked a farm between Walker Road and River Bend Road, he also worked for the Washington and Old Dominion Railroad, which ran from Rosslyn in Arlington County through Fairfax County to Bluemont. He had three children—Vera; Benjamin Oliver, Jr.; and Willard.[23]

Willard Moore Oliver also grew up farming in a house across Walker Road from the Oliver Store. He enlisted in the U.S. Navy in 1916 at the age of 18 and served during World War I. Upon his return, he went back to the farm and eventually married Mary Downey Oliver. They had two children—Willard Eugene Oliver, born on July 13, 1920, and, 17 years later, Mary gave birth to Charles Jesse Oliver, born on October 16, 1937. Willard served a distinguished career in the military and Charles became a respected salesman. Charles Oliver married Carol Robertson and they had three children—Deborah, Nadine, and Willard (the author).

The Olivers have been a part of Fairfax County's history for approximately 250 years, and the history of Fairfax County is, in a way, the Oliver family history. Although many of the farms, store, and homes are long gone, some physical reminders of the Olivers remain—the old Oliver House in Fairfax City, the original log home that James Oliver built, and the Oliver/Thompson cemetery. Despite the fact that many of the Olivers have moved on to other counties, states, and countries, the Olivers helped build Fairfax County and the Oliver descendants continue to shape this great county today.

Endnotes

1. Willard M. Oliver is an associate professor of criminal justice at Sam Houston State University, Huntsville, Texas. He was born and raised in Herndon, Fairfax County, Virginia.

2. *Virginia Military Records* (Baltimore, Maryland: Maryland Genealogical Publishing Company, 1982), 146.

3. Vera Imboden's one-page reference sheet, Oliver family records.

4. Hugh R. and Margaret T. Oliver, *Sketches of the Olivers: A Family History 1726 to 1966* (Greer, South Carolina: Hugh R. and Margaret T. Oliver, 1996).

5. Hugh R. and Margaret T. Oliver, *Sketches of the Olivers.* Lienhard, *The Olivers* (Richmond, Virginia: Virginia Museum of History).

6. Jeannie Yoon, Carol Shupack, and Laura Craig, "Where a Persimmon Tree Once Stood: The History of 1032 Towlston Road." (Fairfax, Virginia: Fairfax County Historical Society, 1989).

7. Verified through the 1850 Census.

8. Elizabeth Miles Cooke, *The History of the Old Georgetown Road* (Annandale, Virginia: Charles Baptie Studios, 1977), 25.

9. Beth Mitchell, *Beginning at a White Oak* (Fairfax County, Virginia: County of Fairfax, 1977).

10. Fairfax County Will Book D-2, 59–60.

11. J. Henry Shannon, "The Rambler Visits," *Sunday Star,* May 26, 1918.

12. Fairfax County Will Book 9, 8.

13. Fairfax County Will Book E-2, 374.

14. Kenneth A. Link, "Courage and Betrayal: The Union Loyalists in Lewinsville," *Northern Virginia Heritage,* 1986, 1–6.

15. Biography of Walter T. Oliver in *The History of Virginia,* Vol. 7, 128.

16. *The Oliver House* (pamphlet); "Notes on the Oliver House," *Yearbook of the Historical Society of Fairfax County, Virginia,* Vol. 23 (1991–1992), 82–6.

17. "Walter T. Oliver Dies," *Fairfax Herald,* November 25, 1932.

18. Based on 1870 Census.

19. Fairfax County Minute Book 1863, 465.

20. Courtesy of Milburn Sanders and his unpublished manuscript titled *Great Falls: A Waterfall and a Community.*

21. Ibid.

22. *Oliver v. Oliver,* Chancery Suit No. 286, April 1, 1918, for the May term, 1916.

23. "Old Resident Dies" (Benjamin Oliver, Sr., obituary), *Fairfax Herald,* May 8, 1936, 1.

Historic Huntley
An Architectural Treasure
By Erica C.A. Hershler, *Alexandria, Virginia*

In southeastern Fairfax County, an empty, early 19th-century dwelling sits on a ter-raced hill, almost in defiance of the late 20th-century townhouses that surround it. Known as Historic Huntley, it was purchased by the Fairfax County Park Authority in 1989 and enclosed in a protective cage of cyclone fencing, topped by barbed wire. The fence offers some protection from vandals who don't care that the National Park Service placed it on the National Register of Historic Homes in 1972, or that the Virginia Landmarks Register and the Fairfax County Historic House Inventory also claim Historic Huntley on their listings.[1]

What makes this 2.75-acre property so special? It was built in 1825 for Thom-son Francis Mason, a grandson of the illustrious statesman George Mason IV of Gunston Hall, author of the Virginia Declaration of Rights. Originally a 1,000-acre plantation,[2] the property extended from its current site all the way down to Huntley Meadows Park, where irrigation ditches can still be seen near the nature path. Today, all that remains of the estate are the Federal-style manor house, multi-seat necessary (outhouse) with a storeroom on either side, an office with a root cellar, and an un-derground 20-foot domed brick icehouse, tenant house, and the ruins of a spring-house. Terraced landscaping still slopes gracefully toward Huntley Meadows Lane and Harrison Lane.

In the preface to *Huntley: A Mason Family Country House* by Tony Wrenn, archi-tectural historian Calder Loth describes Huntley as "one of Virginia's undiscovered architectural treasures."[3] Historic Huntley has architectural similarities with homes designed by Benjamin Latrobe and George Hadfield, both highly esteemed architects of the Federal period, but at this time, Huntley's designer still remains a mystery.[4]

Although eclipsed by his prominent grandfather, Thomson Francis Mason was himself a leader, having held numerous public offices, including several terms as mayor of the City of Alexandria and as justice of the peace, 11 years as president of the Middle Turnpike Company (which developed present-day Route 7), and seven years on the Alexandria Common Council.[5] In 1838, President Martin Van Buren appointed him as the first judge of the Criminal Court of the District of Columbia.[6]

Over the years, Thomson Francis Mason bought and sold many properties in the City of Alexandria, where he maintained permanent residency.[7] Historic Huntley was probably a summer retreat, but at this time research has yet to give a definitive answer on the family's use of the home.

A New Generation Takes Over
The next generation of Masons inherited Historic Huntley in 1859: Thomson Fran-cis Mason's sons John Francis and Arthur Pendleton, who had both enlisted with

the Confederate Army.[8] Ironically, in 1861, the 3rd Michigan Infantry camped on the property while the quartermaster and his wife stayed in the house. The officer's presence may have spared the house from the wartime fate of many nearby homes, including that of Richard Chichester Mason, Thomson Francis' brother. Richard's home, Okeley, was located in Huntley Meadows Park, near the park's rear entrance on south Kings Highway.[9] Taken over as a Civil War hospital, Okeley was deliberately destroyed to prevent the spread of disease.[10]

The end of an era came in 1862. That's when John Francis Mason and Arthur Pendleton Mason defaulted on a loan from a family friend, Benjamin King, and the property became the means to settle the debt.[11] Part of Historic Huntley's land had first been acquired by George Mason IV of Gunston Hall, but about 90 years later it passed out of the Mason family's hands. And as if to underscore this change, the new owner was a doctor with the Union Army. When a newspaper reporter for the *Syracuse (NY) Journal* visited Historic Huntley in the mid 1870s, he found vestiges of the Union camp on the property as well as 30 open graves from which the soldiers' remains had been removed.[12]

Dr. King sold Historic Huntley in 1868 to two farmers from New Jersey, Albert W. Harrison and Nathan W. Pierson, and they, in turn, split the property in 1871. Harrison Lane, on which Historic Huntley stands, is named after Albert W. Harrison, a leader in the agricultural community. The estate remained in his family for the next 78 years, almost as long as the Masons owned it.[13]

Friends of Historic Huntley

Prior to the Fairfax County Park Authority's purchase, there were three more owners, but only one household lived a significant amount of time at Historic Huntley. Ransom Place, Amlong Avenue and Amlong Place are nearby streets that were named after the Ransom Amlong family who resided in the house from 1949 to about 1970. Unfortunately, from that point on, the property stood empty, since the last owners were real estate speculators who didn't inhabit the house.[14]

Normally, a house boarded up and fenced off for years and years would present a forbidding exterior, yet people have always been intrigued by Historic Huntley and want to learn more. That's why a small but active citizens group formed in 1990 to open the mysterious dwelling to the public. The group—Friends of Historic Huntley—holds an open house twice a year in conjunction with the Fairfax County Park Authority.[15] Gates and doors are unlocked, windows are unboarded, and people are invited to explore. Over the years, tours have been supplemented with views of archaeological digs, artwork by local elementary school students, live music, living history performers, slide shows, lectures, games based on the Mason family, farming history and architecture. The puppet show featuring Thomson Francis Mason, some of his family, and even his horse, is a big draw.

For a time, Huntley Meadows Park offered to school groups History Mystery Tours that were conducted by costumed interpreters. One lesson in particular always entertained the students: after a corncob was passed around at the necessary, the students learned to their horror or amusement that the corncob was used as toilet paper in the early 1800s. There may even have been budding archaeologists on some of the tours. During one visit that took place after a heavy rain, a girl found a rusty horseshoe literally at her feet—a true testimony to Historic Huntley's farming past.

Endnotes

1. Friends of Historic Huntley, *Huntley: One of Virginia's Historical Treasures* (Alexandria, Virginia, 1999).

2. Ibid.

3. Tony P. Wrenn, *Huntley: A Mason Family Country Home* (Fairfax: Fairfax County Office of Comprehensive Planning, 1977), vi.

4. Friends of Historic Huntley, *Marker Dedication Ceremony Historic Huntley Mansion* (Alexandria, Virginia, 1994).

5. Mona B. Heath, "Thomson Francis Mason: An Obscure Figure in Alexandria's History," *Yearbook Vol. 17* (Fairfax, Virginia: The Historical Society of Fairfax County, Virginia, Inc., 1981), 1.

6. Ibid., 8.

7. Ibid., 9.

8. Susan Escherich/Friends of Historic Huntley historian, unpublished papers "History Mystery Tour Background Information," 1997.

9. Fairfax County Park Authority et al., "Historic Huntley," *Fairfax County Park Authority—Historic Huntley*, n.d., August 27, 2006, www.fairfaxcounty.gov/parks/histhunt.

10. Escherich.

11. Fairfax County Park Authority et al.

12. Wrenn, 17.

13. Ibid., 53.

14. Escherich.

15. Fairfax County Park Authority et al.

Historic Huntley, taken in 1969 by William Edmund Barrett. (Courtesy the Virginia Room, Fairfax County Library)

Taken on August 15, 1989, this photo of Huntley shows the building after it was purchased by Fairfax County and boarded up. Real estate speculators Kellog Shapiro Limited owned the house from 1970 to 1989, during which time it stood empty and suffered much vandalism. Note the middle gable has been truncated, although the dental molding was retained. The front porch, which used to protrude, was replaced with one flush with the building, and the railing was replaced with one of a different style. (Courtesy the Virginia Room, Fairfax County Library)

Gentleman Jim Robinson
The Family's Story
By Mary Robinson Ewell, as told to Deborah Karen Nagy, *Centreville, Virginia*

James Robinson, my great-great-grandfather, was a widely known and respected free African American in Fairfax County and surrounding areas during the 1800s. Many articles have been written about his life based on records in Prince William County, the Manassas National Battlefield Park Collections, and the Manassas Museum. For the most part, the records support the story that has been passed down to me from my ancestors, but our story also contains details not found in the documents. This is the family's story as it has been told to me.

James was born October 6, 1799, on a plantation in Bull Run owned by Robert "King" Carter, a relative by marriage to Robert E. Lee, according to my family. James' father is said to have been King Carter's grandson, Landon, and his mother an African slave on the plantation. From birth, James (Jim) was granted his freedom along with nine acres of land on what is now Bull Run Battlefield.

Landon Carter's two white daughters, Tasco and Bladen, were tutored by a man from England named Robinson. The young Jim learned to read and write alongside his white half-sisters and later took the name "Robinson." When he became an adult, he was known in the surrounding community as "Gentleman Jim Robinson."

On the land he had been given, Gentleman Jim built a 1½-story log house, from which he operated a drover's tavern. The tavern was a rest stop and watering hole for both white and black travelers who drove wagons on the Warrenton Turnpike (now Route 29) on their way to Alexandria, the local center of commerce. The house was located east of Henry Hill, site of the Henry House, which still stands on the battlefield. Both houses faced Warrenton Turnpike and were across the road from the Old Stone House. Early photographs reveal that the Robinson house had a stone chimney, rather than a wooden one, an indication that Gentleman Jim was already enjoying some prosperity.

From a neighboring plantation owned by John Lee of Manassas (a relative of Martha Washington, I was told), Jim met a slave girl named Susan Gaskins. Together they had six children—two girls and four boys. Gentleman Jim began buying and selling land in what are now Prince William and Fairfax counties, and his landholdings increased.

For years, Susan and the children all remained the property of John Lee. When Gentleman Jim could afford it, he bought his two sons, Bladen and Tasco (named after his white half-sisters). Then, when Lee died in 1847, Susan and their two daughters, Jemima and Etta, were freed. Jemima was my great-grandmother.

According to the family story, the other two sons, James, Jr., and Alfred, were skilled stonemasons. They were sold and sent south to New Orleans to work on plantations, possibly growing and harvesting sugar cane. The story goes on to tell that, after the war, Alfred made his way to Richmond and lived there for a while. He is said to have owned a horse, and when the horse died, Alfred returned home on foot from Richmond.

When the Civil War came to Virginia, the Robinson house was the scene of comings and goings by the armies from both sides. During the First Battle of Bull Run on July 21, 1861, Confederates streamed through the yard in retreat from the Union Army before returning to prevail over the Union advance. The Robinson property sustained little damage at that time.

Before that battle, Jim was entrusted with a set of heirloom silver belonging to the nearby Portici estate. The story goes that Jim sent his family to hide in a neighbor's cellar while he hid with the silver under the stone bridge on Warrenton Turnpike. Being entrusted with the silver reflected how highly he was regarded by the white community.

The Robinson House as a Field Hospital

In August 1862, during the Second Battle of Bull Run, the Robinson house served as a field hospital for the Union troops under the command of General Sigel. After the battle, the Union forces ransacked the Robinson home, taking canned and stored food, moving furniture to the barns and elsewhere, eating the fruit off the trees, and destroying much more. After the war, in 1872, Gentleman Jim sued the federal government for $2,080 in damages. The family records I possess include a transcript of the hearings. In the hearings, Gentleman Jim testified that he was a Union sympathizer, but that it was definitely the Union Army, not the Confederates, who raided his home. He further testified that the troops used or destroyed 20 tons of hay, 60 bushels of wheat, 20 bushels of corn, cabbages, potatoes, barrels of salted herring, 300 pounds of bacon, cattle, two horses, 7 hogs, two beds and bedding, household groceries, kitchen utensils, and two miles of fencing. On March 3, 1873, he was awarded $1,249, a significant sum at that time.

By 1860, Gentleman Jim owned $2,500 in personal property and about 1,700 acres, making him the third largest property holder among the free African Americans in the area. He is said to have used his knowledge and influence after the war to help newly freed slaves find work in the community.

Jim Robinson died on October 16, 1875, and was buried in the family cemetery located near the present-day Fairfax County–Prince William County line. The land he held at his death was parceled among his heirs. His son, Tasco Robinson, received the land on which the house was built, and in 1926, the original log house was dismantled and a 2½-story structure erected in its place. In 1936, Tasco's grandson, McKinley Robinson, sold seven acres and the Robinson house to the National Park Service. This second structure was destroyed by fire on July 26, 1993. It was presumably the work of vandals.

After the destruction of the Robinson house, the grounds became an archaeological dig site. (A former student at Mountain View School in Centreville earned social studies credits by participating in that excavation.) It is an African practice to dig a large hole on the grounds of one's home for the disposal of trash. When it gets full, another hole is dug. So, years later when the archaeologists uncovered these repositories, they discovered hundreds of artifacts. Some of the artifacts are now on display at the Manassas Battlefield Museum; others are stored by the National Park Service at Harper's Ferry, West Virginia. All that remains of the Robinson house today is its stone foundation. Its location is identified by a historical marker on Route 29.

My great-grandmother, Jemima Robinson Harris, gave part of her inheritance of land to Fairfax County Public Schools for the purpose of building a school for young African Americans. The school was built across Route 29 from the site of the present London Towne Elementary School. I attended that school, built on my ancestor's land, during my first year of elementary school in 1951. I remember it had three rooms and a wood stove. An Assembly of God church now stands where my first school used to be.

Each fall during the celebration of Centreville Days, I dress in a period gown and retell this story of my great-great-grandfather, Gentleman Jim Robinson. His life and his legacy comprise an important chapter in the history of Fairfax County.

The Formation of the Mount Vernon Ladies' Association
Dedicated Women Save George Washington's Estate
By Emily Coleman Dibella, *Mount Vernon, Virginia*

George Washington's Mount Vernon Estate is one of the most recognizable landmarks in Fairfax County, and perhaps in the world. But this famous home was almost lost, if not for the courageous actions of a group of pioneering women who saved Mount Vernon from ruin and who continue to maintain this icon of American history.

After the 1799 death of George Washington, the ownership of Mount Vernon changed hands among family members five times. Residing in the home of Washington proved to be more of a hardship than a privilege. Like most Virginia plantations, Mount Vernon suffered from exhaustion of the soil from over-farming and the constant fluctuation of market forces, to the point that profits all but vanished. At the same time, Washington's heirs were burdened by hordes of travelers who arrived at Mount Vernon, eager to see what was rapidly becoming a national shrine.

A National Treasure for Sale

John Augustine Washington III, George Washington's great-grandnephew, owned the estate beginning in 1829. As his funds dwindled and the wear and tear of hundreds of visitors began to take its toll, Washington could do little to maintain the mansion and its surroundings. Several columns on the piazza rotted away completely, so the roof was propped up with old ship masts. Not surprisingly, Washington was approached by speculators who hoped to develop the property into a commercial enterprise. Washington revealed that his best offer for the property was $300,000, yet he could not consent to sell Mount Vernon without an absolute assurance that it would be protected, as is, for future generations.

Washington approached Congress and suggested the government purchase the mansion. But his timing was unfortunate. Factions from the North and South were already immersed in the debates about land and slavery that would eventually lead to the Civil War. Very little attention was paid to Washington's offer. He then changed course and traveled to Richmond, where he made a similar appeal to the General Assembly of the Commonwealth of Virginia. The reaction there was much the same.

The mansion continued to decline. Thus it happened that, on a moonlit evening in 1853, Louisa Dalton Bird Cunningham stared out from the deck of a passing steamer and saw the first president's house in near ruin. She was making the long trip home to South Carolina from Philadelphia, where her 37-year-old daughter, Ann Pamela, was being treated for severe spinal injuries she had suffered when she was thrown from a horse as a teenager. For 21 years, Ann Pamela Cunningham had been "confined to her couch" at Rosemont, a plantation in rural South Carolina. The pain from the injury was ever present, limiting her ability to participate in the active life of plantation society, and she quickly became isolated, depressed, and lonely.

So when she received a letter from her mother (some accounts insist it was soaked in tears) describing the shocking condition of George Washington's home, Ann Pamela was seemingly ill equipped to face such a formidable challenge. But her mother's message was an inspiring one: If the men of America are allowing the home and burial place of its most respected hero to go to ruin, why can't the women of America band together to save it?

In fact, Ann Pamela's unusual circumstances made her take risks that few other women in the 19th century would have considered. In an age when it was scandalous for a woman's name to appear in a newspaper, unless it was to announce her marriage or her death, Cunningham initiated a daring public campaign to rally thousands of women around a noble cause. With few prospects for a fulfilling life as a wife or mother, she made a conscious decision to focus her energies on rescuing Mount Vernon.

Appeals to the Women of America

Cunningham's first hope was to gather enough contributions from patriotic women, primarily in the South, to allow the Commonwealth of Virginia to purchase and manage the property. Her initial letter of appeal was published in December 1853 in the *Charleston Mercury*. Although several other newspapers picked up the letter, the governor of Virginia, Joseph Johnson, was far from an enthusiastic partner in the campaign to solicit funds to purchase Mount Vernon. In all probability, the vast majority of American men quietly disdained this bold appeal initiated by and directed to women. Cunningham correctly judged that, with or without the approval of men, she had gone too far to turn back. As more and more newspapers published her appeals, and a variety of extremely influential women agreed to become the original vice regents, Cunningham found herself a most unlikely celebrity.

Gradually, several men outside the realm of government—including lawyers, judges, and bankers—expressed a willingness to help Cunningham. The most indispensable was Edward Everett of Boston, known as the most respected orator of his time. His résumé was exceptionally distinguished and his lectures were celebrated with great fanfare across the nation. Cunningham convinced the silver-tongued Everett to adopt her cause. Over the next three years, Everett delivered a lecture on Washington 129 times around the country. In the end, Everett's efforts contributed more than $69,000—more than a third of the purchase price.

By the spring of 1858, in large part due to Everett's phenomenally successful speaking tour, Cunningham was so confident the association would reach its goal that she arranged to meet with John Augustine Washington III, hoping to bring closure to the purchase of Mount Vernon. According to Gerald W. Johnson in his book *Mount Vernon: The Story of a Shrine*, Cunningham found Mount Vernon's owner in

Shown on the veranda of Mount Vernon are the first vice regents of the Mount Vernon Ladies' Association, the oldest historic preservation organization in the Unites States.

"the worst of tempers." Washington was cordial but firm in his refusal of Cunningham's offer, and after listening to "all the arguments she could bring to bear . . . with cold civility, he left her and she went to bed in a state of collapse."

Sealing the Deal

After a nearly sleepless night in the historic residence she now envisioned slipping out of her grasp, Cunningham started anew the following day, this time calling upon the sage advice of Washington's wife. The result was inevitable. Several hours later, on April 6, 1858, Washington signed a contract of sale with the Mount Vernon Ladies' Association of the Union for $200,000. According to the association's annual report of 1858, the terms were $18,000 down, with an additional $57,000 to be paid no later than the first of the new year. The remaining balance was to be paid in three annual installments.

Within the next two years, thousands of people donated to the fund, including President James Buchanan. The association paid Mount Vernon's purchase price in full on December 9, 1859—more than two years ahead of the deadline—and took possession on the 128th anniversary of George Washington's birth, February 22, 1860. It was a time when sectionalism threatened the Union and cast a pall over the nation, but despite the tense political climate, Cunningham and her secretary, Sarah Tracy of New York, moved in to begin the process of preservation. The house was completely empty with the exception of a few artifacts from the Washington family. Fortunately, Cunningham possessed the sensibilities of a true preservationist. She immediately dismissed all proposals to tear down Washington's outbuildings or to transform the landscape.

Just a few months after settling into Mount Vernon, Cunningham was forced to return to her home in South Carolina due to the death of her father. Tracy remained at Mount Vernon with Upton Herbert, the superintendent selected at the suggestion of the Washingtons, and a handful of workmen and servants. Little did they know of the drama and adventure that would soon envelop their stoic little staff.

War erupted in April of 1861, preventing Cunningham from returning for six years. Union troops stormed nearby Alexandria and moved within four miles of Mount Vernon. Confederate forces were almost as close to the south. Cunningham was insistent that George Washington's estate be sheltered. She persuaded Tracy to stay at Mount Vernon, believing that ". . . the presence of ladies there would be its greatest protection, even from the unruly." Herbert also agreed to remain on the estate.

Even though Tracy wrote to Cunningham, "This war news has completely unnerved me," she showed no fear when it came to securing Mount Vernon as a "national spot" free from armed conflict. She first demanded an audience with Gen. Winfield Scott in Washington, who agreed to forbid his soldiers from entering the Mount Vernon grounds under arms. Tracy garnered a similar pledge regarding

Confederate troops from the governor of Virginia. Still, Tracy was constantly forced to meet with both armies to remind them of the agreements when officers were replaced with men new to the region.

Surviving the War

Tracy also had to request special passes that would allow her to pass through military encampments just to make ends meet. She raised cabbages on the estate, drove a wagonload to market in the nation's capital and Alexandria, and would return with much-needed meat, salt, and pepper. Simply providing enough food for the table was a full-time occupation, and the continuing restoration of the house was all but abandoned when workmen had to be discharged after the association could not pay them.

Soldiers encamped around Mount Vernon were the only visitors Tracy and Herbert entertained, and the two caretakers frequently found themselves showing them around. Typically, the soldiers were gracious guests, as reported by Tracy in a May 1861 letter to Cunningham:

> Mr. Herbert told the Captain of the Company of soldiers stationed near here your wishes with regard to their not coming here in uniform or armed. They have behaved very well about it. Many of them come from a great distance and have never been here, and have no clothes but their uniforms. They borrow shawls and cover up their buttons and leave their arms outside the enclosures, and never come but two or three at a time. That is as much as can be asked of them.

There were times, however, when bands of soldiers did not adhere to the association's wishes. But Tracy always stood firm. In one instance, large groups of soldiers "refused to stack their arms, but were for over an hour straggling all over the place without any order, their guns in their hands. The colonel said that if the men were to lay down their arms, we must have an order to that effect from General Scott." Tracy recorded that she went directly to Colonel Townsend, who relayed her concerns to General Scott. "He said I should have all I wanted. I received a pass and a written order, signed by General Scott, to show any of his officers who do not wish to obey our regulations."

Taking Risks

On September 13, 1861, John Augustine Washington III, a member of Gen. Robert E. Lee's staff, was killed in a skirmish in West Virginia. Federal officers had learned that a large part of the money the association had paid to assume ownership of Mount Vernon was left in the hands of an Alexandria banker, and the Union had every intention of confiscating the funds as enemy property. The banker tipped off

Tracy of the officers' plans. She took the cash, tucked it snuggly at the bottom of her egg basket during one of her regular runs to deliver fresh eggs, and hurried to Washington, DC, to the bank of George W. Riggs, who served as treasurer of the association. While Riggs counted out the eggs he wanted, Tracy rented a safe deposit box for the cash.

A few months later, Union officers forbade Tracy from crossing into Washington, telling her that Gen. George B. McClellan had deemed her pass null and void. When told that only President Lincoln could overrule McClellan's order, Tracy skirted a blockade, talked her way into the White House, and convinced the president himself to write a note to the general kindly requesting an exemption to his orders. As Gerald Johnson noted, "with what astonished amusement the ungainly giant must have looked down upon this bit of femininity who had burst in upon him bristling with indignation against his field commander, and demanding that he order the United States Army to stand aside while she passed with her groceries."

Never one to back down, Tracy faced serious obstacles in her quest to keep Mount Vernon safe from harm, which she detailed in letters she loyally penned to keep the association informed of events. Crossing army lines and convincing officers to let her pass or escort her to the next company of soldiers ensured that George Washington's house would remain unscathed. In some of this country's darkest hours, Tracy and Herbert protected the estate, paving the way for the Mount Vernon Ladies' Association to preserve Mount Vernon and Washington's legacy for future generations.

Since 1860, more than 80 million visitors have made George Washington's Mount Vernon Estate and Gardens the most popular historic home in America. Through thought-provoking tours, entertaining events, and stimulating educational programs on the estate and in classrooms across the nation, Mount Vernon strives to preserve George Washington's place in history as "First in War, First in Peace, and First in the Hearts of His Countrymen." Mount Vernon is owned and operated by the Mount Vernon Ladies' Association, America's oldest national preservation organization, founded in 1853.

Source

Gerald W. Johnson, *Mount Vernon: The Story of a Shrine.* (Mount Vernon, Virginia: Mount Vernon Ladies Association, 1991, originally published by Random House, New York, 1953).

Elhanan Winchester Wakefield
Methodist Minister
By Mildred M. Moore, *Alexandria, Virginia*

Elhanan Winchester Wakefield was an adventurer, soldier, circuit-riding Methodist minister, and family man. Born in Ohio, Wakefield traveled west as a young man, joined the Massachusetts cavalry during the Civil War, and settled in Fairfax County, Virginia, after the war. Wakefield Chapel, named in his honor, displays a plaque stating (in error) that he is buried across from the chapel. Reverend Wakefield, his first wife, several of his children, and a granddaughter are actually buried in the cemetery of the Annandale United Methodist Church in Annandale, Virginia.[1] Newspaper articles, military records, court records, church records, obituaries, and headstone inscriptions provide insight into the adventures and life of Elhanan Wakefield.

He was born in Proctorville, Lawrence County, Ohio on July 2, 1834.[2] He was the son of Elhanan Winchester Wakefield and Candance Gillette.[3] The 1850 census of Windsor Township, Lawrence County, Ohio, showed E.W. [Elhanan] Wakefield, age 16, living with his parents and seven siblings.[4] In the 1860 census for Windsor Township, Lawrence County, Ohio, Wakefield's parents were still living in Windsor Township,[5] but their son, the adventurer, had begun his journey in life.

Sometime after 1850, Wakefield traveled to Kansas, where he is said to have espoused the antislavery movement and joined John Brown's raiders.[6] Other accounts state that he was also an Indian fighter in the Black Hills of South Dakota, and a miner in Colorado.[7] With Gold Rush fever, Wakefield moved to California before 1860. In the 1860 census for San Jose, Santa Clara County, California, Wakefield was listed as a day laborer, possibly working in a mine.[8]

Civil War Service
Young men on the West Coast followed the Civil War in the newspapers and were anxious for a chance to join in the fight. They knew if they joined a California state unit they would be stationed in the West, fighting Indians, guarding commerce trails, or other duty. Late in the summer of 1862, a group of men originally from the East contacted Massachusetts Governor Andrews with a proposal. The men proposed raising 100 volunteers to form a separate company as a part of the cavalry regiment that was being formed in Massachusetts. The governor agreed to the proposal but told the men they would have to provide their own uniforms and equipment. The young men used their enlistment bounty to pay for their passage and left San Francisco aboard the ship *Golden Age* on December 1, 1862. At the Isthmus of Panama the men left the ship and traveled across the land by rail. Upon reaching the coast, they boarded the *Ocean Queen* and continued their journey. The men arrived at Camp Meigs at Readville, Massachusetts, on January 4, 1863. After basic training,

Elhanan Winchester Wakefield, c. 1913–1920. Wakefield is on the right, with his arm in a sling. The other gentleman is unknown. (Courtesy the Virginia Room, Fairfax County Public Library)

the company was transported to Fortress Monroe, Virginia. On February 22, 1863, they were placed on active duty where Wakefield served in Company F.[9]

Wakefield participated in battles in Gettysburg, Northern Virginia, and the Shenandoah Valley in Virginia. Sgt. Elhanan Wakefield was wounded at Tom's Brook (Fisher's Hill), Virginia, on October 9, 1864.[10] He was discharged on March 28, 1865, in Annapolis, Maryland, as a result of his wounds.[11] In 1903, an x-ray showed that Wakefield still had two pieces of metal in his shoulder.[12] Battlefield wounds continued to plague him for the rest of his life.

Fairfax County, Final Home

Instead of going back to Ohio after his discharge in 1865, Wakefield returned to Virginia and settled in the community of Annandale in Fairfax County. The Annandale Methodist Church (at the time called Annandale Methodist Episcopal Church) was burned during the Civil War. It was rumored that Wakefield was the Union soldier who gave the order to burn the church. However, this could not be verified through military or other records. On returning to Annandale, he became an active member of the community. He helped rebuild the Annandale Methodist Church that he was purported to have burned during the Civil War.

On September 7, 1865, Wakefield married Mary Rebecca Tennison, daughter of Samuel Tennison and Lucinda Marts.[13] They were married in the home of the bride's mother in Fairfax County, Virginia. Mary Rebecca Tennison, a native of Virginia, was born in April 1842. After settling in Annandale and becoming active in the life of the community and the local Methodist church, Wakefield was ordained a Methodist minister. He was involved in church work in Fairfax, Alexandria, and Loudoun counties of Virginia, and in the District of Columbia.[14]

The Wakefields acquired a farm in the vicinity of Annandale in Fairfax County. Wakefield, the restless adventurer, was now a farmer, family man, church leader, and circuit-riding Methodist minister. Ten known children were born to the couple: Malcolm Mallow Wakefield, October 5, 1865/6–August 17, 1944; Blanche L. Wakefield, January 2, 1869–January 3, 1902; Elwin E. Wakefield, born about 1872; Oneita Grace Wakefield, June 1874–March 3, 1920; Mabel Wakefield, born about 1876; Rowell/Roy Wakefield, born about 1879; Theresa May Wakefield, January 24, 1881–October 30, 1886; Jane/Jeanne Winchester Wakefield, born March 1883; Lowell Tennyson Wakefield, March 24, 1885–April 4, 1978; and Harry Harold Wakefield, May 3, 1886–October 5, 1959.

In the early morning hours of November 9, 1907, Mary Rebecca Tennison Wakefield, age 66, died at home.[15] On November 11, she was buried in the cemetery of the Annandale Methodist Church.

In June 1908, Wakefield was injured while trying to catch his horse.[16] This injury, combined with earlier battle wounds, was taking a toll on the elderly man of 74. In October 1908, he rented his farm to a Mr. Hains.[17]

In September 1909, widower Wakefield married Ada C. Haines in Baltimore, Maryland. He was 74 and Ada Haines was 22 at the time of their marriage. At a reception in Baltimore, someone questioned the differences in their ages, to which Ada replied it was nobody's business but hers whom she married, and quickly left the house with Wakefield.[18]

In July 1910, Wakefield visited his relatives in Ohio.[19] Presumably the visit was to introduce his new wife to his family in Ohio. He made several trips back to Ohio to visit family, and in the summer of 1919 he vacationed for several weeks in Wayne County, Pennsylvania. This was reputed to be his first vacation, ever.[20]

Elhanan Winchester Wakefield died on January 21, 1920, at home in Fairfax County. He was buried beside his first wife in the cemetery of Annandale United Methodist Church. On February 20, 1920, Rev. George H. Williams wrote an article in memoriam that included these words:

> In the recent death of Rev. E.W. Wakefield I am free to say, that a good man has gone to his eternal reward. I have known Bro. Wakefield for 45 years or more and having been a member of the Quarterly Conference that gave him license to preach, I have followed with interest his career from that time, and in no small measure, have I known of his untiring labor not only in the church, but among the people who needed his help, for indeed "the night was never so dark or the roads too rough" for Bro. E.W. Wakefield to go to those who were sick or in trouble.[21]

Endnotes

1. Mildred M. Moore, *Annandale United Methodist Church Cemetery*, research of families buried in the Annandale United Methodist Church Cemetery (Annandale, Virginia, March 2005), 130.

2. Obituary of Rev. Elhanan W. Wakefield. This article indicates that Rev. Wakefield was born in 1824, however all other sources and data refer to his birth year as 1834. *Fairfax Herald*, January 30, 1920, 3.

3. Melvin Lee Steadman, Jr., *Falls Church by Fence and Fireside* (Bowie, Maryland: Heritage Books, Inc.), 445–449.

4. Ohio, Lawrence County. 1850 U.S. Census, from National Archives microfilm M432, roll 51, *Heritage Quest Online* PERSI, Heritagequest-online.com/ hqoweb/library/do/census/results : 2005.

5. Ohio, Lawrence County. 1860 U.S. Census, from National Archives microfilm M653, roll 152, digital images. *Heritage Quest Online* PERSI, Heritagequest-online.com/ hqoweb/library/do/census/results : 2005.

6. Obituary of Rev. Elhanan W. Wakefield, *Ironton Register* (Lawrence County, Ohio), February 2, 1920, www.lawrencecountyohio.com/obits/newspapers/vol1/ObitWZ.

7. Obituary of Rev. Elhanan W. Wakefield, *Fairfax Herald*, January 30, 1920, 3.

8. California, Santa Clara. 1860 U.S. Census, from National Archives microfilm M653, roll 65, digital images. *Heritage Quest Online* PERSI, Heritagequest-online.com/ hqoweb/library/do/census/results : 2005.

9. *Second Massachusetts and Its Fighting Californians* online, 2mass.omnica.com/.

10. Obituary of Rev. Elhanan W. Wakefield, *Fairfax Herald*, January 30, 1920, 3.

11. *Second Massachusetts and Its Fighting Californians* online, Roster Company F, M–Z, 2mass.omnica.com/.

12. *Fairfax Herald*, October 2, 1903, 2.

13. Elhanan W. Wakefield and M. Rebecca Tennison, *Marriage Folder—1865*, Fairfax County Circuit Court Archives, Fairfax, Virginia.

14. *Fairfax Herald*, January 30, 1920, 3.

15. Ibid., November 15, 1907, 3.

16. Ibid., June 26, 1908, 2.

17. Ibid., October 30, 1908, 3.

18. Ibid., October 10, 1909, 3. Ada may have been related to the Mr. Hains who was renting the Wakefield farm. Multiple spellings were found for Ada/Ida and for Hanes/Haines. For this story, Ada Haines was chosen.

19. *Fairfax Herald*, July 1, 1910, 2.

20. Ibid., August 1, 1919, 2, and August 29, 1919, 2.

21. Ibid., February 20, 1920, 2.

Was She or Wasn't She?
Antonia Ford: Polite Southern Lady or Confederate Spy?
By Katherine Cooch Rau, *Warwick, Rhode Island*

"A young lady at or near Fairfax Court House, has also been arrested, and some others—all charged with giving information that led to the late raid on the Court House."[1] This young lady in question was Antonia Ford, who was arrested as a Confederate spy on March 16, 1863. Her guilt was confirmed to her accusers when an honorary commission given her by Confederate Gen. J.E.B. Stuart was discovered during a search of her home. As recounted in *The Washington Star,* it read,

> TO ALL WHOM IT MAY CONCERN;
> Know Ye, that reposing special confidence in the patriotism, fidelity and ability of Antonia J. Ford, I, James E.B. Stuart, by virtue of the power invested in me as Brigadier General in the Provisional Army of the Confederate State of America, do hereby appoint and commission her my Honorary Aide de Camp, to rank as such from this date. She will be obeyed, respected, and admired by all the lovers of a noble nature. Given under my hand and sealed the Headquarters Cavalry Brigade at Camp Beverly, the seventh day of October, A.D. 1861, and the first year of our Independence.
>
> J.E.B. Stuart [impression of his signet ring][2]

However, despite this paper evidence, the leader of the raid, John Singleton Mosby, as well as J.E.B. Stuart, always denied that Ford acted as a spy for them. So, was she or wasn't she?

Antonia Ford was born in 1838 in Fairfax Court House, Virginia. Her father, Edward R. Ford, was a successful merchant. As a result, Ford grew up comfortably and was raised "for society." As an adult, she was known both in Fairfax and Washington social circles and was considered to be beautiful and well mannered.[3]

The Fords were staunch secessionists and supported the Confederacy throughout the war. As the war progressed, Fairfax quickly became an area populated by Union soldiers. While the Fords' sympathies to the Confederacy were known, they nevertheless had much contact with Union soldiers and loyalists. They even took in Union soldiers as boarders. Because of this proximity, Antonia Ford was in a good position to gather Union activities information that she could pass to the Confederates. She thus sought information using a unique method: "She seemed to do nothing, talked of everything except actual military affairs, and allowed the other fellow to presume she sided with him."[4] One person commented that she listened, "in an apparently very careless and no-interest-to-me-I-assure-you manner, which quite deceived the men."[5] She then passed on what she knew to her Confederate military contacts.

A couple of stories of Antonia Ford's spying exploits are fairly well known. The first occurred shortly after she had begun gathering documents and subtly soliciting information that would be helpful to the Confederacy. She learned that Union soldiers planned to search local homes for Confederate contraband, so she gathered all her spying materials and put them under her huge hoop skirts and then sat down in a chair. When Union soldiers arrived to search her house she remained seated as they searched. After they finished searching her home, one of the officers who was investigating asked her to stand up. She famously replied, "I thought not even a Yankee would expect a Southern woman to rise for him." She embarrassed the officer enough that he did not force her to stand. The search party left and thus she was able to protect the fruits of her spying.[6]

Spying Exploits

Another famous story of spying involving Antonia Ford was her 20-mile ride before the Second Battle of Bull Run. She had come upon information that the Union forces "planned to use Confederate colors to draw the Confederate soldiers away from their assigned positions"[7] in the forthcoming battle. She couldn't find anyone to deliver this important information to General Stuart so she set out with an aunt on the 20-mile ride to his camp, where she successfully passed along her information.[8]

The most famous of Antonia Ford's spying exploits was her connection to Colonel Mosby's raid, which resulted in the capture of Gen. Edwin H. Stoughton. Ford's brother was a soldier under Gen. J.E.B. Stuart's command. It was this connection that enabled Ford to meet both General Stuart and Colonel Mosby.[9]

James Ewell Brown "J.E.B." Stuart was born in 1833 and grew up on a small plantation in rural Virginia. He did well in school and, with his family's political connections, was able to get an appointment to West Point for the class of 1854. After a successful career in the U.S. Army, fighting Indians in the West, keeping the peace during fighting over slavery in Kansas, and quelling John Brown's uprising at Harpers Ferry, he resigned his commission when his home state of Virginia seceded. He decided he would "go with Virginia. . . . I for one would throw my saber in the scale consecrated by principles and blood of our forefathers—our constitutional rights without which the Union is a mere mockery."[10] He entered the Confederate army as a lieutenant colonel and quickly received a promotion to brigadier general after performing admirably in the first major battle of the war.[11]

John Singleton Mosby's background was much less conventional than Stuart's. He was born in Powhatan County, Virginia, in 1833 and grew up in Albemarle County. As a young man he attended the University of Virginia where he studied Greek literature. He was expelled after he shot a classmate in what he claimed was an act of self defense.[12]

After serving nine months of his 12-month jail sentence, he became a lawyer. He was very opposed to secession and said he would fight for the Union if it came to war. However, once his home state of Virginia seceded, he joined the Confederate army, declaring, "Virginia is my mother, God bless her! I can't fight against my mother, can I?"[13]

Mosby entered the Confederate army as a private at the beginning of the war and rose to the rank of colonel by the end of the war.[14] He came to serve, while he was a private, under J.E.B. Stuart. He greatly admired Stuart and was a very successful scout for him. Eventually, he convinced General Stuart to let him go out on his own to conduct guerilla activities against the North.

A previously discussed, Antonia Ford's brother was also a soldier under General Stuart, and the Fords knew both Mosby and Stuart. Through her social position in Fairfax Court House, Antonia also became friends with General Stoughton. In fact, in a letter that became public after Stoughton's capture, a Union soldier wrote home discussing Stoughton's friendship with a known Rebel sympathizer. He wrote, "There is a woman living in the town by the name of Ford, not married, who has been of great service to General Stuart in giving information, et cetera—so much so that Stuart has conferred on her the rank of major in the Rebel army. She belongs to his staff. Why our people do not send her beyond the lines is another question. I understand that she and Stoughton are very intimate. If he gets picked up some night, he may thank her for it. Her father lives here, and is known to harbor and give all the aid he can to the Rebs, and this in this little hole of Fairfax, under the nose of the provost-marshal, who is always full of bad whiskey."[15]

The actual raid that resulted in General Stoughton's capture occurred on March 9, 1863, and was described at the time in the *Alexandria Gazette:*

> Last night the Confederates, under Captain Mosby, came into this town, dressed in Union clothes took all the pickets and patrols prisoners, one hundred and ten fine horses, General Stoughton, of the Vermont Brigade, prisoner; hunted for Capt. L.E. O'Conner, of the New York 5th, Provost Marshal of the town, but could not find him; they also searched Colonel Johnstone's house for him but he made his escape in his night clothes.
>
> The night was dark and rainy, but these guerillas dashed to and fro in a reckless manner, although their plans, were well matured, as the different squads who went to the different headquarters would indicate.[16]

The raid was considered highly successful both because of what was secured—"General Stoughton, along with close to forty of his soldiers, over fifty of his horses, and all of his weapons"[17]—and because of the embarrassment it caused the Union. Stoughton had been caught alone sleeping and Colonel Johnstone had escaped only by running away in his nightshirt and hiding under the outhouse. Stoughton and several other officers had their reputations and careers ruined as a result.

Mosby's raid was wildly reported in the press. "The *New York Times* called the capture 'utterly disgraceful.' The *Baltimore American* styled Stoughton 'the luckless sleeper at Fairfax' who was 'Caught Napping.' . . . A humorous howl went up, and Lincoln joined in by making a statement to the reports. He said that he did not mind losing a brigadier as much as the horses, 'For I can make a much better Brigadier in five minutes, but the horses cost a hundred and twenty-five dollars apiece.'"[18]

Less reported on, but still speculated about, was the involvement of local sympathizers in giving Mosby the information necessary to carry out his plan. The Secret Service was brought in to investigate and fairly quickly Antonia Ford became the prime suspect. She was known to have been friendly with both Mosby and Stoughton. An undercover female agent posing as a Southern sympathizer got Ford to show her the commission from Stuart, as well as to discuss how she had gathered information about "the number of our forces there [at Fairfax Court House] and in the neighborhood, the location of our camps, the places where officers' quarters were established, the precise points where our pickets were stationed, the strength of the outposts, the names of officers in command, the nature of general orders, and all other information valuable to the rebel leaders"[19] and passed it to Mosby before the raid.

Ford was promptly arrested. "At her home were found letters which indicated she had been corresponding with Confederate authorities at Richmond."[20] The Secret Service also found her honorary commission.

Ford was imprisoned in Old Capitol Prison. It is unclear exactly when she was released, although she was definitely out of prison a year after the raid. At this time she married one of her Yankee jailors. When asked by a friend in a letter how such a staunch Confederate could marry a Northerner, she replied, "I will tell you truly, Sallie, I know I could not revenge myself on a whole nation, but felt very capable of tormenting one Yankee to death, so I took the Major."[21]

So, was she or wasn't she? While Ford's involvement in the raid has been questioned, it does seem clear that Ford was involved in spying. Ample evidence in her confession to the undercover Secret Service agent, the correspondence found in her home between her and Confederate authorities in Richmond, and the open secret of the Fords' support of the Confederacy would seem to indicate it.

As for the raid, it seems less clear what her involvement was. On the pro side is Ford's own confession to the undercover female agent. On the con side was the behavior of Stuart and Mosby, who always denied her involvement. During the war, General Stuart tried to her release from prison by soliciting from Mosby a letter saying she had nothing to do with it. While Stuart died during the war, Mosby lived until the age of 81 and always maintained Ford's innocence. In fact, he famously wrote in a letter to a friend in 1900, "That he met Ford when he was a private on picket duty early in the war but did not communicate with her again until after the war: 'She was innocent as Abraham Lincoln.'"[22]

Photographic portrait of Antonia Ford by O.H. Willard, 1200 Chestnut Street, Philadelphia. (Courtesy Library of Congress)

Endnotes

1. News Bullet, *Alexandria Gazette,* March 16, 1863.

2. Ibid., March 18, 1863.

3. Larissa Phillips, *Women Civil War Spies of the Confederacy* (New York: The Rosen Publishing Group, Inc., 2004), 52–5.

4. Harnett T. Kane, *Spies for the Blue and Gray* (New York: Doubleday & Company Inc., 1954), 169–70.

5. Ibid., 170.

6. Larissa Phillips, *Women Civil War Spies,* 59.

7. Ibid.

8. Harnett T. Kane, *Spies for the Blue and Gray,* 171.

9. Larissa Phillips, *Women Civil War Spies,* 55.

10. Thom Hatch, *Clashes of Cavalry: The Civil War Careers of George Armstrong Custer and Jeb Stuart* (Pennsylvania: Stackpole Books, 2001), 1–14.

11. Robert J. Trout, *They Followed the Plume: The Story of J.E.B. Stuart and His Staff* (Pennsylvania: Stackpole Books, 1993), 3.

12. James A. Ramage, *Gray Ghost: The Life of Col. John Singleton Mosby* (Kentucky: The University Press of Kentucky, 1999), 11–22.

13. Ibid., 32.

14. Kevin H. Siepel, *Rebel: The Life and Times of John Singleton Mosby* (New York: Saint Martin's Press, 1983), 135.

15. Virgil Carrington Jones, *Ranger Mosby* (North Carolina: The University of North Carolina Press, 1944), 98.

16. "Raid Upon Fairfax Court House: Fairfax Court House March 9," *Alexandria Gazette,* March 9, 1863.

17. Elizabeth D. Leonard, *All the Daring of the Soldier: Women of the Civil War Armies* (New York: W.W. Norton & Company, 1999), 46.

18. James A. Ramage, *Gray Ghost,* 71.

19. Elizabeth D. Leonard, *All the Daring of the Soldier,* 48.

20. Virgil Carrington Jones, *Ranger Mosby,* 98.

21. Elizabeth D. Leonard, *All the Daring of the Soldier,* 50.

22. James A. Ramage, *Gray Ghost,* 74.

Robert Gunnell of Langley
An Emancipated Slave
By Henry C. Mackall, *McLean, Virginia*

On September 18, 1849, Margaret Adams Brooke signed a paper acknowledging receipt of $300 from Benjamin F. Mackall of Langley in Fairfax County, Virginia, representing payment in full for her Negro man "Robert known by the name of Robert Gunnell" and all of his possessions.[1] In addition to Gunnell's household furniture and farming implements, this personal property included three horses, one cow, one cart, and two wagons.[2]

One year later, he and his family were living at Langley. Although he was still a slave, Gunnell's household was enumerated in the U.S. Federal Census (not the slave census) taken on September 19, 1850:

Robert Gunnell	54-year-old mulatto male
Harriet Gunnell	43-year-old mulatto female
Mary Gunnell	20-year-old mulatto female
Sarah Gunnell	16-year-old mulatto female
Ludwell Gunnell	11-year-old mulatto male
Ida Gunnell	5-year-old mulatto female
Florida Gunnell	4-year-old mulatto female
Nancy Gunnell	3-year-old mulatto female
Richard Gunnell	2-year-old mulatto male
David Curtis	12-year-old mulatto male

Robert's occupation was listed as farmer. Neither he nor Harriet was able to read or write. Everyone in the household was Virginia born.[3]

On November 6, 1851, just two years and two months after the purchase, Benjamin F. Mackall executed a document by which he "emancipated and set free from slavery my negro man named Robert otherwise Robert Gunnell." The deed of manumission was not recorded in Fairfax County records until June 3, 1856.[4] Years later one of his descendants stated that Robert had bought his freedom for $300, paying $50 per year.[5] He had obviously received special and unusual treatment even prior to the conveyance to Mackall. Proof of this is evidenced by the accumulated personal property mentioned in the conveyance.

The slave, later known as Robert, was inherited by Margaret Brooke from her father, Samuel B. Adams, who died in 1840.[6] Adams owned a plantation on Difficult Run near Hunter Mill. "Bob" was listed in Adams' estate inventory. On June 25, 1844, Margaret Adams and Benjamin Brooke entered into a marriage contract now commonly referred to as a prenuptial agreement. The contract listed many items of property owned by Margaret, including slaves named Ellie, Robert, Verlinda, Fanny,

Maria, Louisa, Frederick, Darcas, and Philip. All the slaves were "presently employed on the said [Difficult Run] plantation" under the control of her brother, Gabriel Adams.[7]

On June 16, 1856, Robert Gunnell registered as a free Negro with the clerk of the court of Fairfax County. In the registration certificate he was described as 60 years of age, five feet four and a quarter inches tall, with straight hair, and scars on the back of each hand.[8]

Shortly after he was freed, Robert Gunnell acquired from the Lee family title to 6½ acres at Langley adjoining the Mackall farm:

> I have this day surveyed a lot of land at Langley, Virginia, for Robert Gunnell, of which the above plat is a correct representation and on which he has been living for the last 15 years[9] to my knowledge. Boundaries etc.: Beginning at the south east corner of this lot in the boundary of the Turnpike road and running thence with the boundary of a lot of land belonging to G.F.M. Walters, N. 18 deg. W. 60 poles to the line of E. Mc-Nerhany; thence with his line S. 71 deg. W. 18 poles to a platened stone; thence S. 18 deg. E. 60 poles to the turnpike road; thence with said road N. 71 deg. E. 18 poles to the beginning containing 6½ acres of land. I have surveyed this lot of land once before by the request of B.F. Mackall but the plat and survey were lost in the beginning of the war.
>
> Fairfax, Va. June 18, 1864
> B.D. Carpenter, Surveyor

> Washington City, DC, July 26, 1864
> I believe that all the heirs of my mother Elizabeth Lee, were willing to give a deed to the annexed described land to Robert Gunnell. And I do by these presents convey all my right, title, and interest in the foregoing described 6½ acres of land to Robert Gunnell.
>
> [Signed] Mrs. A.M., Washington[10]

Richard Bland Lee, who at the time owned both Langley Farm and Sully Plantation, conveyed both properties in trust on January 1, 1809, to secure a debt owed to Bushrod Washington. At the same time he conveyed in trust for the benefit of his wife, Elizabeth:[11]

> . . . the following slaves namely John and his wife Alice & their children Patty, Betty, Henry, Charles, Johnny, Margaret, Milly and Frank; [Beaver] Ludwell and his wife Nancy and their Children Caroline, Harriet, Frederick, Ludwell & Barbara; Henny and her child Ealenor; Rachel and her child Rachel; two sisters Kitty & Letty and their Brothers Alexander and

Alfred and the following Men: George a Blacksmith, Henry a carpenter, Henry Butler a Waggoner, Tom a Carter, Thornton a Cook & Saml. a smith and Jack a plow boy.[12]

The elder Ludwell was referred to on several occasions in Lee family correspondence dating back to December 24, 1803. By a deed of emancipation dated February 1, 1817, in the name of Richard Bland Lee but signed by his wife, Elizabeth, the slave Beaver Ludwell was set free on the condition that "Beaver undertakes to keep my present woman, Nancy, his wife, who is in an infirm state of health." Shortly thereafter Richard Bland Lee, who was then living in the District of Columbia, executed a note and gave as security his slaves:

> . . . Peter—commonly called Peter Jones—Alexandar, Henry and Thomas, valuable young men; Frank, a valuable boy; Kitty and Caroline, young women; Harriet and Betty, valuable girls, and Letty and her two sons William and Albert; . . .[13]

The child Harriet was undoubtedly the person who lived with Robert Gunnell and later married him in the District of Columbia on January 15, 1866.[14]

In the 1859 personal property tax records for Fairfax County, Robert Gunnell was shown as a free male with two slaves over the age of 16 and two over the age of 12. He had five farm animals valued at $180 and furniture worth $50.[15] In 1861, he had only two slaves over the age of 12 with seven farm animals worth $200 and furniture worth $50. He was also shown as owning some type of horse-drawn vehicle valued at $25.[16]

During the Civil War, Robert and Harriet may have moved for a time into the District of Columbia. On April 16, 1862, the United States Congress passed an act freeing slaves in DC and providing for compensation to their owners. On May 26, 1862, Robert Gunnell of Fairfax County filed a petition including claims for the value of 10 slaves he owned, who had been freed. The petition was witnessed by Benjamin F. Mackall and E.C. Morgan. The names, approximate ages, and identifications of those listed in the claims with the dollar amounts claimed for each were as follows:

Name and Age	Identification	Amount Claimed	Description
Paulina Booth, 24	Wife of William Booth of Georgetown	$1,000	Quite black
Sarah Fairfax, 26	Widow of John Fairfax	$1,000	Brown
Florida Gunnell, 17		$900	Brown
Anna Gunnell, 12		$800	Brown

William Fairfax, 8	Child of Sarah	$500	Black
Frank Fairfax, 4	Child of Sarah	$250	Black
Thomas Fairfax, 3	Child of Sarah	$200	Black
Joseph Fairfax, 1	Child of Sarah	$100	Black
Sally Booth, 1	Child of Paulina	$100	Brown
Charles Gunnell, 4 mos.	Child of Florida	$50	Brown[17]

Gunnell claimed that "these persons always lived in the District of Columbia and are still in the District of Columbia."[18] He further stated that:

> He [had] purchased Paulina Booth of E.C. Morgan Esq. Attorney at law at Washington DC and Evelina his wife as per bill of sale, Sept. 20th 1858 for seven hundred dollars which bill of sale is recorded in the Deed Records of Washington Co. in Liber J.A.S. No. 161, fol. 153 and he has mislaid the original bill of sale, so that he cannot produce it. He purchased the said Sarah Fairfax with her child William, then a small infant and Florida and Anna of Major Richard B. Lee[19] then of the U.S. Army, in Washington, DC in the year 1854 for the sum of six hundred dollars, very cheap, but Florida and Anna were both small at the time—the Bill of sale is in the possession of B. F. Mackall Esq. who has mislaid it. The said Frank, Thomas, Joseph, Sally and Charles have been born of the said Paulina, Sarah and Florida since their said purchase by this petitioner.[20]

Paulina Gunnell and John Anderson obtained a marriage license in DC on January 14, 1867.[21] Pursuant to a marriage license issued in DC on August 16, 1862,[22] Sarah Gunnell Fairfax married William Lucas Ashton, who came to Virginia in 1861 from Baltimore as a cook in the Bushtail Regiment of the Union Army. Following the marriage, they lived on the upper part of the farm at Langley owned by Benjamin F. Mackall under an arrangement with him whereby they took care of the house during the war so that the U.S. Army would not tear it down.[23] A marriage license was issued in the District of Columbia on July 30, 1864, to David Thompson and Flinda Grinnell [Florida Gunnell].[24] On April 25, 1867, a marriage license was issued in DC to Ludwell Gunnell and Elizabeth Dixon.[25]

A 1912 newspaper article titled "Lost by Emancipation: Many Negroes Who Owned Slaves were Reduced to Poverty by the Civil War" cited Robert Gunnell as:

> . . . a free blooded African Virginian who married a slave wife, but bought her of her master before their first child was born, becoming the legal owner of her and her children and of their daughter's children.[26]

Deed of manumission, dated 1849, made by Benjamin F. Mackall freeing his slave, Robert Gunnell. (Courtesy Mackall family collection)

Road district warrant ordering the treasurer of Fairfax County to pay Robert Gunnell "ninety five cents" for working on a road. (Courtesy Mackall family collection)

After the Civil War

Following the war, Gunnell filed a claim in the amount of $1,715.50 for losses he had suffered. In 1871, a report was filed by the Commissioners of Southern Claims allowing him $1,058.99 for forage and fuel. The remainder was disallowed.[27]

The census taken on July 15, 1870, showed Robert and Harriet residing in Providence Township, Fairfax County, at Langley Post Office.[28] They were aged 70 and 60, respectively. Robert was a farmer who owned real estate valued at $1,000. Harriet's occupation was "keeping house." Neither one could read or write. Living with them were their daughter Anna and her husband Peter Fossett, who had been married the preceding December. Anna, a domestic servant, was 19 and Peter, a farm hand, was 30. While Peter could not read or write, it appears that Anna could.[29]

In 1866 the black members of Nelson's Chapel began to worship at Robert Gunnell's house, which was said to be the first place a black could worship freely in Fairfax County.[30] They then erected a simple, two-story building where Gunnell's Chapel was later constructed. This building "was also the first Negro school house in the area."[31] By deed dated December 17, 1879, Robert and Harriet conveyed a half-acre to the trustees of the church[32] and "On Sunday, June 25, 1899, construction began on what became Gunnell's Chapel."[33]

Robert and Harriet executed a deed of trust dated November 22, 1873, conveying the 6½-acre property at Langley to Russell Barr in trust to secure Caroline Shaw, Harriet Gunnell, Barbara Butler, and Ludwell Lee—heirs at law of the late Ludwell Lee. Each held a note for $90 made by Robert.

Harriet died on June 23, 1883, of old age (age 83). Her death was reported to the county by her husband.[34] On October 18, 1883, Robert conveyed to Richard Payne a half-acre adjoining Langley farm, now owned by W.W. Mackall (son of Benjamin). Robert's mark on the deed was witnessed by Ludwell Gunnell and William L. Ashton.[35]

Aside from his farming activities, Robert Gunnell obviously had a number of vocations. On September 19, 1865, he was ordered "with his hands, to work on the road from Lewinsville to Langley."[36] For serving as an overseer of road work during the period 1872 to 1873, Robert Gunnell received payment of $8.14 from the Providence Township clerk, George W. Hawxhurst.[37] For the year ending July 1, 1874, he received a $5 payment for burying Renah Hawley, a pauper.[38] A warrant for 95¢ in favor of Robert Gunnell was issued on September 10, 1887, by C. Money, clerk of the Board of Road Commissioners of Providence District.[39]

On October 25, 1888, Robert Gunnell conveyed the remainder of his land to Florida Thompson and Annie Fossett.[40] The deed recited the consideration as love and affection, past support, and the agreement of his two daughters to henceforth clothe, support, and maintain him. Robert Gunnell died on October 28, 1890.[41]

In September 1891, his son, Ludwell Gunnell, filed suit in the Circuit Court of Fairfax County against Florida Thompson, David Thompson, Annie Fossett, and

Peter Fossett to enforce a judgment lien on the land that had been owned by his father.[42] In the suit he alleged he had personally paid the creditor, Miss Mary Jones, and that the lien had been assigned to him.[43]

From the depositions that were taken at the offices of Mackall & Maedel in Washington, DC, it appears that Robert Gunnell had leased a farm from Mary Jones, who obtained a judgment against him for unpaid rent. In October of 1879 Robert Gunnell had filed a petition in the District of Columbia to collect a sum owed him by Brooke Makel [Mackall] for work Robert had performed for him. This money—$800—was paid by Brooke Mackall and, through a series of lawyers, found its way to Miss Jones. For some reason the judgment lien was assigned to Ludwell Gunnell, who claimed he had paid it with his own funds. In her testimony given on October 14, 1893, Florida Thompson, a 47-year-old widow living at 1642 10th Street, N.W., Washington, DC, stated that her father said he paid the judgment with his money. She testified that she was living at her father's place about 1880 and that she had been there all her life.[44]

The case was settled in 1894 when Sarah Ashton (and William L. Ashton, her husband); Richard Payne, a grandson of Robert Gunnell; and Ludwell Gunnell, heirs at law of Robert Gunnell,[45] conveyed to Annie Fossett and Florida Thompson the land previously deeded to them by Robert Gunnell.[46] Following this there were several lawsuits culminating in a deed from Thomas R. Keith, Special Commissioner of Sale, to Richard Payne.[47] Payne was still living on his property when the census was taken in 1930. He was a 75-year-old head of household with no other persons listed.[48]

While no descendants of Robert Gunnell still live in the area of his home, there are undoubtedly many in the metropolitan area of Washington, DC. Perhaps some of these descendants will be able to share family stories that will help resolve or explain some of the inconsistencies found in the records that have been cited. Robert Gunnell's house at Langley is no more, but the building next door, which was known as "Gunnell's Chapel," is still standing as it has for many years, serving, as The Rambler stated in a 1927 article, "in memory of that worthy old man."[49]

Endnotes

1. Original document in possession of the author, great-great-grandson of Benjamin F. Mackall.

2. Ibid.

3. U.S. Federal Census, 1850.

4. Fairfax County Deed Book X3, 339.

5. "Spirited Debate in Congress Preceded District Emancipation," The Rambler, July 3, 1927.

6. Fairfax County Will Book T1, 202–6; Fairfax County Will Book U1, 279–81.

7. Fairfax County Chancery Final File #1847-032. Not long after the marriage contract was signed, Margaret and Benjamin were married. They soon began to have problems and

Margaret filed a suit "by Joshua Gunnell, her next friend" to clarify and reform the marriage contract. The court appointed Joshua Gunnell as trustee to take possession of all her separate assets and to hold them for her benefit. The conveyance of Robert Gunnell to Benjamin Mackall was also signed by Joshua Gunnell as trustee and by Benjamin Brooke who acknowledged having received the money paid by Mackall.

8. Donald Sweig, *Registrations of Free Negroes: Commencing September Court 1822, Book No. 2 and Register of Free Blacks 1835, Book 3* (Fairfax, Virginia: Clerk of the Courts, 1977).

9. Since 1849.

10. Ann Matilda Lee Washington, daughter of Richard Bland Lee and his wife, Elizabeth Collins, was the widow of Dr. Bailey Washington, who died in Washington, DC, on August 14, 1854. *Lee of Virginia 1642–1892: Biographical and Genealogical Sketches of the Descendants of Colonel Richard Lee* (Philadelphia, Pennsylvania: Edmund Jennings Lee, Maryland, 1895), 371.

11. Daughter of Stephen Collins of Philadelphia. *Lee of Virginia 1642–1892,* 370.

12. Fairfax County Deed Book J2, 106.

13. The Rambler, November 12, 1916, 3.

14. Wesley E. Pippenger, *District of Columbia Marriage Licenses* (Westminster, Maryland: Family Line Publications, 1994–1996), 120.

15. Fairfax County Personal Property Tax Book, 1859, 31 (line 29).

16. Ibid., 1861, 18 (line 29).

17. "Petition of Robert Gunnell," Records of the Board of Commissioners for the Emancipation of Slaves in the District of Columbia 1862–1863, Microfilm Roll 2, No. 442, National Archives, Washington, DC.

18. Ibid.

19. Son of Richard Bland Lee and Elizabeth Collins. *Lee of Virginia 1642–1892,* 41.

20. "Petition of Robert Gunnell," Records of the Board of Commissioners for the Emancipation of Slaves in the District of Columbia 1862–1863, Microfilm Roll 2, No. 442, National Archives, Washington, DC

21. Pippenger, *District of Columbia Marriage Licenses,* 5.

22. Ibid., 7.

23. William L. Ashton, Claim No. 20.471, March 31, 1877, Southern Claims Commission, National Archives, Washington, DC

24. Pippenger, *District of Columbia Marriage Licenses,* 290.

25. Ibid., 120.

26. *Washington Post,* December 1, 1912, M1.

27. Gary B. Mills, *Southern Loyalists in the Civil War: The Southern Claims Commission* (Baltimore, Maryland: Genealogical Publishing Co., Inc., 1994), 242.

28. U.S. Federal Census, 1870.

29. Ibid.

30. "Gunnel's *[sic]* Chapel Methodist Church, Langley, Virginia" in *Yearbook Volume 15* (Fairfax, Virginia: Historical Society of Fairfax County, Virginia, Inc., 1978), 71.

31. Ibid., 71–2.

32. Fairfax County Deed Book A5, 428.

33. "Gunnel's *[sic]* Chapel Methodist Church, Langley, Virginia," 72.

34. Elizabeth R. Frain, *Fairfax County, Virginia, Death Register, 1853–1896* (Westminster, Maryland: Willow Bend Books, 2002), 78.

35. Fairfax County Deed Book E5, 253.

36. Fairfax County Minute Book 1863, 244.

37. *Fairfax News,* July 4, 1873, 2.

38. *Fairfax News,* June 26, 1874, 3.

39. Road District Warrant, September 10, 1887. Original document in possession of author.

40. Fairfax County Deed Book H5, 238.

41. Fairfax County Chancery Final File #1894-028.

42. Ibid.

43. Miss Mary Jones was the daughter of General Roger Jones.

44. Fairfax County Chancery Final File #1894-028.

45. Ibid.

46. Ibid.

47. Fairfax County Deed Book D7, 199–200.

48. U.S. Federal Census, 1930.

49. "Spirited Debate in Congress Preceded District Emancipation," The Rambler, July 2, 1927.

My Dear Son
Letters from Gray's Hill Near Woodlawn
By Susan Hellman, *Herndon, Virginia*

Morris and Sarah Wilkinson started a new life in Fairfax County, Virginia, in March or April of 1886.[1] When they relocated to Virginia from Cecil County, Maryland, four out of five of their adult children joined them. Their eldest son, William C. (Willie, b. 9-26-1853), a grain broker with the Philadelphia Bourse, lived in Philadelphia with his wife, Eva. The four children who came to Virginia with their parents were Caleb Kirk (Calie, b. 9-22-1855), Anna Mary (b. 12-30-1858), Sarah R. (Sallie,[2] b. 1-6-1861), and Francis Hilary (Frank, b. 3-29-1864). Like many people of the period, the Wilkinsons were prolific letter writers. Their letters offer an intriguing glimpse of life in Fairfax County near the turn of the 20th century. In a letter to Willie, Morris described the purchase of the family's new home in Virginia:

> We got home from Va last evening—had a very nice time. Ma enjoyed it immense. Stopped in Washington a day . . . attended the President's[3] reception. Ma shook hands with him.
>
> Well we got a farm at last, the Grays Hill property near Mt. Vernon, had a sweat over it, the man hung for $3,300 and I told him I would not give it. So . . . we struck a Bargain—$3,000—$1,000 cash, $1,000 in 3 years and $1,000 in 5 years. Mr. Gillingham said to me, "Well I don't know how good a day's work you have made but I think that is the best one you ever made." It is a much better property than I thought, a long pretty water view. You can see the Steamers & Boats at all times. Pretty good Buildings. House has 9 or 10 Rooms. The parlor is large & it takes 40 yards of carpet to cover it. The Buildings are not old but solid and substantial. We get possession January 1st. I paid $100 on it. The Bal of $1,000 to be paid 1st of January.[4]

Gray's Hill was located near Woodlawn, on a bluff overlooking Dogue Creek. The land was part of the original Woodlawn plantation that George Washington gave to his foster-daughter, Nellie Custis, when she married his nephew Lawrence Lewis. In 1846 the Troth-Gillingham lumber company purchased the 2,030-acre Woodlawn plantation from Nellie Custis Lewis' heirs. Partners Jacob Troth and Chalkley Gillingham sold some of the land to fellow Quakers from New Jersey, while retaining timber rights. Thomas Wright, who originally scouted the land for Troth-Gillingham, constructed Gray's Hill between 1846 and 1848 on 99.56 acres that he had purchased from Gillingham.[5]

Morris wrote to Willie about preparations for the move:

Well Frank just got home from Va, he put in 12 acres of wheat & 2 acres of rye for early pasture. He says the grass is sit elegantly on about 20 acres of last year wheat—likes the land and the neighborhood, in fact I think as every one down there seems to say that we have a bargain—land easy to work & production—has been raising the best crops in that neighborhood. . . . My article says to get possession Jan 1st 86 but I think we will try and move most of the things down about 1st Dec & just lock them up in the house or one of us go down & take part of the stock. I don't know which. Farming commences there about 1st of Feb & there will be so many things to do I feel as though we ought to be there as soon as possible to be getting fixed up . . . it will take $100 to move—$300 or $400 to fix up house such as building a Porch and fencing yard &c. The kitchen is not much & we will have to build one. Aside from this, the house is good, 8 rooms, ceilings 9 ft down and 8 feet upstairs.[6]

Once the Wilkinsons arrived in Fairfax County, the locals immediately welcomed them into the community. The Wilkinsons, also Quakers, quickly became valued participants in the area's vibrant social life. As is often the case, the family's children increased the opportunities for social interaction. Sarah wrote about some of the regular community events: "The Farmers Club meets next 7th day at John Ballinger's.[7] The Literary Club meets 3 of the 7th days in the month, and the Farmer's Club on the 4th one, so every 7th day is taken up, and parties between whiles, they keep things moving down here."[8] She described a fairly typical week:

The children were invited to John Ballinger's last evening to tea. . . . On 5th day the children were invited to Lukens' to tea, next 4th Lukens' young folks are coming here to tea. Norman Gibbs and wife are coming the same evening to spend the evening and set a day for the children to go there to tea. Next 7th day night there is a party at Moons'. On the 21st of March Charlie Lukens is going to have a party, it will be his 21st birthday. Next 7th day the farmers club was to have met at Valentine Baker's, but he and his wife both died within a week of each other, so there will not be any club until the 8th of March at Courtland Lukens'. We are all invited to John Ballinger's day after tomorrow to the "Sewing circle."[9]

In addition to the social whirl, other more serious events also gripped the community. Sarah kept Willie and Eva informed of all the neighborhood happenings. Soon after the Wilkinsons arrived, one of the local youths went missing:

Francis (Frank) Hilary Wilkinson, his son Charles Kirk Wilkinson, and his wife Mary Alice Ballinger Wilkinson in a photo taken about 1907. (Courtesy Wilkinson family collection)

Taken at Gray's Hill on May 20, 1906, this photo shows, in the front row, left to right, an unknown black child, Anna Mary Wilkinson Brosius, her mother Sarah Haddock Kirk Wilkinson, and an unidentified man. Standing in the back row, left to right, are Caleb Kirk Wilkinson, Samuel Martin Brosius, and Sarah R. Wilkinson. (Courtesy Wilkinson family collection)

. . . a boy come to the door and asked if we had seen anything of Jane Doe, John Doe's daughter. Said that Walter Walton's folks had been there, and had taken her out driving as she has not been well for a few days. They found she was out of her mind, and Walter told her father that they must not lose sight of her. She went upstairs, her father went up pretty soon, and she was lying on the bed, he thought she was asleep. When he went up the second time she was gone. They think she jumped out of the window, it was a little before sunset. Some of the neighbors saw her go by, the whole neighborhood are out in search of her. Pap was out, it is 12 o'clock. The men have gone to get a boat to search the creek. They think she has made way with herself.[10]

The next night, Sarah continued her letter:

Lewis Gillingham and Mr. Mero's son found Jane Doe this morning about 3 o'clock, in that big pine woods south of our house. There is 2,700 acres of woodland in that tract. She was sitting on the ground entirely naked. They put their coats around her and carried her home. They have her in the parlor today, the windows fastened, and several of the neighbors staying with her. She took a spell today and wanted to go away again. . . .[11]

Another interesting incident took place a few months later:

The night you went away I was out in the kitchen about 10 o'clock. Something commenced to knock on the side of the kitchen, it thumped harder and harder. I began to get frightened & called Pap to come there; he ran to the front door, and said the noise was there, when he got to the kitchen it was stopping off. I then went up to bed. Grand Ma[12] called me into her room, and said, "What is the matter? I have been tossed from one side of the bed to the other, and back again." Then it just occurred to me that it was an Earthquake. We got a Washington paper next day with the account of the destruction of Charleston in it, was it not terrible?[13]

In June of 1887, Sarah wrote about the Moon girls being in a serious buggy accident:

Last 1st day, Jessie and Lutie Moon drove down to meeting, going home, as they went down "Gum Spring" hill, the horse got to trotting, Jessie grabbed the lines out of Lutie's hand, and the horse ran off the bridge, upset the buggy and threw both girls into the creek. Lutie scrambled out,

Looking in 1887 from Gray's Hill toward the Potomac River in the background are Anna Mary Wilkinson Brosius, on the left, and her sister, Sarah R. Wilkinson, on the right. Rex is on duty at their feet. (Anna Mary Wilkinson married Samuel Brosius in June 1911.) (Courtesy Wilkinson family collection)

In an undated photo taken at Gray's Hill and standing left to right are Sarah R. (Sallie) Wilkinson, Caleb Kirk Wilkinson, Anna Mary Wilkinson, and Carrie Pennock (a relative). (Courtesy Wilkinson family collection)

and saw Jessie's overskirt in the water. She got hold of it and with great effort pulled her ashore, but she was insensible, and her face cut, and nose broken, she was terribly hurt. There was a colored man coming along, he caught the horse, and got on him, rode to Moons' for some of the family, told them one of the girls was badly hurt, and the other one killed. He thought that Jessie was dead.[14]

Social and Religious Life

Generally, Fairfax County life was less dramatic. Running a family farm was an exhausting business, but community members managed to find plenty of time to enjoy themselves. Skating parties on the frozen Potomac River, sleighing, fishing, frequent teatime visits, horse and buggy expeditions, picnics, and other miscellaneous activities kept everyone very busy and closely connected with the community as a whole.

Intellectual pursuits were very popular. Frank was elected president of the debate society in 1886, just a month or so after moving to the area. The topic of debate on May 1, 1886, was "Resolved: Which was the greenest, a country man in the city or a townsman in the country?"[15] The following week's topic was: "Resolved that the inventive genius of this age is in advance of the requirements of the people, and is therefore detrimental to good society." Sallie and Buckman argued on the affirmative side, while Harry Gillingham and Jessie Moon argued the negative. Although the general belief of the group lay with the negative side, Sallie and Buckman had the more persuasive argument and won the debate.[16]

Large evening parties occurred with frequency, some more elaborate than others. In 1890, Fred Snowden hosted one of the more elegant parties the Wilkinsons attended:

It was like a fairy land there on the River, the lawn extends to the river. It was filled with Chinese lanterns and hammocks. They have a wide porch facing the River, the musicians sat in one corner of the porch, it is about 15 ft. wide and runs the length of the house. They danced on the porch, and I was honored with the first invitation to dance, but I declined. Eva and the girls seemed to enjoy it. I wish you could have seen the moon rise out of the River, it was magnificent, it threw a broad path of silver across the River. There at River View, right opposite on the Maryland side the electric lights were all lighted, and about 30 lanterns on the lawn. I never saw such a beautiful place. The new steamboat *Macallister* came up from Marshall Hall about 11 o'clock. When it got to River View it threw the search light over on us and everything was as bright as noon. Then they came nearer they threw the light again, saluted us, and the boys hurraw'd and the girls waved their hdkfs [handkerchiefs]. Stacy Snowden (Fred's father) went down off the porch and rung the big bell. The music went on all the time. About 12 o'clock we had sandwiches and coffee, then all kinds of cake and bananas, lots of ice cream for the last course. Well we had an elegant time and the night was perfect, we got home at 2:30.[17]

Attending weekly meeting was another important component of Quaker life. Sallie described one somewhat unusual meeting: "Anna Mary, Pap, Frank, and I went to meeting yesterday morning. It was cool and there was not any fire on the men's side so they all came over and sat *on our side.* There was a little girl sat in front of us, who sat there and amused herself by stuffing green leaves in her mother's ears and nose, which made us more than smile."[18]

Life continued in this manner for many years. Frank married a local girl, Mary Alice Ballinger, on November 25, 1891. Their son, Charles Kirk Wilkinson, born in 1894, was the only Wilkinson grandchild. Frank, Alice, and Kirk lived at Sherwood, the house Alice's father, Charles, had built in 1859.[19] In January 1897, the Wilkinson family suffered a severe blow. Morris lay dying:

> Dr. Klipstein has just been here . . . he examined Pap, and says, "He is in the last stage of Brights disease [inflammation of the kidney], and no medicine can reach his disease." We cannot arouse him, he sleeps all the time, only when we give him whiskey & milk, he swallows it, but makes no sign of knowing anything. He cannot last long. I wish thee could come home. Dr. Nevitt was here last night, said that his pulse was stronger, left him no medicine. Dr. Klipstein said to not worry him, let him lie quietly, that he considered him Sinking. So the end is near, & it is hard to bear. I cannot see to write.
>
> 4 o'clock—I have just come down from Pap's room, he breathes very short. I am afraid he cannot last long. I wish thee was home.[20]

Morris R. Wilkinson ("Pap" to his children) died soon after, three months shy of his 72nd birthday. Sarah and some of her children remained at Gray's Hill until Sarah's death at age 85 on July 29, 1910. In 1911, Anna Mary married Samuel Brosius; they lived on Newton Street, in the Mount Pleasant area of Washington, DC. Calie and Sallie, both talented artists, never married.[21]

On March 20, 1917, Caleb, Sarah, Frank, and Alice Wilkinson, and Anna M. and Samuel Brosius sold ". . . that certain farm or tract of land adjoining the 'Woodlawn' property, known as Gray's Hill. . . ."[22] Hugh and Frances Keneipp converted the home to Gray's Hill Inn, which they advertised as "overlooking the Potomac," and "formerly a part of Mount Vernon."[23]

As neighboring Camp A.A. Humphreys (later renamed Fort Belvoir) expanded, the federal government condemned nearby farms for army use. Gray's Hill was no exception. The Keneipps lost 58½ acres to the army in 1921 and the rest of the farm in 1941.[24] The army tore down the house in the 1940s to make way for a new housing project, Gray's Hill Village, which has since been demolished as well. On March 18, 2006, the army completed an archaeological survey of the area in preparation for construction of the U.S. Army Museum. Due to the presence of the 1940s housing, they found virtually no evidence of the original Gray's Hill house. The only reminder of the home is a line of cedars that formerly led to it from what is now Route 1. The new museum will be located on Gray's Hill property, near Dogue Creek. The site of the house itself will most likely be roads and/or parking.[25] Although Gray's Hill now exists only in memory, the Wilkinson letters vividly recall a bygone era in that hospitable home.

Endnotes

1. Most of the information in this story is from family papers in possession of the author. Pre-1886 letters pertaining to Cecil County, Maryland, were donated to the Historical Society of Cecil County and can be viewed at their library/headquarters in Elkton, Maryland. Letters are transcribed as written, with minor changes such as sentence breaks.

2. Both mother and daughter were named Sarah and nicknamed Sallie. For the sake of clarity, the mother is referred to as Sarah and the daughter as Sallie.

3. Grover Cleveland, inaugurated March 4, 1885.

4. Morris R. Wilkinson to William C. Wilkinson, September 27, 1885. Wilkinson finalized the purchase of Gray's Hill from Walter and Anna Walton on March 1, 1886. See Fairfax County Deed Book F-5, 305. "The man" in this letter is probably Walter Walton. Anna Walton's father, Thomas Wright, built Gray's Hill, which stood southeast of the Woodlawn Baptist Church on Route 1.

5. Dorothy Troth Muir, *Potomac Interlude: The Story of Woodlawn Mansion and the Mount Vernon Neighborhood 1846–1943,* n.p. 1943, 38–9, 52. See also Fairfax County Deed Book X-3, 47, April 10, 1855, Chalkley Gillingham to Thomas Wright. Fairfax County Deed Book O-3, 395, November 17, 1848, divides the Woodlawn property between Troth and Gillingham. Excepted from the division is Lot 1, Thomas Wright's farm, "heretofore sold to one T. Wright."

6. Morris R. Wilkinson to William C. Wilkinson, October 31, 1885.

7. John Ballinger built Union Farm in 1857. His wife Rebecca was Walter Walton's sister. Union Farm is still standing and is listed on the Fairfax County Inventory of Historic Sites.

8. Sarah H.K. Wilkinson to Eva Wilkinson, January 30, 1887.

9. Sarah H.K. Wilkinson to William and Eva Wilkinson, February 27, 1887.

10. Sarah H.K. Wilkinson to William and Caleb Wilkinson, April 18, 1886. The family name was changed here to Doe out of respect for the woman's descendants. The Wilkinson children referred their father Morris as "Pap."

11. Ibid. Apparently, Jane made a full recovery. She later married, and lived for at least 50 more years.

12. Sarah Wilkinson's mother, Ann Langtry Haddock Kirk, was visiting from Cecil County, Maryland.

13. Sarah H.K. Wilkinson to William Wilkinson, September 5, 1886. This was the largest earthquake to ever strike the southeastern United States. It rocked the coastal plain near Charleston, South Carolina, on August 31, 1886, at approximately 9:50 p.m. Charleston sustained heavy damage and 60 or so people were killed. See South Carolina Seismic Network, Department of Geological Sciences, University of South Carolina, scsn.seis.sc.edu/html/eqchas.html.

14. Sarah H.K. Wilkinson to Eva Wilkinson, June 26, 1887. Jessie Moon recovered; she married John and Rebecca Ballinger's son, David Walton Ballinger, in 1889. Lutie Moon may be Louise Moon, who married Walter and Anna Walton's son, Edward, in 1892.

15. Sarah H.K. Wilkinson to William Wilkinson, May 9, 1886.

16. Sallie Wilkinson to William Wilkinson, May 17, 1886. She does not give Mr. Buckman's first name.

17. Sarah H.K. Wilkinson to William Wilkinson, August 3, 1890. Stacy Snowden built Collingwood, which is listed on the Fairfax County Inventory of Historic Sites. River View, now gone, was a bit north of Collingwood, just south of Wellington, current headquarters of the American Horticultural Society. Wellington is listed on the Fairfax County Inventory of Historic Sites.

18. Sallie Wilkinson to William Wilkinson, May 17, 1886.

19. Charles Ballinger was John Ballinger's younger brother. Like Union Farm, Sherwood is still standing and is listed on the Fairfax County Inventory of Historic Sites. To confuse the reader further, John's and Charles' mother, Jemima, married David Walton in 1844, a second marriage for both. John Ballinger married his stepsister, David's daughter Rebecca, in 1857. Walter Walton, David's son, married Anna Wright. They sold Gray's Hill to the Wilkinsons. Ann Walton, David's other daughter, married Jacob Troth, son of Troth-Gillingham partner Jacob Troth. Jacob and Ann lived at Grand View, adjacent to Woodlawn and also listed on the Fairfax County Inventory of Historic Sites.

20. Sarah H.K. Wilkinson to Caleb Kirk Wilkinson, January 10, 1897.

21. All Wilkinsons mentioned in this article, including Willie and Eva, are buried in the Woodlawn Friends Cemetery.

22. Fairfax County Deed Book D-8, 185, grantee Harry Barger. Fairfax County Deed Book D-8, 186, March 23, 1917, Barger to Hugh and Frances Keneipp.

23. Gray's Hill file, Virginia Room, Fairfax City Regional Library, Fairfax Virginia.

24. Fairfax County Deed Book M-10, 428; A-15, 138; B-15, 2.

25. Derek Manning, Cultural Resources, Specpro, US Army Garrison, Fort Belvoir, Directorate of Public Works, interview by author, March 20, 2006.

Fairfax County's Poor House
Caring for the Poor for Almost 70 Years
By Martha Robertson, *Springfield, Virginia*

The first Poor House to be administered by the Fairfax County Board of Supervisors was built just outside Clifton in 1842. The land on which the new Poor House would stand was sold to the county by George and Mary Dent Chichester for $1,500. That parcel, which George Chichester inherited from Daniel McCarty Chichester, contained 150 acres. The parcel's description, found in Fairfax County Deed Book H-3, includes a detailed listing of the boundaries, including references to runs, poles, and the large stump of a red oak. This site would triple the size of the 50-acre parcel on which a previous Poor House had been built and would also move the Poor House from its previous location of Providence (the county seat at the time) to an area just outside of modern-day Clifton. The county's poor would be housed at this site until 1911, when the land was sold at public auction.

The Poor House provided "indoor aid" or institutional aid to the destitute, aged, and those residents unable to physically care for themselves. This was considered to be separate from "outdoor aid," assistance provided to paupers who lived on their own outside the Poor House, which was administered by the overseers of the poor. Besides housing the poorest of county residents, the Poor House occasionally also provided shelter for the unsound of mind. An entry in the Circuit Court minute book for September 2, 1869, includes the following:

> Ordered, that the Sheriff of the County remove _____ Hicks, a supposed lunatic of unsound mind from the Jail of the County to the Poor House.

While maintenance of the poor farm and the care of its residents, who were referred to as inmates, were the responsibility of the superintendent of the poor, the duties were, in truth, divided between the superintendent and his wife, who was referred to as the matron of the Poor House. The matron dealt with normal domestic duties of cleaning, cooking, disinfecting, and doing laundry, but would also tend to the bathing and treatment of sick or frail inmates.

While she attended to these duties, the superintendent dealt with the fertilizing, planting, and harvesting of crops, feeding and caring for the farm animals, maintaining farm tools, and ordering supplies for farm maintenance and the sustenance of inmates.

Since public monies were spent for the maintenance of the Poor House and its inhabitants, the superintendent had to provide quarterly expenditure reports to the Fairfax County Board of Supervisors. This quarterly report was submitted to the board for their review and approval.

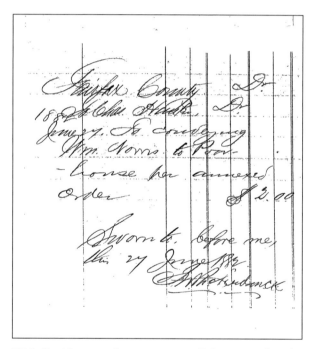

F.M. Smith served as overseer of the poor for the Providence District of Fairfax County from 1882 to 1889. This note, at top, dated June 27, 1882, requests that "Charly Hunter . . . Will please transport William Norris to the Poor House and charge Fairfax County." The note at bottom is a request for reimbursement of $2.

All expenditures were to be "supported by proper vouchers" detailing who provided the needed goods and services to the Poor House and farm. This quarterly account became especially important if the superintendent overspent the quarterly allocation of county funds.

Failure to provide sufficient documentation for purchases could mean the board might refuse to pay for the additional expenditures, leaving the superintendent to deal with any businesses demanding payment.

The overseers of the poor were responsible for administering "outdoor aid" to the poor living outside the Poor House. Each district's overseer could order residents of their district who were unable to provide for themselves to be taken to the Poor House. Inmates, however, were not compelled to remain at the Poor House and a few who were physically able left of their own free will. Many residents, however, due to advanced age or delicate physical condition, were unable to leave this institution and continued to reside there until their death. Albert B. Harrison, superintendent of the poor, observed in 1888 that, "The paupers at present at Poor House are made up of old, infirm, and children who are unable to perform labor—worthy of attention."[1]

Resident Population Fluctuations

The population of the Poor House rose and fell within a given year. Statistics from quarterly and annual reports of the superintendent of the poor show as many as 29 inmates in residence during the April–June quarter of 1885, and as few as four inmates in 1906 for the period of January through September. These same reports show the greatest total number of inmates received at the Poor House within a given year was 35 in 1895. These fluctuations in total Poor House inmate population inevitably led to overcrowding at various times. An unusually high Poor House population in 1877 resulted in the following resolution being passed by the Board of Supervisors in November of that year:

> Resolved . . . that the Poor House is filled to its utmost capacity, it is recommended to the several Overseers in this County that in case of paupers wholly or partially unable to support themselves, that instead of sending them to the Poor House that they shall, in conjunction with the Supervisor of his district, contract with a suitable person or persons for their support on as reasonable terms as they can obtain. . . . This shall continue in force until sufficient buildings [to be added to the Poor House] are provided by the Board.[2]

Although these contracts for the maintenance of "outside paupers" continued for many years, the Poor House was still used to house and care for the county's neediest residents.

The years following this resolution saw increased building activity at the Poor House. A Board of Supervisors minute book shows that on August 17, 1878, the board actually met at the Poor House and viewed a recently completed building, the exact purpose of which was not indicated. In August of 1881, C.F. Ford appointed a committee "to have a new porch built to the house occupied by paupers on the Poor House farm of this County."

Further improvements were initiated in November of 1882 when supervisors Davis and Ford were appointed as a committee to receive proposals to build a stable. They reported to the board the following February they had contracted with J.W. Ashford to build the said barn for the sum of $250. The Board of Supervisors met yet again at the Poor House in September of 1883. At this meeting, F.C. Davis appointed a committee to make repairs on the paupers' quarters at the Poor House and supervisors Davis and Hawxhurst were appointed to receive proposals for building a kitchen. The contract for the kitchen was subsequently awarded to H.G. Simpson for the sum of $229.

Further improvements were ordered at yet another board meeting held at the Poor House on September 4, 1886, when the board resolved, "that the east chimney to the male quarters be taken down and a chimney with a stove be built instead."

In addition, the superintendent of the poor was instructed to:

> purchase four large coal stoves and fuel for same for use in the male and female quarters, and to have the gable ends of said quarters lathed and fastened and to present the bill for this work at the board at its next meeting.[3]

Additional improvements continued in 1894 when supervisors Davis and Simpson were charged with the advertising and receipt of proposals for additional buildings. The following month, a contract was awarded to J.W. Ashford with a low bid of $418.97 for building a house on the Poor House property. It was a return trip for Ashford, who had previously built a barn on the Poor House property in 1883. This new dwelling was completed and inspected by the board in November 1894.

Caring for the Dying and Contagious

While all of these projects enhanced the facilities at the Poor House, one aspect of caring for the county's aged and infirm population had not yet been addressed, that being the caring for the terminally ill or those with contagious diseases. A physician to the poor at the Poor House was established in the early 1870s when Dr. R.L. Simpson was appointed and allowed the sum of $60 per year for administering to Poor House inmates. It was not until January of 1899, however, that a medical situation is mentioned that forced the board to deal with the quarantining of inmates with terminal diseases. At that time the board directed Supervisor Williams to:

[H]ave an inmate of the Poor House suffering with an incurable disease be removed from the Poor House to the Town of Vienna and to rent a house for him and hire an attendant to take care of and feed him in case his family declines to receive him and present the bill for all expenses to this board for payment.[4]

It would be mid-August of 1899 before the board passed the motion of Supervisor Pearson to "build a Pest House in which to keep paupers afflicted with infectious or contagious diseases, at the Poor House farm." This structure was most certainly put to use in 1904 when smallpox patients were quarantined at the Poor House. The February 5th issue of the *Fairfax Herald* for that year included the following citation on page 4 under news from Clifton:

The smallpox patients that were sent to the Poor House farm from here have been released. There are no new cases developed. The cases were very light. No one need be frightened over this kind of disease.

Paupers were not the only people to spend their last days at the Poor House. The only superintendent of the poor to die while still holding that position was A.B. Harrison, who died in 1901 after serving as superintendent of the poor for 24 years.

His sister and executrix, Nancy Harrison, submitted his last quarterly report, for the period ending September 30, 1901, to the Board of Supervisors. She was well aware of Poor House finances because she had also served as the matron of the Poor House during her brother's tenure as superintendent.

More Buildings, More Food

Frederick M. Ford was subsequently appointed as the new superintendent of the poor and his wife, Mary, became matron of the Poor House. In 1903, Ford seemed to feel the board should be made aware of less than desirable conditions at the Poor House.

He subsequently made the rather unusual request that a committee of board members be appointed "to go to the Poor House and to look into the general treatment by said Superintendent of the inmates thereof, and report to the Board." The committee report—dated May 4, 1903, and signed by supervisors Franklin Williams and R.S. Spindle—stated:

[T]hat some of the buildings are old and need some repairs to make them in a degree comfortable. The . . . house is in a very bad condition and the roof ought to be removed as soon as possible. We found one of the stoves used by the inmates was perfectly worthless and will have to be replaced before winter. We were informed that there was an insufficiency of blankets and under clothes, also of vegetables but no scarcity of such food as they now had. The superintendent stated there were plenty of blankets which could be had if requested, also there was a scarcity of vegetables at this time but during the winter they had peas, beans, and potatoes and he would like to have a small appropriation to supply such vegetables as are now in season and we will also state while viewing the rooms we saw clothing hanging on the wall, while the inmate had before stated that he had no underclothing.[5]

The Board of Supervisors began to consider building a new Poor House structure in late May of 1906 when "Mr. Triplett was appointed as a committee to view a site on Mr. G.H. Burke's land for a Poor House and to report at the next meeting."[6]

In late March of 1908, the board made the motion to appoint a committee of two—supervisors Pearson and Harrison—who were to investigate what kind of structures should be built to house the county's poorest residents as well as the superintendent and his family and to ascertain the cost of these buildings. It would take another two years, however, before further progress was made toward establishing a new Poor House.

A suitable parcel of land for a new Poor House was finally located and was brought to the board's attention in June of 1910, when Auld and Pearson reported they had located a tract of land:

> ... at Jermantown owned by James H. Langley containing 14 and 63/100 acres, which in their opinion, is suitable for the purpose of erecting thereon, the proposed new Poor House and necessary out-buildings and that the same could be purchased for $1,000 cash, which they regarded as a reasonable price and agreed to purchase same. Whereupon on motion said committee was directed to purchase said land for said amount. . . .[7]

The board further directed the county clerk to "advertise for sale at a public auction before the front door of the courthouse building the present Poor House Farm and land in Centreville District for cash, or on terms he thinks advisable and that he state in said advertisement that possession of said farm will be given on January 1, 1911."[8]

Thus, the county Poor House and farm, located just outside Clifton, was sold at public auction to Mary F. Burritt for the price of $3,001, a little more than twice the original price paid by the county in 1842.

Endnotes

1. Annual Report of the Superintendent of the Poor of Fairfax County for the Year Ending June 30, 1888.

2. Minute Book, Fairfax County Board of Supervisors, Vol. 1, 122.

3. Ibid., Vol. 2, 51.

4. Ibid., 403.

5. Franklin Williams and R.S. Spindle, "Report of Committee to the Poor House" Miscellaneous Papers, Fairfax County Board of Supervisors, May 4, 1903.

6. Minute Book, Fairfax County Board of Supervisors, Vol. 3, 199.

7. Ibid., 296.

8. Ibid., 297.

The Metropolitan Western Railroad
Approved But Never Built
By Mildred M. Moore, *Alexandria, Virginia*

John Frederick Bauch owned land in the Chesterbrook area south of Pimmit Run in northeastern Fairfax County. When Bauch died, he left 15 acres to his brother, William Bauch, and the balance to his wife, Henrietta Hager Bauch. When Henrietta Bauch died, her son, John Frederick Hager (my great-grandfather), inherited her land. This land was eventually deeded to my grandfather, father, and others. Research on this land led to an interesting discovery.

In August 1892, John Frederick Hager sold a small section of land to the Metropolitan Western Railroad Company.[1] The deed described the land as being near Pimmit Run and joining properties of Luch and Bauch. Having grown up in the area, I knew that a railroad had never been constructed on the land.

On February 4, 1890, the Virginia State Assembly approved the construction of a railroad by the Metropolitan Western Railroad Company.[2] The railroad was to run through properties located in Fairfax and Prince William counties, beginning at a point on the Potomac River that the board of directors selected. The act further stated that construction of the railroad was to begin within two years of the date of the passage of the act, and the main line was to be completed within four years of the passage of the act.

Seven men were listed as representing the Metropolitan Western Railroad Company: Gen. W.W. Mackall, William S. Smoot, T.D. Moncure, Mathew J. Laughlin and D.S. Mackall—all of Virginia, and L.D. Whitaker and H.F. Lofland—of Maryland.[3]

The company proposed changes to the railroad almost immediately. Beginning on February 16, 1892, and every two years thereafter through 1902, the Virginia General Assembly approved amendments for Section 3 and/or Section 12 of the original act of February 4, 1890.[4] Section 3 of the original act included Fairfax and Prince William counties; amendments to Section 3 added Stafford County in 1892 and Loudoun County in 1902. Amendments to Section 12 changed the start and completion dates for the railroad construction.

Beginning in 1890, the Metropolitan Western Railroad Company obtained more than 70 deeds to lands in Fairfax County. Many transactions between citizens of Fairfax County and representatives of the Metropolitan Western Railroad Company are recorded in Fairfax County deed books from August 1890 to January 1894.[5] In most cases, citizens sold their land, but at least 14 transactions were condemnations of land.

In a March 1894 article, the *Washington Post* stated the Metropolitan Western Railroad was a subsidiary of the Baltimore and Ohio Railroad Company (B&ORR), which had not been mentioned in the original act of 1890. Further, the article discussed plans for building an extension of the B&ORR on the Virginia side of the Potomac River.[6] Congress would not consent to bridge construction across the Potomac River within the boundaries of the District of Columbia, so the company came up with another plan. They proposed crossing the Potomac River from Maryland to Virginia north of Chain Bridge at a point near the upper end of Little Falls, known as High Island. In Virginia, the railroad was planned to pass over a level stretch of land, through a quarter-mile tunnel, and come out at Pimmit Run. The railroad was to continue along the north bank of Pimmit Run, crossing the Washington and Ohio division of the Richmond and Danville Railroad at Dunn Loring, to Fairfax Court House, and southward to a point that had not been determined. The *Hopkins' 1894 Map of the Vicinity of Washington, DC*[7] implied the railroad had already been built.

Trestle Construction is Begun, then Halted

The 1894 article also indicated that sometime in the past Georgetown had granted the B&ORR a right-of-way along the canal towpath. Construction on a trestle had begun at a point about a mile west of the Aqueduct Bridge, but had ceased suddenly. The company now expected railroad construction to be completed. When the train crossed the Potomac into Virginia it would become the Metropolitan Western Railroad.

The railroad was never built and original property holdings were transferred from person to person. Original railroad stockholders died off during the time amendments were being presented and approved by the Virginia General Assembly. One of the original stockholders, Gen. W.W. Mackall, died on August 19, 1891.[8]

There is a record of the transfer of lands in Fairfax County from one set of directors of the Metropolitan Western Railroad Company to another in December 1942.[9] The deed between George E. Hamilton, Sr., and James S. Murray, surviving directors of the Metropolitan Western Railroad Company, in liquidation, granted "all the real estate, appurtenances and every part thereof" belonging to the Metropolitan Western Railroad Company and situated in Fairfax County, Virginia, to E.A. Kummer and R.S. Duncan, both of the City of Baltimore, State of Maryland. Persons involved in the transaction of December 1942 lived in Maryland and were involved in various occupations related to railroad work.

In the 1940s and 1950s, notices in the *Fairfax Herald* were posted in an effort to contact persons with information on current names and addresses of any officials of the Metropolitan Western Railroad Company. Quit claims or clear title to properties had to be obtained by property owners before they could sell or build on their properties. In some *Fairfax Herald* notices during the 1950s, property owners were seeking clear title to land they had obtained about 1914 and 1920 "under color of title."[10] (*Black's Law Dictionary* defines color of title as "a written instrument or other evidence that appears to give title, but does not do so.")

Notices in the *Fairfax Herald* repeatedly listed E.A. Kummer, R.S. Duncan, and R.E. Kennedy as persons of interest connected to the Metropolitan Western Railroad. Robert E. Kennedy was a civil engineer for a railroad and lived in Baltimore County, Maryland.

In April 1946, R.S. Duncan and E.A. Kummer, still representatives of the Metropolitan Western Railroad Company, did "release and forever quit claim" a certain piece of land that the Metropolitan Western Railroad Company had purchased from William Bauch on July 12, 1892. William Bauch died and his sons inherited the property,[11] which adjoined the property of John Frederick Hager.

Hager sold about 10 acres to a son in 1924.[12] The son then sold that piece of property to C.B. Ellis in 1927.[13] In January 1958, a quit claim was filed between R.S. Duncan, sole surviving trustee of the Metropolitan Western Railroad Company, and Mrs. Ellis, heir to the estate of C.B. Ellis. A statement at the end of the 1958 transaction indicated that when C.B. Ellis purchased the property in 1927, the Metropolitan Western Railroad Company had issued a quit claim. The statement continued: "the same property its right, title, and interest in which the Metropolitan Western Railroad Company by deed dated June 21, 1927, released and forever quitclaimed unto Challen B. Ellis . . . which deed is not to be found among the land records of Fairfax County, Virginia."[14]

For many years, people experienced much frustration over a railroad that was never even built.

Endnotes

1. Fairfax County Deed Book M-5, 697–8.

2. *Acts and Joint Resolutions Passed by the General Assembly of the State of Virginia, During the Session of 1889–'90.* (Richmond: J.H. O'Bannon, Superintendent of Public Printing, 1890), 242–4.

3. Ibid.

4. *Acts and Joint Resolutions Passed by the General Assembly of the State of Virginia, During the Session of 1892,* 392–3; *Acts and Joint Resolutions Passed by the General Assembly of the State of Virginia, During the Session of 1893–1894,* 666; *Acts and Joint Resolutions Passed by the General Assembly of the State of Virginia, During the Session of 1895–1896,* 239; *Acts and Joint Resolutions Passed by the General Assembly of the State of Virginia, During the Session of 1897–1898,* 705; *Acts and Joint Resolutions Passed by the General Assembly of the State of Virginia, During the Session of 1899–1900,* 110–1; *Acts and Joint Resolutions Passed by the General Assembly of the State of Virginia, During the Session of 1901–1902,* 145–146.

5. Fairfax County Deed Book J-5, 262, 264, 267 and 270; Book M-5, 621, 624–5, 648, 650, 652–4, 660, 662–3, 689–90, 692, 697–8, 700, and 702–3; Book N-5, 13–4, 17, 19, 22, 24, 27, 29, 42, 47, 49, 56, 71, 96, 115–6, 121, 123, 126, 129, 131, 154, 156–7, 165, 170, 177, 219, 237, 269–70, 295–6, 328, 330, 380, 579, 588, 694; Book O-5, 170, 255, 259, 564; Book Q-5, 8.

6. *Washington Post*, March 19, 1894, 8. Digital image. *ProQuest Online.* (proquest.umi. com/pqdweb:2005). This lengthy article presented projected plans of how the railroad could eventually build, grow, and expand in the region and possibly on into other states.

7. Richard W. Stephenson, *The Cartography of Northern Virginia Facsimile Reproductions of Maps Dating from 1608 to 1915* (Fairfax County, Virginia: Office of Comprehensive Planning, 1983), 109. Plates 95–8 are of a map published by Griffith M. Hopkins in 1894.

8. *Fairfax County, Virginia, Gravestones.* Vol. VI. (Fairfax, Virginia: Fairfax Genealogical Society, Inc. 1999), MI–125.

9. Fairfax County Deed Book 399, 66–7.

10. *Fairfax Herald,* January 20, 1950, 2; August 25, 1950, column 3.

11. Fairfax County Deed Book 488, 472–8.

12. Ibid., L-9, 422–3.

13. Ibid., Z-9, 445–8.

14. Ibid., 1735, 205–6.

The Family History of John Bell and Clarence Raymond Summers, Sr.
A Baileys Crossroads Family
By Houston M. Summers, Jr., *Falls Church, Virginia*

John Bell was born into slavery in 1825 in North Carolina. Because he was the son of a plantation owner, he was able to acquire an education. John Bell's father was not only a planter, he was also a politician who made many trips to Washington, DC. My great-grandfather, John, was trained as a carpenter and a coachman. He made these trips with his father.

We don't know much more about John Bell's life as a slave other than he married his first wife before the Civil War. She died without birthing any children. By 1866, he had left the plantation and come to Washington, DC. He was employed by the federal government in the U.S. Patent Office. He also was an evangelist minister. In 1866, he married Margaret Cole. From this union the following children were born: Clara Bell, Lillie Bell, Risetta Bell, Abner Bell, Lawrence Bell, Eston Bell Lee, Janie Bell, Anne Bell, and Margaret Bell Furrell.[1]

On August 29, 1876, the Bells purchased from Miles Munson 50 acres of land in the Baileys Crossroads area of Falls Church at a cost of $2,500. This parcel of land was part of the Oakton track lying south of Columbia Pike.[2] They were able to purchase the land from Miles Munson because Munson's son died in a house fire on the property. After that tragic occurrence, he no longer wanted the property.[3] The Munsons were not aware that John Bell was an African American because he could pass for white. The Bells' house was built where Barcroft Apartments are located (as of 2006). Abner Bell lived in this homestead house, which stood until 1960.

John and Margaret's daughter, Clara Toliver Bell,[4] was my grandmother. She was born at Baileys Crossroads in 1877. She grew up here and graduated from a normal school with a major in education. At that time, a normal school was equivalent to a four-year university today. Clara married Clarence Raymond Summers, Sr., on October 17, 1903.[5] On June 7, 1906, in consideration of the sum of $10, John and Margaret Bell granted Clara B. Summers a five-acre parcel of land located in Baileys Crossroads.[6]

Clarence worked as a plasterer in residential construction. He later worked for the federal government at the Washington Navy Yard. Clara was a housewife, and she also taught in her home local children who wanted an education. From this union the following children were born: Clarence Raymond Summers, Jr.; Helen S. Smith; Elsie S. Smith; Houston Maxwell Summers, Jr.; and Aubrey Bernard Summers. These five offspring were each given a parcel of land within the original five-acre tract, which is located on the south side of Summers Lane. Of that land, ¾ of an acre was deeded to my father, Houston, Sr., by Clara and Clarence on July 23, 1936.[7]

Education

In 1870, Fairfax County established a segregated public school system and 408 African American children were enrolled in school. The school population increased to 1,150 by 1899. A teacher's salary in 1870 was about one dollar per day. The average time school was in session was six months. At that time, schools went to grade six or seven. African American students were not able to attend high school in Fairfax County until Luther Porter Jackson High School was completed in 1954 for African American students.[8]

John Bell was interested in education as well as religion. He was active in the Freedman's Bureau, a federal government agency that was formed in 1865 by Congress to protect, care for, and educate formerly enslaved persons. Confirmed by the U.S. Supreme Court in 1896 and reinforced by the Virginia Constitution of 1902, black citizens of Virginia were provided "separate but equal" tax-supported facilities that kept them apart from white citizens. This continued until Fairfax County desegregated its school system in 1965.

John Bell provided a five-acre tract of land near Columbia Pike for a public school in the 1880s. One of Fairfax County's first public schools, this small, wood-frame building was used for several years by black children until it was closed and the tract reverted to John Bell's ownership as his deed specified.

During the early decades of the 20th century, no local school was provided for black students in Baileys Crossroads. For a few years, children walked to a one-room school at Mount Pleasant, where a youthful Lillian Carey was principal and the only teacher. My grandmother, Clara T. Bell, acted as substitute teacher whenever it was necessary. In the 1920s, graduations for the colored children were held at Warner Baptist Church in Baileys Crossroads. Later, school was held in a small, wood-frame building, which was built and operated by the county until it was closed in 1948. That same year Fairfax County opened James Lee, a new elementary school for colored children in Falls Church. This was the first school built for African Americans using the same standards as those schools built for white children. The brick Lillian Carey Elementary School was built in 1956 (using those same standards) on a portion of John Bell's original homestead on Summers Lane.

Life for the children who attended colored one-, two-, or three-room schools was far from easy. Many had to walk long distances to reach them. The colored school, built in Baileys Crossroads by Fairfax County, had three rooms. The first and second grades were in one room; third and fourth grades in the middle room; and fifth, sixth, and seventh grades were in the third room. Fairfax County did not deem it necessary for colored children to have an education past the seventh grade. Each room had a coal stove. Water came from a well with a pump. The bathroom facilities were outhouses. There was one bathroom for girls and one for the boys. During cold weather, the boys kept the fires going by carrying wood or coal and kept the stoves clean. They also had to clean the outhouses and make certain they were supplied with lime. The girls were responsible for keeping the school bus and the classrooms clean.

In the colored schools during the 1930s and 1940s, social activities involved daily recess sessions, during which students played baseball, horseshoes, dodge ball, and double Dutch jump rope. The school celebrated May Day, or Field Day, on May 1. Many years ago, May Day was a magical time to welcome spring. This was a day of fun and enjoyment. Everyone in school participated. Games went on for the entire day and climaxed by the wrapping of the Maypole. During non-school hours the school was used for dances. Music was played from recordings and, on special occasions, a local, live band played. Typically, the foods served were hot dogs, sodas, and potato chips.

Health care was provided by the county. Students were screened for vision, hearing, and dental problems. Every student received a cod liver oil soft gel daily.

Warner Baptist Church

In the 1800s, a group of families composed of former slaves and freedmen settled in Baileys Crossroads. This group of families had learned to rely on God for their well-being, for the road they traveled was extremely difficult. This deep belief in religion made them realize that only by working and worshipping together could they survive in their new surroundings.

In 1881, B.H. Warner, a white citizen of Washington, DC, donated to the African American citizens of Baileys Crossroads an acre of land to be used for a church or school. The deed stipulated that the building erected should be named after the donor.[9] Therefore, it was named Warner Baptist Church. In the early days, the worshipers communed together under a small group of trees on the site where the present church stands. Presiding at these meetings in the grove were various speakers from different walks of life. When temperatures did not permit outside services, they were held in an old store on Columbia Pike near Seminary Road.

Almost 40 years later, in 1919, a committee was formed to organize, break ground, and build a church. Lumber for the building was shipped from a sawmill in Herndon to Barcroft by freight train. From there, it was transported to the church site by horse and wagon. The Warner Baptist Church was completed in 1920. Clarence Summers, Sr., was a member of the construction committee. His daughter, Helen Smith, was one of the first members baptized.

In 1962, groundbreaking for the present edifice occurred. Church members and volunteers from the community performed most of the labor, including bricklaying, carpentry, and painting. Rev. Milton Sheppard drew the blueprints and acted as an overseer of the construction. In 1964, the new church was completed and dedication services were held in November of the same year.

In 2001, Warner Baptist Church experienced a major renovation, which I coordinated. It included an addition to house an elevator, handicapped-accessible rest-

Clarence Raymond Summers, Sr.

Clara Toliver Bell Summers

Lawrence Bell

Aubrey Bernard Summers

(All photos courtesy Summers' family collection)

Back row, left to right, Anne Bell and Clara Toliver Bell Summers. Middle row, left to right, Margaret Bell Furrell and Helen Summers. Front row, left to right, Elsie Summers and Clarence Raymond Summers, Jr. (Courtesy Summers' family collection)

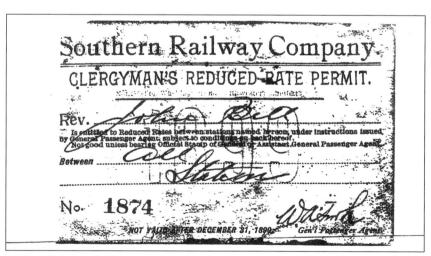

Issued in 1899 by the Southern Railway Company, this clergyman's reduced rate permit, number 1874, documents John Bell's life as a traveling evangelist minister. He used this discount pass to travel between Baileys Crossroads (from Falls Church's Barcroft Station) and North Carolina. (Courtesy Summers' family collection)

rooms, air conditioning in the basement, electrical services and panel, interior and exterior lights and receptacles, painting and interior trim, a new sound system, exterior brick steps, and heating and air conditioning in the sound control booth. A dedication service for the completed renovation was held on October 9, 2005.

Music—a Gift to the World

Music is a very important part of the African American worship service. The most prevalent types of music today are hymns, Negro spirituals, and gospel music. Negro spirituals were created by African Americans and are their gift to the world. These songs were born out of the struggles of slavery and African American life. They tell stories about struggles, strife, and exile as well as about faith and hope. Gospel music came about during the latter part of the 19th century. Many of the texts were taken from the first four books of the New Testament. Thus, these songs were given the name "Gospel." The text dealt with the teachings of Jesus and the Christian church. This music is very popular today and has evolved to include many of the popular secular musical styles while maintaining a religious text.

Because of segregation, African Americans could not socialize with whites, so most of their social activities were centered on the church. Church members then, as well as now, held Sunday worship services, weekly prayer meetings, visitation between churches, all-day worship services, and yearly homecoming worship celebrations. The preparation of food, its consumption, and the fellowship created at these meals were important parts of the gatherings. I can still remember those dinners that were served between worship services. The food came from local fields, gardens, and farmyards of church members. Menus consisted of fried chicken, baked ham, corn pudding, macaroni and cheese, string beans, mashed potatoes and gravy, sweet potatoes, and homemade bread. Desserts included cake, pie, block ice cream, with iced tea or fruit punch served as beverages.

Sunday school classes were held before church services every Sunday morning. These classes taught children about the Bible. By participating in the activities organized by the Sunday school, children developed self-confidence and enhanced their communication and leadership skills. The children always looked forward to taking part in plays, talent shows, pageants, candlelight services, as well as gifts at Christmas, Easter programs, and summer outings at the beach. For the summer outings, we went to Sparrows, Carrs, or Longview state beaches in Maryland—all segregated beaches for colored people. However, federally owned beaches were not segregated and anyone could use them. Nearby in Maryland these included Sandy Point, Fort Smallwood, and Beachwood, which we also visited. The church would rent a bus and everybody carried along a bag lunch from home. Because no one had coolers back then, only non-perishable dishes, such as fried chicken and sandwiches made with mustard instead of mayonnaise, were carried.

The Children of Clarence and Clara (Bell) Summers

Four of the five Summers' descendents built homes on their parcels of land where they lived and raised their families in Baileys Crossroads. Helen S. Smith had one daughter, Clarabel, who died at age 19 in 1951. Aunt Helen worked for Woodward & Lothrop in Washington, DC. She was a seamstress and worked in the china department until she retired. Aunt Helen didn't drive, so she used public transportation. At that time, buses stopped only in Culmore or at the intersection of Route 7 and Columbia Pike. Both of these locations were more than a mile and a half from her home. I can still picture her walking across the local baseball field late in the evening, struggling with the weight of several bags, trying to make it home. But no matter how tired she may have been, she always stopped to give you a treat from one of those bags. When I was in college, Aunt Helen always gave me money when I came home on holidays.

Clarence Raymond Summers, Jr., the oldest son, grew up in the Mason District. He attended Armstrong Technical High School in Washington, DC, and he learned the plastering trade from his father. He also worked in the grocery business during the Great Depression. Later he worked at the Washington Navy Yard as a plumber's helper and plan operations assistant.

Uncle Raymond was married twice; his first wife was Carlye Adams. They were married in 1928 and lived at 19th and M Street, N.W., in Washington, DC. During the 1930s Georgetown, as well as Foggy Bottom, was populated mainly by black people. All of Raymond's brothers and sisters lived with him at one time or another. Carlyle died in 1934, and Raymond later married Louise Washington and finished building his home in Baileys Crossroads. From this marriage two children were born—Wanda and Clarence. Uncle Raymond was a deacon at Oakland Baptist Church in Alexandria. He was a hard worker and very thrifty. He always paid cash for everything, including new cars. He was also an avid vegetable gardener. Everyone in the family enjoyed the fruits of his labor from the garden and fruit trees in his yard.

Houston M. Summers, Sr., my father, was born in 1910. He grew up in Baileys Crossroads with his brothers and sisters. They all attended the one-room colored elementary school in Mount Pleasant. My father talked about how strict and demanding his teacher, Lillian Carey, was and that he didn't like her or school very much. He did, however, complete the eighth grade. Like his older brother, Raymond, Houston also learned the plastering trade from his father. As a boy he helped build the first Warner Baptist Church in 1919. He was a lifetime member of the church. He was a deacon, and served as chairman for many years. Houston was a people person. He worked well with individuals as well as groups. He was a true leader, able to evaluate and assess people's strengths and weaknesses. He provided counseling and always offered a helping hand. Whenever he needed assistance for a project or asked for help, people came and stayed until the job was done.

Houston was a very hard worker and was very strong physically. From the age of 18 he worked as a truck driver for various companies. From 1942 through 1945, he worked as a general helper at the Naval Powder Factory in Indian Head, Maryland. By 1945, he had completed building his home in Baileys Crossroads, where he lived the rest of his life. He met and later married Ethel Ewell in 1932. I am their son. He worked as a plasterer and retired from National Motors as an assembly-line worker, rebuilding Ford engines.

What Houston lacked in formal education, he made up for in hard work. He taught me at a very young age to work. Like his brother, Raymond, he, too, was an avid gardener. I had to cultivate the plants with a hoe and pick the vegetables when they were ready to eat. While living on my uncle's farm, I helped care for hogs, cattle, chickens, and horses. Dad and Uncle Raymond took me on their plastering jobs and taught me how to plaster. Houston was a devoted father who spent time with his family. We all attended church on Sundays. We visited relatives and remained in close contact with his immediate family who built their homes on the land given them by their parents.

Aubrey Bernard Summers was the youngest of the five children. He grew up in Baileys Crossroads and also attended the one-room colored school in Mount Pleasant. He completed grammar school in 1928 and studied carpentry at Armstrong Technical High School. After graduating, he got his first job working for Fossetts, a grocery retailer in Georgetown, where he stocked shelves. In 1936, he met and married Elizabeth Fields. They had two daughters—Juanita White and Cheryl Sneed. Aubrey entered the government as a crater's helper and was promoted to head crater-packer supervisor. He held a high government clearance. He was responsible for the crating and packing of crashed military aircraft. He traveled to the crash sites and had the plane's parts shipped to Langley Field, Andrews Air Force Base, or the Naval Air Station (adjacent to Bolling Air Force Base), for further evaluation. While working as a crater's helper and living at 1164 19th Street, N.W., in Washington, he completed the construction of his new home and moved back to Baileys Crossroads in 1945. Aubrey was a devoted father and husband. He always worked and provided for his family and was a supportive parent. He believed everyone could experience success in life. Aubrey never caused problems; he was a problem solver. He loved to socialize with his friends and family and was a free spirit who loved to travel and enjoy the fruits of living.

The Grandchildren of Clarence and Clara (Bell) Summers
The descendents of Clara Bell and Clarence Summers' five children also grew up in the Baileys Crossroads.

Juanita White was born at Freedman's Hospital in Washington in 1937. She spent her early years living at 1164 19th Street, N.W., in Washington. She attended St. Phillips Wormley in Georgetown. She liked to stand in rationing lines during World

War II because she could talk to people while waiting to get sugar, nylons, and cigarettes. The family moved back to Baileys Crossroads when their new house was completed in 1945. Juanita entered the second grade and was very disappointed that she had to attend the old, three-room, wood-frame colored school. In 1948, James Lee Elementary School opened, consolidating all the substandard colored schools located in Baileys Crossroads, Mount Pleasant, Lincolnia, Chesterbrook, and Falls Church. Juanita graduated from James Lee Elementary School and attended Dunbar High School in Washington.

Juanita married Burton White in 1956; they had two children—Burton, Jr., and Elaina. Like her father, Juanita is a very social person and loves working with people, especially children. In 1960 she organized a club named the Burtons for the teenagers living in the Baileys Crossroads community. The Burtons was the first black group to go on the televised Milt Grant Dance Show. As a result of her work with the teen club, she was hired by the county recreation department as director of the Teen Center at Lillian Carey Elementary School. In 1978, Juanita worked at the Bailey's Community Center supervising the summer and after-school programs. In 1992 she was elected president of the Bailey's Social Seniors.

I, Houston Summers, Jr., was born at Freedman's Hospital in 1943. I grew up in Baileys Crossroads, then a black community of about 75 single-family residences. The community had no paved roads, storm drainage, sidewalks, gas, sewer, or public water. Electricity and telephones were the only services available. Residents without wells got their water from a spring located in the community. I can remember going to the spring with other kids in the summer. We watched crawfish, baby frogs, and tadpoles swimming in its streams. One could always find trees bearing fruit, blackberries to pick, mulberries to eat, birds, rabbits, and squirrels to hunt. The only dogs that were tied were hunting dogs; the rest of the dogs were allowed to run free because the environment was safe and everyone in the community knew one another. When you left home, your dog was there and was there to greet you upon your return.

In 1950 I entered first grade at James Lee Elementary School. I already knew my alphabet and could read the Dick and Jane books because my mother had taught me how to read. After I completed third grade, my parents and I moved to Thorofare, Virginia, in Prince William County near Gainesville. There I experienced life on a farm and attended a three-room, wood-frame colored school for one school year. I remember only that no one talked in class unless the teacher asked you something. It seemed to me we had recess all day. Because of the distance, we arrived at school early and played while we waited for school to start. After school we played more while we waited for the bus to arrive. We had a morning recess and a whole hour for lunch. The next year a new school, Antioch, was built across the road from where I lived. The holiday was over. My mother was a supervisor in the cafeteria. My cousin, Evelyn, taught first grade. I was now in the spotlight. My mother, a very smart woman, told me she could no longer help with my homework and I would have to pay attention in class and ask questions if I didn't understand something. Oh brother, my crutch was gone!

After I graduated from seventh grade, my parents and I moved back to Baileys Crossroads so I could attend Luther Jackson High School in 1957. Fairfax County finally built a Negro black public high school that was equal to the area's white school. The principal, Taylor Williams, ran a tight ship. The instructional staff was excellent. They nurtured us as students, setting high expectations for achievement; developed high self-esteem; and provided a curriculum that met the needs of the students. While attending Luther Jackson, I lettered in football and basketball, played first trumpet in the band, took bricklaying and maintained a B+ average in an academic curriculum. I graduated in 1962 and entered Hampton University the following fall.

I received a grant-in-aid, played football, and worked construction as a brick mason during the summers to help to pay for my education. I majored in industrial education. Hampton's academic programs were extremely difficult. The dean of men informed us freshmen that football was an extracurricular activity; we were attending Hampton University to obtain a degree, not to play football. I understood what he meant when only seven freshman football players returned for their sophomore season. Hampton not only prepared us with the skills necessary for a career, it also developed in us a desire to work in one's community. A line in our alma mater states: "Let our lives do the singing." As graduates, we felt we could compete with anyone, anywhere, at any time. Hampton was my home by the sea then, as well as now.

I graduated in 1966 and worked for 33 years for the Fairfax County Public School system as a teacher and administrator. While working as a teacher, I received a master of arts degree from the College of New Jersey in 1973, and later acquired more than 45 graduate hours in various disciplines in public school education. I met my wife, Joyce Bradby, in 1966 and we were married in 1968. Our daughter is Ashley Summers. We built our home in Baileys Crossroads in 1976. Since that time, I have served as president of the Springdale Civic Association; served on numerous boards, panels, and committees; been a spokesman for the community at countless open hearings; and have received many awards. I have "let my life do the singing."

Wanda Louise Summers was born in 1948 at Freedman's Hospital. She grew up in Baileys Crossroads in a segregated society where she played with her cousins, visited Aunt Hazel and her family daily and attended church on Sundays. In 1955, Wanda entered first grade at James Lee Elementary. Lillian Carey Elementary School opened in Baileys Crossroads the next year, and she graduated from there in 1961. During this time, schools were still segregated in Fairfax County but African American families could, if they chose to, send their children to white-only schools. Wanda was one of the first African Americans to attend Glasgow Intermediate School in 1961. She graduated from J.E.B. Stuart High School in 1967.

Wanda is a very intelligent person and a problem solver. She acts as an advisor and counselor, often placing others' problems before her own. She is a devoted mother and family supporter. In 1967, she entered Monroe College in Middletown, Virginia, and graduated with a business degree. After graduation, she worked for the federal government. As of 2006, she is division supervisor for the Department of State, Bureau of Diplomatic Security Services. Wanda married Jerome Barnett in 1972. They have two daughters—Melissa and Hillary.

Clarence Raymond Summers, III, was born at Freedman's Hospital in 1950. He grew up in Baileys Crossroads in a segregated community. During his childhood, he played with his cousins and neighbors. He remembers eating mulberries, blackberries, and pears from his grandfather's yard. He also worked in his father's garden. Clarence entered first grade at Lillian Carey Elementary School in 1958. He then attended Glasgow Intermediate School, graduated from J.E.B. Stuart High School in 1969, and went on to the University of Maryland and George Mason University. While at Stuart, he played football, basketball, and ran track. Unlike many other African American students, Clarence assimilated with the white students attending J.E.B. Stuart High School.

Clarence is the adventurer of the family. He loves outdoor activities and, as a world traveler, has backpacked through Central America, Nepal, India, and Europe. While still in high school, he spent summers working in Glacier Bay National Park in Alaska. Dedicated to youth sports, Clarence coaches youth basketball, soccer, and baseball and is a Boy Scout leader. He is also a very compassionate and caring person. He cared for his father in his home for 10 years until his death in 2004. Clarence has worked for the Department of Interior as a federal park ranger and supervisor since the early 1970s. He presently lives in Anchorage, Alaska, with his wife, Janice Morkto, whom he married in 1992. They have one son—Clarence, IV.

Cheryl Summers was born in 1952 at Freedman's Hospital. She grew up in Baileys Crossroads and attended Lillian Carey Elementary School, Glasgow Intermediate School, and graduated from J.E.B. Stuart High School in 1971. She then attended Northern Virginia Community College. Cheryl is a hard worker and is employed by the federal government. She began her career as a clerk typist and is presently a senior human resources manager in the office of the Secretary of Defense at the Pentagon. She is married to Waver L. Sneed and has two sons—Aubrey and Brian.

In 2006, I am the only descendent of John Bell presently living on his original land designated in the property deed books of Fairfax County as Bell Estates.

Endnotes

1. Fairfax County Deed Book X-7, 349.
2. Ibid., U4, 319–21.
3. Told to the author by his father, Houston M. Summers, Sr.
4. Family genealogy prepared in 1994 by Elaina White West.

5. Marriage License, Fairfax County, Virginia, October 17, 1903, Circuit Court Archives, Fairfax, Virginia.

6. Fairfax County Deed Book T-6, 698–700.

7. Ibid., G-12, 467–8.

8. Guinevere Jones, *African American Landowners, Churches, Schools, and Businesses: Fairfax County, Virginia, 1860–1900* (Fairfax County, Virginia: 2000).

9. Fairfax County Deed Book D-5, 364–6.

A Brief History of the Fairfax Education Association
Teachers and Administrators Bring About Change
By Dennis Joseph Pfennig, *Springfield, Virginia*

In 1886 Milton Dulany Hall began his 42-year career as school superintendent in Fairfax County. He was 37 years old. When his administration began, there were 73 schools operating; 64 of them had no outhouses. Only six of these had more than a single room, less than 35 percent of the county's youth attended, and teachers' salaries averaged about $27 a month. Hall's annual salary was $420. The school system cost the taxpayers approximately $40,000 annually. That year, Fairfax County's school population was 6,237; by 1890 it was 6,403. Fairfax received $1,984.93 from the state to educate the children. That was 31¢ cents per pupil.

Hall was an innovator for his day. A change he made in 1890 that was near revolutionary for its time was giving teachers a six-month employment contract. Hall's administration also saw for the first time teachers retiring and receiving a pension. The first teacher retired in 1909, receiving a quarterly pension of $27.56. Another retired in 1916. Her quarterly pension was $100.

Another of Hall's innovations was summer Peabody institutes for teachers. (The educational innovation of Georgia-born philanthropist George Foster Peabody, today these would be called teacher in-services.) These institutes lasted five days, and in addition to the reading of essays, public addresses, and a general discussion by the teachers and the county superintendent of the most approved methods of teaching, model classes were organized to demonstrate new methodology. To ensure the new methods he stressed were being employed, "Colonel Hall," as he was affectionately called, wearing a top hat, traveled in his horse and buggy from school to school. Anxious teachers made sure their pupils were well scrubbed, classrooms were swept, and student spelling bees were conducted to impress the superintendent.

At the same time, the Virginia State Board of Education established the State Teachers Association, urging counties to establish local associations as well. Hall melded this state mandate for local associations with his institutes. By the spring of 1897, Hall had established two associations—one for the white teachers and one for the black. He attended meetings of both organizations regularly, took part in discussions, and gave advice as to work in the schools. While Hall served as president of the white association, the colored association had its own president. In 1897, it was A.T. Shirley. All county teachers were described in May 1897 by *The Virginia School Journal* as poor and having to depend "solely on their meager salaries." Both black and white teachers begged in 1897 that they needed to be paid on time, have better pay, and have a longer school year.

The white association eventually evolved into the Fairfax Education Association (FEA), recognized as an existing entity by the Virginia State Teachers Association as early as 1902. (That year the state organization noted in its journal that 42 jurisdictions, including Fairfax, had local teacher associations.) By 1914 annual Virginia educational conferences were held in Richmond, and Fairfax was assigned to State District 8 along with Alexandria County (now Arlington), Culpeper, Fauquier, King George, Loudoun, Louisa, Orange, and Stafford counties. In 1920 the state association journal listed for the first time a president of FEA—Mary M. Snead. By that time Fairfax had 100-percent membership in the state association. The reason for that was quite simple: Membership was a requirement for employment. The county school board took state and local association dues directly out of teachers' salaries.

Moving Ahead with Vision

Throughout the next half-century, FEA remained essentially a company union, one in which membership is a requirement for employment, dues are taken out of paychecks by the employer, and management pre-approves elected leaders. But even in this era of complacency, there were ripples. One young teacher in the 1910s complained that the only equipment provided her by Hall's leadership was a broom and a box of chalk. She lamented that if she wanted anything else she had to get out and get it. Her one-room, wood-frame school had neither electricity nor running water. The students performed upkeep on the school. The boys brought shovels and rakes to level the ground and plant trees. She further complained that Superintendent Hall "was of the old school . . . and I don't think I saw him but several times the whole time I taught." Still the job had its bright side as the same teacher noted that during the four years she taught in the county she never had one problem in discipline; never had one act of vandalism.

After World War I, many an FEA member read with interest an article in the May 1928 edition of the *Virginia Journal of Education,* the voice of the state association renamed the Virginia Education Association (VEA). The article proclaimed, "The teachers . . . of Virginia have . . . hardly realized the power . . . [that] could be exercised if . . . [they] chose not to endure . . . perpetual bullying by ingnoramuses *[sic].* The teachers will be slaves if they act like slaves. Weakness always tempts the bully. If they cower, they will be bullied. . . . Nothing can excuse or explain away spinelessness." This may have inspired Fairfax teachers meeting in Falls Church in 1930 as part of VEA's District H to have the courage to call for, among other things, "a more adequate retirement," a nine-month school term, and free textbooks. The following year, the same group moved that "sex education be included as a regular part of teacher training courses at the state teacher colleges." Individual activism also appeared. In November of 1940, one FEA member wrote to Superintendent W.T. Woodson challenging the automatic deduction of $2.10 in VEA/FEA dues from his salary. Woodson responded with surprise that anyone would challenge the practice, admitting "to my knowledge yours is the first instance where the question has been raised." But he did urge the writer to take the matter to the school board.

By 1930 Fairfax teachers were doing a superb job with the children of the county. The illiteracy rate among students had fallen in just five years from some 11 percent to 4.3 percent. Teachers began to think "outside the box." Elizabeth Minor of Baileys Cross Roads School had her students write to four Indian schools in Arizona "for first-hand information concerning the Hopi and Navajo" tribes. The class got a reply from one of the four. They answered by sending pictures of Washington, DC, and stories of their home life, while in return received a Navajo doll, a blanket, a piece of the Petrified Forest, two pieces of pottery, and colored corn. Elizabeth Minor proudly reported to her charges: "Indians . . . are no longer characters found only in books but real people."

The outbreak of World War II saw FEA members supporting the troops. While FEA's executive committee set a goal of $100 for the National Education Association's War and Peace Fund Drive, by September of 1943, members contributed a total of $130.30. But the war did not stop FEA from urging members to vote; to maintain professionalism in relations with students, principals, and each other; and to continue interest in the affairs of the VEA.

After World War II

The postwar years witnessed a flurry of activism on the part of FEA. Veterans of the war were not as docile as those who preceded them in the classroom. The organization severed its last ties with the school system. It was independent. It rented office space in downtown Fairfax. In 1956, FEA leaders established the Fairfax Education Association Federal Credit Union, now independent of the FEA and known as the Apple Federal Credit Union. With assets in excess of $700 million, the institution serves more than 60,000 clients.

The youth movement of the 1960s and its assault on authority added to the restlessness of teachers. In 1962 FEA hired its first executive director, Paul Peter. This one-time radio announcer and teacher was an effective leader in desegregating the profession (in 1963), having the FEA incorporated under state law, and negotiating the first collective bargaining contract within the state of Virginia. But many saw him as a "tea-and-crumpets" man, one too much in the pocket of the superintendent. Thus, Allerton H. Barnes replaced him in 1968. The fact that Barnes had recently organized a strike in Denver, Colorado, caused concern among county leaders. He negotiated contracts that provided for a grievance procedure, full release time for the FEA president, a sick-leave bank, and a joint school administration/FEA commission to work on matters of mutual concern. The most lasting success of his tenure was achieved in 1973 when, along with the strong championing of association leaders such as Walt Mika and Gloria Thorpe, he successfully got the school board to agree to a county retirement plan to supplement the existing state program.

By 1971, the FEA had grown so that it purchased an 8.5-acre tract on Little River Turnpike to expand its once rented headquarters. (This was sold at a profit in 1988 when the organization purchased its present building near downtown Fairfax.) That same year, FEA's encouragement of teachers running for public office paid off as James H. Dillard, II, a Republican and one-time member of the FEA board of directors, successfully entered the state House of Delegates. (Dillard rose to be chair of the House Education Committee. He retired from public service in 2005.)

The 1980s and 1990s saw the FEA struggle with issues of pay for performance, more stringent teacher evaluation programs, changing demographics, and complacency on the part of the Reagan-Me-First generation. The organization had to face these and other issues without collective bargaining, which the Virginia State Supreme Court declared unconstitutional in 1977. But even without this, the FEA got the school system to agree to a new communications procedure, gained additional salary for its members by successfully getting the school board to improve salaries and add longevity steps to the scale, and blocked attempts to eliminate Monday early closing on the elementary level. With the use of newspaper advertisements, monetary contributions to political action committees, and one-on-one lobbying both locally and on the state level, FEA members supported political leaders who were pro-education. In the most recent local elections, 11 of the 12 successful candidates for school board won with FEA endorsement.

Superintendent Hall never really envisioned back in the 1880s that the simple teachers association that he incorporated as part of his annual institutes would one day play the role it does in the formulation of local and state education policy.

It Began with the 1898 Spanish-American War
Filipinos and Other Asian Americans in Fairfax County
By Corazon Sandoval Foley, *Burke, Virginia*

The Spanish-American War was a milestone for Fairfax County because it helped develop Dunn Loring and it triggered the migration of Filipino Americans, some of whom settled in Fairfax County along with other Asian Americans. Four hundred years after Jamestown was settled, Asian Americans have become the largest minority group in Fairfax County—in 2005, 153,000 residents (15 percent) of the Fairfax County population are of Asian heritage.

Camp Alger and Dunn Loring
On February 24, 2006, the Virginia legislature passed Senate Joint Resolution No. 191 on the occasion of Dunn Loring's 120th anniversary. It stated: "During the Spanish-American War, the founding of Camp Russell A. Alger brought growth and prosperity to Dunn Loring, and among the troops trained at Camp Alger was the celebrated author-poet Carl Sandburg, after whom the present Sandburg Street was named."

Following the sinking of the battleship *Maine* in the Havana harbor in February 1898 and the declaration of war against Spain in April, a call for volunteers was issued. Overnight the army's quota was filled and President William McKinley selected a site between Falls Church and Vienna for the assembly point. The site was intended to be symbolic of a reunited North and South dedicated in a common cause. Further, it was handy to Washington, connected both by steam railroads and electric trolley lines. On May 13, 1898, Camp Alger was established in honor of Secretary of War Russell A. Alger, who, coincidentally, had served in Fairfax County with the Union Army during the Civil War. More than 23,000 soldiers from 16 states entered the camp's gateway—the railroad hamlet of Dunn Loring. In the end, Camp Alger barely fulfilled its purpose before it had to be closed in August 1898 after an epidemic of typhoid fever. The War Department began the sale of land in September 1898, as Falls Church and Dunn Loring settled back into a more leisurely way of life.[1]

Filipino Americans and Asian Americans in Virginia and Fairfax County
Meanwhile, the Spanish-American War led to the Philippines becoming an American territory and Filipino Americans began permanent settlements in America.[2] They first came to Hawaii in 1906 as farm laborers. They later immigrated to other states, including Virginia, as nurses, doctors, and other professionals. The 1930 census found 45,208 Filipinos in the 48 mainland states, with more than 100 living in Virginia. By the 2000 census, Filipino Americans had grown to some 2.4 million, or

about 20 percent of the Asian American population. Filipino Americans represent the second largest Asian American group after Chinese Americans.

Filipino Americans have valued integration as active contributing members in the American society; many have chosen interracial marriages. In Virginia, Congressman Robert C. Scott of the 3rd District and Secretary of Public Safety John W. Marshall are of both Filipino and African American heritage.

In November 1992, Congressman Robert Cortez Scott became only the second African American from Virginia to be elected to the United States House of Representatives, and the first since Reconstruction. Having a maternal grandfather of Filipino ancestry also gives Congressman Scott the distinction of being the first American with Filipino heritage to serve in the United States Congress. Congressman Robert Cortez Scott chaired the Civil Rights Task Force of the Congressional Asian Pacific American Caucus.

John W. Marshall served with distinction as Virginia's secretary of public safety starting in 2002. He began his public safety career as a member of the Virginia State Police, earning promotions from the rank of trooper to special agent to sergeant during his 14 years of service. Between 1994 and 1999, he served as a U.S. marshal for the eastern district of Virginia. In 1999, he was appointed by President Bill Clinton to be the head of the U.S. Marshals Service. Secretary John Marshall, his brother, his father (the late Supreme Court justice Thurgood Marshall), and his mother—Cecelia Suyat Marshall, a Filipino American originally from Hawaii—lived in Fairfax County.

Changes in U.S. immigration laws, the Korean War, and the Vietnam War increased immigration from Asia to the U.S. By the 2000 census, Fairfax County had become one of the top 25 counties in the U.S. in terms of the proportion of Asian American residents. The Asian American population in Fairfax County totaled 126,038, or 13 percent of the county population. The group included Korean Americans (28,028, or 2.9 percent), Asian Indian (25,700, or 2.7 percent), Vietnamese Americans (23,044, or 2.4 percent), Chinese Americans (17,756, or 1.8 percent), and Japanese Americans (2,892, or 0.3 percent). Filipino Americans ranked fifth, with 11,632 Filipino Americans who constituted 1.2 percent of the Fairfax County population.

Asian Americans have become the largest minority group in Fairfax County. By 2005, Fairfax County was home to 152,830 Asian Americans (15.2 percent of the county population of more than one million). This group represented 46 percent of Virginia's total Asian American population of 329,529 (4.4 percent of 7.6 million Virginians).

Camp Alger in Dunn Loring and Falls Church, 1898. (Courtesy Fairfax Historical Commission)

The Foley Family of Burke, Virginia. From left to right, the author Corazon, Michael, Melinda, and Joshua.

Fairfax County Population by Race and Ethnicity, 2000

Race	Non-Hispanic		Hispanic		Total	
	Number	Percent	Number	Percent	Number	Percent
White alone	624,296	72.4	53,608	50.1	677,904	69.9
Black or African American alone	81,287	9.4	1,811	1.7	83,098	8.6
American Indian or Alaska Native alone	1,834	0.2	727	0.7	2,561	0.3
Asian alone	125,585	14.5	453	0.4	126,038	13.0
Native Hawaiian and Other Pacific Islander alone	616	0.1	75	0.1	691	0.1
Some other race alone	2,473	0.3	41,546	38.8	44,019	4.5
Two or more races	26,700	3.1	8,738	8.2	35,438	3.6
Total	**862,791**	**100.0**	**106,958**	**100.0**	**969,749**	**100.0**

Source: U.S. Census Bureau, 2000 Census of Population and Housing, Table P7.

Asian Americans in the Fairfax County Landscape

The Edgewater neighborhood on Burke Lake Road has many reminders of the ways Asian Americans have been integrated into the life of Fairfax County. The Korean American Church—The Happiness Presbyterian Church of Washington—meets in the church built in 1891 by an African American congregation. The Little Zion Baptist congregation moved to a new building at 10185 Zion Drive.

In addition to changing the demographic composition of Fairfax County, the influx of Asian American residents has changed the landscape. Aging suburban strip malls have been reinvigorated by businesses catering to Asian customers and restaurants offering a variety of Asian cuisines. Weekend language and culture schools have sprung up to broaden the American education of Asian Americans and other interested students.

The growth of the Asian American population also has influenced cultural life, with a proliferation of traditional arts associations, many of them affiliated with churches or temples. Many communities have sponsored annual festivals to celebrate the diverse cultures, traditions, and talents from Asia. In 2006, 17,000 visitors joined the third annual Reston Asian Festival showcasing cultures from the Philippines, China, Japan, Vietnam, Korea, India, and Thailand. All these have enriched the Fairfax County lifestyle.

The commercial landscape of Fairfax County has been a particularly active arena for Asian American contributions. Fairfax County has more Asian-owned firms than any other locality in the Washington area and Virginia, and more of these businesses than 37 states. Fairfax County accounts for about 47 percent of all the Asian-owned businesses in Virginia, and 35.6 percent of the Asian-owned businesses in the Washington area.

On May 16, 2006, the U.S. Census Bureau reported that 14,313 Asian-owned businesses operated in Fairfax County in 2002, a 34.7-percent increase since 1997 when the last count was taken. The Fairfax County increase is larger than the 24-percent national increase noted by the Census Bureau.[3] The 2002 Economic Census found that Asian-owned firms in Fairfax County employed 25,075 people in 2002, up 49 percent since 1997; had $2.7 billion in sales and receipts; and had payrolls totaling more than $922 million. Such business growth helps Fairfax County fund public services such as a top-ranked public school system and library, public safety, social services, and park systems.

Fairfax County School Board Chairman Ilryong Moon
Fairfax County elected its first Asian American official in 1995. Ilryong Moon moved from Korea to the U.S. with his family in 1974. He arrived as a 17-year-old rising junior, but repeated the 10th grade to learn English as an ESL student.

Ilryong Moon went on to become a cum laude graduate of Harvard and then to law school. He is now a partner of Moon, Park & Associates in Fairfax and his main practice area is in business law. He has held key positions, including at-large commissioner on the Fairfax County Planning Commission; vice president of a local Rotary Club; and member of the Virginia Advisory Committee of the U.S. Civil Rights Commission. His wife, Haewon, is a coordinator of the piano department at the Duke Ellington School of the Arts. He has two sons; both graduated from Thomas Jefferson High School for Science and Technology.

Ilryong Moon believes "the diverse communities in Fairfax should all work together to build a better community and they can certainly build a better community by working together. Although the county enjoys the best reputation as a model of education in the whole country, we need to improve what we have. As Fairfax has the most diverse student body and an increasing population, I want to hire more bilingual staff and teachers. I want to get more resources to raise the standard of teachers' training and pay them better. I want to decrease class size as class sizes are a factor in success and a key to reduction in disparity." He wants his children to grow up and live here not just as "hyphenated" Asian Americans, but as "full-fledged" Americans.

Changes in the Law
In 1967, the Supreme Court abolished the barrier that made it impossible for my family to enjoy life as Fairfax County residents. Before 1967, state governments were able to deny marriage licenses to interracial couples and punish them with fines, imprisonment, and hard labor. As an example, Richard and Mildred Loving were

Congressman Robert Cortez Scott of Virginia's 3rd District is the first American with Filipino heritage to serve in the United States Congress.

Ilryong Moon, Fairfax County School Board chairman in 2006.

dragged out of bed by Virginia police and arrested for being married outside of their race. When the Supreme Court ruled in their favor in *Loving* v. *Virginia* (June 12, 1967), interracial relationships were legalized nationwide.

I was born in Manila, Philippines, and moved to the U.S. in 1970. I met Michael Daniel Foley, a fourth-generation Irish American from California, in 1972, and we were married in 1973 in Alexandria, Virginia. Our family moved to Fairfax County in 1980, after serving overseas with the U.S. Department of State in Port-au-Prince, Haiti; Cebu, Philippines; and Leningrad in the former Soviet Union. Our children, Joshua Daniel and Melinda Corazon, graduated from West Springfield High School and Joshua also graduated from George Mason University. Michael, Joshua, and I are federal government public servants, and Melinda is a writer living in Los Angeles, California. Mike and I moved in 1996 to the Burke, Virginia, community of Edgewater, which was developed by Stanley Martin from 1990 to 1998. The community is located in the area in which an international airport was proposed but never built, due to vigorous Burke community protests in 1958. The Dulles International Airport was built instead.

Endnotes

1. (Steadman, Falls Church) from Industrial and Historical Sketch of Fairfax County, Virginia, 1907, as quoted in *Fairfax County in Virginia: A Pictorial History* by Ross and Nan Netherton, 1986.

2. Filipinos were the earliest Asians to cross the Pacific Ocean for the North American continent because they were pressed into service in the Manila galleon trade between Mexico and the Philippines from 1565 to 1815. Some jumped ship and in 1763, "Manilamen" settled in what became Louisiana. (Source: *Filipinos: Forgotten Asian Americans* by Fred Cordova, 1983.)

3. May 16, 2006, press release by the Fairfax County Economic Development Authority.

The Neck
Memories of a Woodburn Road Community
By Jennifer Santley, *Falls Church, Virginia*

In 1990, a longtime landmark of the Annandale area became history, the victim of progress, development, and improvement. For 66 years, a one-lane, wood-plank bridge carried Woodburn Road over the Accotink Creek, gradually becoming an anachronism in suburban Northern Virginia. The bridge earned dubious fame whenever heavy rains swelled the Accotink to flooding. High water washing over the bridge occasionally caused Woodburn Road to be closed to traffic. In 1981, Everett Robey, a lifelong Fairfax County resident who spent his childhood near the creek, described it this way:

> I've seen the Accotink look like the Potomac River. Lots of times, you'd lose your crops because they'd flood so. I've seen that creek in flood, when you can't get over that bridge. You wouldn't believe it. It looks like the Potomac River. They actually need a better bridge down there than what they've got. It's a wonder they haven't washed that away.

Well, they got a better bridge down there—a smooth, modern, two-lane paved span, which is resistant to all but the worst of flooding. We've gained efficiency and convenience, but we've lost some local charm and a link to our rural past.

The old rustic bridge is already only a memory, but even more headed for obscurity is the history of the community before the growth of modern housing developments. A few houses dating from the early 20th century and a couple of streets—Tobin Road and Robey Avenue—named after families who farmed the area, are among the only reminders.

In 1981, a few years before his death, I had the opportunity to talk to Everett Robey, a member of one of these farming families, in a series of informal interviews that provide a vivid picture of this characteristically rural area and its close-knit relationships.

Robey was born in 1901 in a log house on Woodburn Road to the north of Accotink Creek. He was the oldest of four children. The growing family soon outgrew the original house, and when Robey was about six years old, his father built a frame house alongside the log house. The family used both houses for a while, but eventually the log house was torn down. The frame house still stands and, until about 1990, remained the property of the Robey family. The Robeys' closest neighbors were relatives: Grandfather Ned Robey and his wife lived next door; second cousin Jasper Robey lived next to them; Andrew Kidwell and Randolph Kidwell, cousins on Robey's mother's side, lived further up the hill (Robey's recollection of the relationship was vague, but he admitted to the family being "mixed up with Kidwells");

great-uncle John Robey lived across the road. John Robey bought about 40 acres, from whom the other relatives acquired strips of land, each stretching down to the creek. Thus each household had access to water for farming. According to Robey's memory, the other neighbors (unrelated) who completed the community were Edgar Scott, William Walker, Lemuel Tobin, Oscar Thompson, and Tom Eskridge, whose children seem to have been Robey's principal playmates—a total of 11 households. For no reason Robey could remember, the community referred to its geographical location as "the Neck," a nickname that was later abandoned as inappropriate and re-placed by "Woodburn," after a school was built where the Woodburn Village apart-ments now stand.

The first school Robey attended was at Ilda, the neighborhood where Woodburn Road and Prosperity Avenue reach Little River Turnpike, and where Dove's Store once stood. Ilda was reached by crossing the log footbridge across Accotink Creek. The nearest drinking water to the school was about a mile away, at a spring down in the woods. The students, up to pranks, would ask the teacher if they could go fetch water. "Kill a little time," said Robey with a laugh. In the school building itself, there was a water bucket and a tin cup, out of which everyone drank. There were also a couple of wash basins for washing hands or feet.

Getting Water for the Household

Household water, now taken so much for granted by urban populations, was a highly valued commodity as Robey was growing up. At the Woodburn Road farm, his par-ents had no well, so they had to haul their water from his grandfather's well, up the road. As Robey told it:

> We had a slide, we called it. It had a 50-gallon barrel. So we had a cou-ple of horses. Well, we hooked one horse up to this barrel, slide, and go to my grandfather's and wind it full of water, 50 gallons. And we used that for watering the chickens and the pigs and so forth and washing the dishes and things like that. Drinking water, we usually went up there and brought it down to the house in buckets.

One barrelful lasted two or three days. The effort involved in transporting water to the house resulted in very little indulgence in washing or bathing. "Didn't do too much of that," said Robey. "We had a wash tub, you could take a bath in it, if you wanted to. Didn't have a bathtub. We didn't do it too often, I tell you."

While listening to Robey's narration, I became aware of how much of his recol-lected history was concerned with sheer physical survival, the effort involved in ob-taining water being one instance. Fortunately, not all his activities were as hazardous as one that gave rise to an incident clearly remembered for its narrow escape:

We had a meat house and we smoked meat. And so I went in there when the meat was smoking, and my brother thought he'd bait me, shut the door and turned the knob, and boy, I couldn't get my breath. When he did open it up, I was just about passed out. He'd a waited a little while longer, I'd have been dead.

Yet another chore that devolved on him as a boy was cutting firewood and stacking it in the wood box in the kitchen. A couple of weeks before Christmas, they laid in extra firewood so none had to be sawed or chopped over the holidays, leaving ample time for celebration. Schools also were heated with wood-burning stoves. According to Robey, "a plenty good-sized student" would be paid to come out early in the morning and get the room warm for the day. There was a high danger of fire inherent in such methods of heating and cooking, particularly when sparks leaving the chimney ignited the wooden roof shingles. Robey recalled several buildings that succumbed to fire, including his in-law's house, the one-room school he later attended in Merrifield, and the Methodist Church at Merrifield. The all-volunteer fire companies were few and far between for combating such disasters. Local historian Nan Netherton wrote it was not until the 1920s that electricity was made available to the majority of households and communities in Fairfax County.[1] In fact, in 1920, only about 145 of the more than 2,000 farms in the county had electricity, and only 75 of them had running water. Most of them had telephones before they had these other amenities.[2]

Taking Goods to Market

The families of the Neck lived by truck farming, in common with a large proportion of the residents of Fairfax County. *Chataigne's Gazetteer* of 1897 states, "the land throughout the county is generally good, producing corn, wheat, rye, oats, potatoes, etc."[3] In 1900, most of the county's 18,580 residents were living on farms,[4] and in Annandale, described by the Board of Supervisors in 1907 as a "promising village, having a church, school, and blacksmith shop," most people made their livelihood from dairying, trucking, and general farming.[5] The board also reported, in 1907, "Improvements in transportation, roads and railroads, spurred increased local activities in dairying . . . , fruit, vegetable and flower growing, to supply the increasing needs of Washington, DC."[6] Robey's father kept some livestock to supply their own needs: cows, pigs ("We had hogmeat nearly every meal."), chickens, and horses to pull wagons.

However, it was his strawberry crop that kept most of his attention. The Robey children and other neighborhood youngsters were paid 1½¢ a quart for picking strawberries. During the strawberry season, Robey's father hauled not only his own crop but those of his neighbors to market three times a week. This was one of Robey's most vivid memories from his childhood. He accompanied his father in their Dayton wagon, leaving home at 8 p.m. and arriving at the market at Fifth and K streets in downtown Washington at 1 a.m. He then slept for three or four hours on hay in the back of the wagon, before the first customers arrived, and by the time they returned home, "It was getting pretty dark," the journey taking five hours in each direction. In winter, the trip to market, to sell such things as pigs and potatoes, was made only once a week.

It is not surprising the journey into Washington took so long. The condition of Fairfax County roads in the early 1900s was so poor automobiles were not considered a viable alternative to horse-drawn transportation.[7] Nan Netherton, in her *Fairfax County, Virginia: A History,* quotes resident Charlotte Corner as saying, in 1906, county roads were "just rivers of mud."[8] Even as late as 1917, Harry B. Derr, the county agricultural agent, complained, "There were very few miles of hard roads in the county and much of the work had to be done with horse and buggy."[9] However, by 1925, he was able to report, "During the past three years over 100 miles of hard-surfaced roads have been built," keeping pace with the increased number of motor vehicles in the county, which reached 2,775 in 1923.[10]

Robey attested to the poor condition of the roads in the early century. When he was a boy, he and his friends used to take their bicycles to Leesburg Pike (Route 7) on a Sunday, because that was the closest paved road, and it was easier to push the bicycles there. Little River Turnpike, a mile from the Robeys' house, had a cobblestone surface and was, therefore, better than most. Almost everywhere else one ran the risk of being stranded in mud when it rained. Robey's father purchased a Model-T Ford in the early 1920s and, on one occasion, Robey remembered helping his father push and shove their car up to the top of Woodburn Road, leaving it parked there overnight so as to avoid the risk of being bogged down the next morning. According to Robey, Merrifield had a particular reputation for the state of its roads. Apparently there were several sawmills in the vicinity of Merrifield and, as Robey explained,

> You know when you saw lumber, and the slabs come off the side? Well, the roads was so bad out there, that they, in the winter time, they couldn't hardly get on their horses and wagon. They made a slab road. And so they called Merrifield "Slab Town."

After Merrifield got its own post office, the local residents objected to the pejorative sobriquet. "Boy," said Robey, "they'd get mad if you called it Slab Town."

Fortunately, there was an alternative to traveling on these deplorable roads. In 1897, *Chataigne's Gazetteer* stated that Fairfax County "transportation facilities are of the very best, there being hardly a place, even the most inaccessible, more than six or eight miles from some one or other of the several railroads which traverse the county,"[11] and the county Board of Supervisors reported a spate of suburban home-building in 1907, due, in part, to accessibility to the railroads.[12] Tying in with the railroad system was the electric trolley network that served commuters in the Northern Virginia area. For instance, Washington and Old Dominion (W&OD) trains connected with Capital Traction cars and resulted in the W&OD lying "somewhere between a true railroad and an electric interurban trolley system."[13]

Taking the Train to Washington and Glen Echo

The Washington and Virginia Railway Company operated two lines—one ran out to Mount Vernon, and the other connecting Rosslyn with Fairfax via Clarendon and Vienna.[14] It was this second line the Robey family used for excursions to Washington. They thought nothing of walking the three and a half miles from home to the depot at Dunn Loring on a Saturday evening. After the movie in town, they caught the last car about midnight and made the long walk home. Robey also recollected outings to the Glen Echo amusement park, out McArthur Boulevard. These excursions involved such planning and excitement, he said it "was like taking a trip to Europe." First, they traveled by horse and wagon to Falls Church, where the horse was left at Nourse's livery stable for the day. Then they would take "the trolley car, go down to Georgetown, walk up a pair of steps, get on another trolley car and go to Glen Echo."

Judging by a photograph in Robey's possession showing the East Falls Church station in the early 1900s, the services of the two livery stables in town were much in demand.[15] The scene shows many horse-drawn vehicles gathered at the station. Looking at that photograph, Robey described some of the different kinds of wagons and carriages in use during his youth. His father drove a Dayton wagon to market. "It looked like a buggy really, only it was longer. People used it more for their hauling, going to market and stuff like that. It was kind of a commercial-looking deal with room for four people to ride." It was not as fancy as a carriage, which, as he said, "was more of a Sunday deal, and it had a fringe on them, and all dressed up."

The stake-body truck was another farm vehicle. "People would use them around farms to haul cattle and stuff on them, they just got a flat platform and some things shoved in there, like a fence." Stake-body trucks were put to grim use during the flu epidemic at the end of World War I. According to Netherton's *History*, the epidemic killed more than 11,000 Virginians, among whom were 531 Fairfax County residents, the second highest county figure in the state.[16] The previously quoted resident, Charlotte Corner, said, "You couldn't bury people 'cause they didn't have enough coffins. . . . And there were not enough doctors, there were not enough nurses."[17] Robey corroborated this information with his own recollection of being told at Camp Humphreys, the training center for the Army Corps of Engineers, now known as Fort Belvoir,[18] "They were hauling soldiers out of there, that died so fast, pulled them out of there in a stake-body truck, piled one on top of the other. They was dying so fast down there." Apparently the Robey family heeded the plea such as the one published in the *Fairfax Herald,* on October 18, 1918, urging "the people ... stay away from ... Washington and Alexandria."[19] Certainly, he said he "never had it, 'cause we didn't go anywhere once we knew the epidemic was going. So we stayed kind of close. Didn't any of my family get it." The epidemic brought public activity to a standstill, closing schools and churches and canceling community gatherings, including the county fair.[20]

Doctors and dentists paid their house calls by horse and buggy, and Robey remembered one occasion when the dentist came all the way from Herndon to Woodburn Road. To make the journey worthwhile, he pulled teeth from Robey's grandmother, mother, and aunt all in one day. Wagons, then, of one sort or another, were a vital form of transportation in Robey's childhood. In the post-Civil War era, in spite of the growth of the railroads, "wagons continued to carry the bulk of Fairfax farm goods to Washington markets," even though, according to Netherton, roads were often impassable,[21] and even as late as 1916, a U.S. Department of Agriculture study found while "the men on the larger farms [were] beginning to use motor trucks" to deliver produce to Washington markets, "the common practice for the farmer [of 10 to 40 acres was] to do the hauling himself with his farm horses and wagons."[22]

Robey recalled his first time in an automobile when, as a boy, he rode with the doctor into Falls Church to fetch some medicine. He conveyed the excitement of the occasion thus:

> That was the first time I ever rode in a automobile. Nobody around had a automobile, and he had a automobile. I thought that was great, riding out there in a automobile.

When Robey's father bought his Model-T Ford, it greatly simplified his way of making a living, and Robey himself owned a car from the time he first went to work for Thompson's Dairy in Washington in 1920.

Plenty of Work; No Time for Mischief

Robey's father attached great importance to the performance of work, and set the example by his own diligence. "Oh, he worked hard, I tell you. I don't think you could get anybody to work like that these days." When his father went to market alone, he left his son "enough work for two days," so much work, in fact, it was discouraging. "Boy, he always seen that you wouldn't run out of work. We didn't have time to get into mischief." As he said, "Sunday was about all the vacation we had," and even then, when he and his friends rode their bicycles on Route 7, his father complained he was "no good on Monday and I was played out." Other times, the farm work still had to be done after day excursions to Glen Echo, so Robey remarked, "You really paid for all your pleasure."

In spite of this burden of work, Robey and his friends managed to have fun. Robey particularly remembered the annual county fairs and the summer ice cream festivals. The first county fair was held in 1912,[23] when Robey was 11. Ice cream festivals were church fundraising events that seem to have raised religious eyebrows in 1916. In that year, the United States Census of Religious Bodies revealed "many county residents may have preferred ice cream and social gatherings to churchgoing on Sundays."[24] Some of the local supply of ice cream came from people named Mason who then owned the Walnut Hill mansion on Annandale Road. Robey said, "They done it with a treadmill, with a bull in it, turned the ice cream pretty good." Because of the lack of refrigeration, "They had to get it and sell it pretty quick," and indeed, a blue law was passed in 1916 that provided, "Ice cream made on any day other than Sunday, can be delivered on Sunday on the ground of necessity."[25] Robey related how, on one occasion when a thunderstorm threatened, ice cream was being given away in order to dispose of it. One small boy was sick for a couple of days afterwards from overindulgence.

Christmas appears to have been the most important time for celebration in the Robeys' year. Although not much visiting was done the rest of the year, on Christmas morning, "We'd go house to house, and they'd give you some cake and wine and stuff like that." But the highlights of the season were the square dances that took place almost every night during Christmas week. Each family in the small community took it in turn to host the dance. They had "a couple of violins and a banjo to make the music, and they'd pass the hat around and pay off the musicians." At intermission, the ladies served coffee and cake. Routine chores were cut down to a minimum during this week of celebration.

The women of the Neck engaged in quilting bees in the winter time. In Robey's words,

> They had these quilting frames, and they put them up in one house, and they'd all come round during the day and work on a quilt. And they got the quilt made, and someone else would take it home with them. Then they'd all go get together and make quilts at *their* house. They kept that frame going pretty much during the winter months. Either one house or another.

Robey continued the story of his life with anecdotes about his working life, particularly his 46-year employment by Thompson's Dairy (originally making his rounds with horse and wagon), and about his marriage and the purchase of his own home on Annandale Road where he and his wife lived from 1929 until his death in 1984. His property is now the site of Roundtree Estates, near the intersection of Annandale and Graham roads.

For the purpose of learning the history of the Neck and its farming community, Robey's stories relating to his childhood are the most relevant. As a child, he inherited some family anecdotes that referred to even earlier times. One such anecdote about the War Between the States was told to him by his grandmother. His great-uncle, watching cows in a field, unwittingly gave information to a Southern soldier, and as a result, a Yankee soldier was killed. As Robey said, "He didn't have no idea what [the Southern soldier] was looking for [the Yankee] for," but the boy was left with a feeling of guilt that became part of the family story. Neither the place nor the exact date is given, but Robey's great-grandparents were prominent farmers at Merrifield, so it is likely the event occurred in that vicinity.

Soldiers in the Neighborhood

Easier to pinpoint are the circumstances surrounding Robey's grandmother's recollections of the Spanish-American War in 1898. Evidently, more than 35,000 troops were stationed at Camp Alger, near Merrifield, by August of that year. According to Charles Alexander Stewart, in *Virginia Village: Historical Sketch of Falls Church and the Old Colonial Church,* published by J.H. Newell in 1904, there was great activity at the camp, what with "troop trains arriving or departing, drills . . . , marches . . . , martial music from army bands, reveille and taps," all of which "contributed to impress [local] folk with the fact that the country was at war." He adds "The houses of the citizens were thrown open to soldiers . . . , and the ladies . . . vied with each other in contributing to the comfort of sick soldiers at the camp."[26] Apparently Robey's grandparents were among those offering comfort to the troops. As Robey put it, "My grandfather and them that lived round here and close by, they tell me they used to bake cakes and pies and things, and run over and sell them to the soldiers." It is to be hoped his grandfather was not one of those described by an eyewitness, in the *Terre Haute (IN) Express.* He reported he saw "imitation pastry sold as pies" by local peddlers. More appealing is the conjecture that the "company of midwesterners [who] reported tasting their first corn pone at a farm house near camp,"[27] may have been offered it by the Robey grandparents.

At any rate, we do know the Robey well on Woodburn Road never stopped turning, supplying drinking water to the soldiers trudging up and down the road to the Accotink Creek. As Robey said, they were "going down there *all* day long. And a lot of recruits who come here, they didn't have any, I guess, any place for them to take a bath or shower or anything. They'd go down there and they'd take their new uniform down there and go in and bathe. And then leave them laying on the bank and go, their old clothes laying on the bank, so their clothes were strung all up and down the branch here."

Such stories lend character to the community of the Neck, a community that identified itself largely by family relationships, common livelihood, and the geographical boundary of Accotink Creek. One more anecdote illustrates the importance of the bonds among the farming families of the Woodburn Road area, but perhaps it also marks a turning point in the Neck's self-containment. During Robey's childhood, the only way to cross the creek was to ford it with horse and wagon, or later by car, or to use the "crossing log."

> They cut an old tree down and let it fall across and trimmed it up, and they tacked a kind of hand-pole on to it you could hold to, and that's all we'd get across with, by walking that log.

However, in 1924, Cameron Station in Alexandria, wanting to dispose of a bridge they were replacing there, offered it to the Woodburn Road community:

> So all these neighbors around, all these people I'm telling you, they got together and went down in their horse and wagons and hauled that bridge up here.

Later that same year, the Board of Supervisors advertised for bids to build approaches to the bridge. Mr. Minor beat out Mr. Hummer and Mr. Tobin with his lowest bid of $181.50.[28]

So the one-lane bridge was installed, expanding the boundaries of the Woodburn Road community, and becoming a familiar landmark in the Annandale area for 66 years. By now, much of the community has gone, along with its farming way of life, and the bridge itself has passed into history. No longer do commuters have to slow down to take their turn over the clankety wooden planking. But while they cross over Accotink Creek, they also unwittingly pass by a segment of the county's history that might have been lost were it not for the willingness of Robey to share his memories. His contribution to the historical legacy of Fairfax County is a rare gift.

Endnotes

1. Nan Netherton et al., *Fairfax County, Virginia: A History.* (Fairfax, Virginia: Fairfax County Board of Supervisors, 1978), 464.

2. Ibid., 529.

3. *Fairfax County in Virginia: Being a Random Selection From Rare Sources Relative to the County's Historic Development, as Described in Statute, Gazetteer, Atlas and Directory, 1742–1973* (Fairfax County, Virginia: History Program Office of Comprehensive Planning, 1974), 15.

4. Netherton, *Fairfax County,* 541.

5. *Fairfax County in Virginia,* 38.

6. Ibid., 22.

7. Ibid., 525.

8. Ibid., 526.

9. Ibid.

10. Ibid., 528.

11. *Fairfax County in Virginia,* 15.

12. Ibid., 17.

13. Jeremy F. Plant and Edgar R. Connor, III, "Before Metro: A Brief History of Rail Commuter Service in Northern Virginia" in *Northern Virginia Heritage,* Vol. II, No. 3 (October 1980), 12.

14. Ibid., 12.

15. Photographs printed by Yates Printing Co., Falls Church, Virginia.

16. Netherton, *Fairfax County,* 499.

17. Ibid., 497.

18. Ibid., 495.

19. Ibid., 499.

20. Ibid.

21. Ibid., 460.

22. Ibid., 528.

23. Ibid., 515.

24. Ibid., 504.

25. Ibid.

26. Ibid., 464.

27. Ibid.

28. Minute Book, Fairfax County Board of Supervisors, July 2, 1924.

Source

Jennifer Santley, "Mr. Everett Robey: A Life Story," 1981. An oral history, including tape recordings and transcriptions of four interviews, on deposit with the Northern Virginia Folklife Center, George Mason University, Fairfax, Virginia.

Ivakota Farm, 1915 to 1962
The House of Another Chance
By Lynne Garvey Wark, *Clifton, Virginia*

Ivakota Farm is a heart-wrenching, yet heart-warming success story. Its characters include hundreds of lost women, hundreds of their babies and children, nurses, social workers, doctors, congressmen, judges, evangelists, philanthropists, and one very uncommon, energetic woman—Dr. Kate Waller Barrett. It is a story of lives saved, healed, and redeemed. It is a story of vision, commitment, hard work, Christian spirituality, and community compassion.

America's Progressive Era (1890–1920) knows no other story quite like Ivakota Farm. Its opening chapters unfolded at a time when other significant stories of vital social reform were being told just miles away—also in Northern Virginia. Here, then, is the story of shame, disgrace, redemption, care, and a return to America's mainstream by her lost female children and adults. It is a story of lessons learned that are timeless.

Ivakota was the name given to a farm purchased in 1907 and owned by Frank and Ella Shaw five miles outside the town of Clifton, Virginia. Established after the Civil War, the town had once been a plantation. The owner, William E. Beckwith, bequeathed to his family and slaves a large expanse of 1,200 acres of land upon his death. With the presence of railroads, a beautiful hotel, and four stores, Clifton became a growing island of commerce. In 1869, elementary and Sunday school classes were taught in the home of Susan Reviere Hetzel, a founding member of the Daughters of the American Revolution (DAR). By the summer of 1890, residents built a new elementary/high school and by 1903, enjoyed telephone and electrical light service. The town emerged as a socially and culturally sophisticated key player in the history of Fairfax County.[1]

Land around Clifton was farmed and used for dairy farms. Other land fueled the goal of the Progressive Era. About 1,155 acres of land, 10 miles away from Clifton, were dedicated to the Lorton prison for the District of Columbia men in 1908. President Theodore Roosevelt envisioned a place were inmates could be rehabilitated though a hard day's work, as part of his plan for humane treatment of all Americans. This rehabilitation could be facilitated if prisoners were provided with fresh air, natural light, and a place to live and work that would instill a sense of order and responsibility. For many years, his dream was an astounding success—including rehabilitated prisoners who had worked an on-site foundry producing fire hydrants and manhole covers still in use in the District of Columbia today. Animal husbandry, farming techniques, and architectural design were skills taught the prisoners, who lived without locks and cell blocks.[2] About 23 miles from Clifton, a progressive school for women was founded in 1906 in McLean by Lucy Madeira, who resolved to provide young women with an education that was as rigorous as that offered to young men. "Knowledge comes, but wisdom lingers," she was fond of saying.[3]

Dr. Kate Waller Barrett Plants the Seeds

Ella Shaw was a woman with a passion for social causes; indeed, her cousin was Mrs. Billy Sunday, wife of former Chicago baseball player turned Presbyterian evangelist (1863–1935). Ella had lived in various locations across the United States: Iowa, Virginia, and North Dakota—hence, the blended syllables to form the word "Ivakota" for the name of their farm. On July 3, 1913, Frank E. Shaw deeded Ivakota to his wife, Ella, for the sum of $10. In 1914, Dr. Kate Waller Barrett—a resident of Alexandria, Virginia, and president of the National Florence Crittenton Mission (NFCM) since 1898—began writing articles for the *Washington Times* on the social evils of unwed mothers and prostitution. Her daily writings were read by Ella and impressed her so much that on May 3, 1915, she deeded her property to the NFCM: a 264-acre farm, residence (completely furnished, including a piano), and 800 fruit jars. Later Ella donated a neighboring farm resulting in a farm of more than 400 acres.[4] The seeds of Ivakota's decades-long success were now firmly planted.

Dr. Kate Waller Barrett often told the story that was her "epiphany" to launch a movement to protect and rehabilitate lost young women and their children. Kate was born on January 24, 1857, at her family estate, Clifton, in Stafford County, Virginia.[5] Her father was a wealthy plantation owner. On July 19, 1876, Kate married Episcopal minister Rev. Dr. Robert South Barrett.[6] During the infancy of their first son, Robert South Jr., a young woman with an infant appeared late one night at the Barrett doorstep, wishing to see the minister. She was cold and wet, "clasping in her arms a fatherless child." Kate invited her in and visited with her, marveling at the deep bond she felt for both her and the child, and noting their similar situation. Kate stated, "She, too, was a country girl. She, too, had loved, but alas! For her, she had loved unwisely while I had loved wisely; she had loved a bad man and I a good one. That seemed to me about the only difference in our stories in the beginning, but how different the end." From that moment, Kate continues, "There entered a God-given purpose in my heart which has never left me from that day to this, that she should have a chance." She developed a conviction to spend her life "trying to wipe out some of the inequities that were meted out to my sisters who were so helpless to help themselves."[7]

Supportive of her vision and sharing her compassion, her husband encouraged her to attend the Women's Medical College of Georgia. She graduated with a medical degree in 1892 and an honorary degree of doctor of science in 1894.[8] In 1893, Dr. Kate Waller Barrett joined a team of women in her hometown of Atlanta, Georgia, to open a home for unwed mothers. While the community was opposed, she visited Atlanta's town council and received approval for the home. Lack of funding

Dr. Kate Waller Barrett (1854–1925), founder of Ivakota Farm.

caused a delay in the opening of the residence and so, Dr. Kate Waller Barrett wrote to Charles Crittenton of New York requesting funding on behalf of her group.

Crittenton was a wealthy pharmacy businessman and philanthropist who had lost his four-year-old daughter, Florence, in 1882. Blinded by grief, he sought comfort in attending noon prayer meetings near his New York City business office. Preacher Smith Allen also preached on the streets of New York at night and invited Charles to accompany him on his rounds of the vice district where they encountered prostitutes. The minister tried to persuade the prostitutes out of their lifestyle and the more practically minded Crittenton wondered where they would find shelter if they, in fact, changed their lifestyle. His curiosity resulted in his discovery that homes for such destitute girls were like prisons: unsuitable for any type of spiritual help or awakening.

"The Millionaire Evangelist" and "Brother of Girls"

Crittenton gathered a group of like-minded men interested in helping such women; a daring undertaking, as such topics were not discussed in private/public social conversation at the time. Previous reformers ended up being similarly scorned as the victims they attempted to help, but this group of New York businessmen succeeded and on April 19, 1883, the Florence Crittenton Night Mission home was opened in New York City.[9] This home was the first in a chain of homes for unwed mothers located internationally and still in existence today. Crittenton came to be known as the "millionaire evangelist" and "Brother of Girls." By 1909, the chain of homes for unwed mothers had grown to 78[10] and in April 1918, the organization was incorporated by the 55th Congress of the United States as the National Florence Crittenton Mission, to "aid and encourage destitute, homeless, and depraved women. . . ."[11] Thus, the public awareness and respectability required to launch an honorable campaign against said "social evils" was born.

In 1893, Crittenton received his letter from Dr. Kate Waller Barrett. Impressed with their similarity on views of women in need, he contributed $5,000 to support Barrett's request.[12] In 1894, Dr. Barrett's husband was given a new assignment and the family moved to the Washington, DC, area, where Crittenton lived. Joining forces, they located the national headquarters of the NFCM in the nation's capital. Shortly after, Dr. Barrett was made the organization's director and her husband died, leaving her a widow with six children.[13] In November 1909, Charles Crittenton died and his position as head of the NFCM was succeeded by Dr. Barrett.[14]

When the NFCM received the gift of Ivakota, Dr. Barrett saw an opportunity to provide young women with the same type of rehabilitative nurture as the nearby Lorton prison. By 1917 the gates of Ivakota were thrown wide open and, as the whole country was girding itself for the World War I struggle in Europe, the slogan "Food will Win the War" was chanted and so the NCFM Ivakota was fueled now with a labor force and a wholesome focus.[15] Girls covered with syphilis rash or gonorrhea

The barn and a meadow on Ivakota Farm.

The main house at Ivakota Farm.

chancre sores; girls who had spent years on the streets selling their bodies for survival; innocent girls who had been raped (an unfortunate misperception of this era was that a man infected with syphilis could be cured by having sex with a virgin[16]); girls who had succumbed to thievery, assault, and even murder now had a "second chance" at a wholesome life—learning a trade and putting their "heart in their hand" as they learned to till the fields and gardens of Ivakota.[17] Minnie Wilcox, 19, dubbed by the *Washington Post* as the "bobbed-hair bandit," guilty of holding up and robbing a taxi cab driver[18] was sent by a Fairfax County judge to Ivakota.

At Ivakota, the girls found their second chance. Here they could attend school, learn domestic skills—canning, cooking, gardening, farming, nursing—and play. Many had come from such sordid backgrounds that they never had a childhood. Baseball and basketball became invigorating forms of entertainment, as did writing and presenting their own plays. Here they could sleep safely, develop wholesome friendships, grow spiritually, and heal.

The devastation of venereal disease at childbirth and its evil passage to the newborn was a daily reality at Ivakota. However, the girls took comfort in burying their sisters and babies with dignity and respect in the property's cemetery, decorated with flowers and gardens. "It is one of the joys of the girls to plan and execute the beautification of the grounds—including a rose garden enclosed by a rock-wall, a bell tower, a number of large stone pillars, a stone arch over the gateway, and significant cement paving."[19]

A Day in the Life of a Girl at Ivakota

Working, playing, and learning were the three great occupations filling a day at Ivakota.[20] The canning plant was a busy summer facility, turning out annually more than 7,000 cans of tomatoes; 1,400 cans of beans; 1,000 cans of apples; 1,500 jars of pickles, jellies, preserves, catsup, and relishes; and three barrels of sauerkraut! With some 60 girls and 10 to 20 babies a year, the Ivakota "homestead" was truly one large family.[21] In 1923, it accommodated a high of 137 women and as many as 160 were cared for on a daily basis.[22]

Morning began with devotions, flag-raising, and calisthenics. Breakfast followed and, as with all other meals, was prepared and served by the girls. Classes or farm work followed and the evening was devoted to plays, entertainment, or music and on two nights a week, Bible study was held.

Six months to three years of this varied and wholesome life was deemed sufficient to provide a young woman with a second chance.[23] Buoyed by the success of the farm, welfare workers came in numbers; doctors and nurses heartily volunteered. The Public Health Service provided lessons in sanitation and hygiene and the county farm demonstration agent made frequent visits.[24] An abandoned three-week-old infant was left on the doorstep of an Alexandria, Virginia, home. "Baby Mary" was sent to Ivakota under the care of Dr. Barrett.[25]

Although Dr. Barrett died in 1925, in 1933 the Virginia DAR donated a four-room schoolhouse with an auditorium on the second floor. John Barrett designed and built "The House that Jack Built" for Ivakota's "least troublesome," while the Shaw-Colo Cottage housed the "most difficult" girls. The on-campus school replaced the nearby Crouch schoolhouse and provided education for local Clifton schoolchildren.[26]

In 1926, the NFCM published the pamphlet *What Happened to the Girls Who Leave Ivakota?* The leaflet included case histories of some 50 girls who "graduated" and went on to live productive and successful lives. Ivakota's practical nursing program graduated 15 women that year and some 53 percent married within six months of their departure—matching Dr. Kate Waller Barrett's conviction that, "A girl who does not marry misses one of the greatest things in life." The girls' slogan became, "I am an American girl and I am going to make the world know that I am worth something."[27]

However, as the 20th-century story unfolded, the need for NFCM homes decreased. By 1948 penicillin was widely used to successfully treat venereal disease, eliminating the long-term care for women and children so infected.[28] Ivakota continued to serve its "disadvantaged girls who were wards of the court" until 1957.[29] At that time the Salvation Army leased it from the Ivakota Foundation (headed by John Barrett) for use as an alcoholic rehabilitation center. With the changing winds of the 1960s, war protests, and introduction of the birth control pill, there soon resulted a drastic reduction in the need for NFCM homes.

The Ivakota story does not end in the 1960s, however, when the property was used for a senior citizens center.[30] For the thousands of women and children who were the characters in this story and who survived society's harshest treatments—abuse; sexual assault; venereal disease; abandonment by family, friends, and church—Ivakota gave them back a life that otherwise would have been lost. Through those reclaimed lives, an infinite number of others have been touched by the understanding and wisdom wrought from an experience—not an education—but a way of life. A shared and productive and wholesome life that taught the lesson: "Keep Your Face to the Sunshine, and the Shadows Will Fall Behind."[31]

Endnotes

1. Nan Netherton, *Clifton: Brigadoon in Virginia,* 1980.
2. www.fairfaxcounty.gov.
3. www.madeira.org.
4. Otto Wilson, *Fifty Years Work With Girls* (in conjunction with the National Florence Crittenton Mission), 1933.
5. Katherine G. Aiken, *Harnessing the Power of Motherhood,* 1998.
6. Ibid.
7. Regina G. Kunzel, *Fallen Women, Problem Girls: Unmarried Mothers and the Professionalization of Social Work, 1890–1945* (New Haven, Connecticut: Yale University Press, 1993).

8. www.alexandria.lib.va.us/pdf_docs/barrett_bio.pdf.

9. Kunzel, *Fallen Women, Problem Girls.*

10. Ibid.

11. Library of Congress, 1918.

12. Aiken, *Harnessing the Power.*

13. Ibid.

14. Kunzel, *Fallen Women, Problem Girls.*

15. Wilson, *Fifty Years Work.*

16. *Victorians Uncovered,* www.channel4.com/history.

17. Aiken, *Harnessing the Power.*

18. *Washington Post,* September 28, 1924.

19. Wilson, *Fifty Years Work.*

20. Ibid.

21. Ibid.

22. *Northern Virginia Heritage,* October, 1988.

23. Wilson, *Fifty Years Work.*

24. Ibid.

25. *Washington Post,* June 24, 1924.

26. Netherton, *Clifton.*

27. Aiken, *Harnessing the Power.*

28. Ibid.

29. Netherton, *Clifton.*

30. Ibid.

31. Wilson, *Fifty Years Work.*

Suffragists at the Occoquan Workhouse in Lorton
Protests, Arrests, and Hunger Strikes
By Bernice S. Colvard, *Annandale, Virginia*

Alice Paul and Lucy Burns, students in their early 20s, met in 1909 in a police station in London. They had been arrested for picketing with Emmeline Pankhurst and her radical followers to gain the vote for women in England. While in prison serving 30-day sentences, they were force-fed to break hunger strikes. Alice Paul, a zealot to her cause, was a brilliant organizer and strategist. Lucy Burns was an accomplished speaker. They returned to the United States as veteran suffragists and joined the National American Woman's Suffrage Association (NAWSA). In 1917, Alice Paul and Lucy Burns broke with Carrie Chapman Catt, president of NAWSA, and formed the National Woman's Party to create a more strident, national-level effort to force President Woodrow Wilson to back the push for women's enfranchisement. The president believed that such matters were best left to the states, but Paul saw that, as the leader of the party in power, Wilson's support was critical for passage of the 19th Amendment, guaranteeing voting rights to all citizens.

The strategy they then set was to picket the White House—for the first time ever. Many found this shocking and even offensive, especially the banners referring to the president as "Kaiser Wilson." America had just entered World War I and anti-German sentiments were running high in the country. The suffragists intentionally created an embarrassing situation for the administration at the gates to the White House.

Over a period of several months in 1917, about 100 suffragists were arrested for disturbing the peace, obstructing traffic, or unlawful assembly, and fined. They had set out to make a political statement and, although well able to do so, refused to pay the fines, knowing the result would be incarceration. It was. Confinement for most ranged from 30 to 60 days. As the ringleader, Paul was kept at the DC jail but many others, including Burns, were sent to the Occoquan Workhouse in Fairfax County.

Those well-educated, respectable, middle- and upper-class, normally law-abiding women were an anomaly to DC law enforcement personnel, who really didn't know what to do with them. So, they were treated as ordinary misdemeanants; requests to be treated as political prisoners were ignored. In the female division of the workhouse they lived in one-story buildings with neither wall nor fence around them. Although there were no bars, no cells, no locks, as the workhouse superintendent proclaimed, life inside was not pleasant.

Treatment became harsher as time went on, the picketing continued and more arrests were made. Reports leaked out of rough physical treatment as well as the general condition of workhouse life—unwashed blankets, unpalatable food, coarse and uncomfortable uniforms, enforced silence at meals (one of the most difficult rules to observe), stringent restrictions on contact with the outside, and dull and monotonous work assignments.

Hunger Strikes Bring Worse Treatment

The worst treatment of all was brought about by prisoner hunger strikes when all forms of nourishment were refused. No penal authority wanted to be held responsible for the death of an inmate by dehydration. They resorted to force-feeding. The prisoner was physically restrained and a tube was forced through a nostril and run directly down the throat to the stomach. Liquid nourishment was then poured through the tube. It was painful and possibly medically dangerous.

The suffragists managed to smuggle out word of their treatment to the press, which helped sway public opinion to support their cause. The president capitulated, and by 1920 the 19th—or Suffrage—Amendment was ratified by the states and became part of the U.S. Constitution. It states:

> The right of citizens of the United States to vote shall not be denied or abridged by the United States or by any State on account of sex. Congress shall have power to enforce this article by appropriate legislation.

Upon passage of the 19th Amendment, Carrie Chapman Catt and her followers converted NAWSA into the National League of Women Voters to further nonpartisan political education and leadership. This was a field unoccupied by any other group. Moreover, nothing like the efficiency of the suffragist organization, founded by Susan B. Anthony et al., had been built from volunteer forces before. Thousands of loyal workers objected to disbanding the organization at the height of its usefulness. They began by expanding their schools for citizenship.

In 1982, the League of Women Voters of the Fairfax Area erected a Virginia state historic highway marker on Route 123 in Lorton at the site of the Occoquan Workhouse to honor those brave women. It reads:

> In the nearby Occoquan Workhouse, from June to December, 1917, scores of women suffragists were imprisoned by the District of Columbia for picketing the White House demanding their right to vote. Their courage and dedication during harsh treatment aroused the nation to hasten the passage and ratification of the 19th Amendment in 1920. The struggle for women's suffrage had taken 72 years.

The first American Women's Rights Convention, called by Elizabeth Cady Stanton and Lucretia Mott, had been held in Seneca Falls, New York, in July 1848, 72 years prior to passage of the Suffrage Amendment. None of the principals who attended that meeting lived to see the outcome of what they had started.

The "Lorton Marker" was taken down and stored for safety by Fairfax Water during major construction at the site. It was reinstalled and re-dedicated on Saturday, July 15, 2006, and now stands at the entrance to the Griffith Water Treatment Plant, near the site of the original Occoquan Workhouse across Route 123 from the Workhouse Arts Center. A memorial bench, inscribed to former League of Women Voters members, is to be added.

We do, indeed, "stand on the shoulders of giants."

This photo, although not dated, could have been taken in the 1920s or later. This is probably how the Occoquan Workhouse appeared in 1917 when the suffragists were held there. The Women's Division was the first building on the right, in a direct line from the pine tree on the right. (Courtesy DC Department of Corrections)

Camp Andrew A. Humphreys, 1917 to 1919
Fort Belvoir's Origins
By Gustav J. Person, *Fort Belvoir, Virginia*

The colonial history of Col. William Fairfax's plantation, known as Belvoir, in south-eastern Fairfax County, is fairly well documented. In the early 19th century, the Fairfax lands were all sold off to local landowners and farmers. By the early 20th century, the peninsula on which the modern Fort Belvoir is now located was overgrown and covered with dense forest.

By 1911, the District of Columbia had acquired approximately 1,500 acres on the Belvoir peninsula for the construction of a workhouse (reformatory). Community opposition, however, soon put an end to that idea, and by the following year the land was turned over to the War Department for use by the troops at the engineer school at Washington Barracks in the District for marksmanship and tactical training. The troops bivouacked at a small camp, known as Belvoir, in the southern end of the peninsula.

Shortly after the United States declared war on Germany in April 1917, it became evident to Maj. Gen. W.M. Black, the chief of engineers, that a large central camp was needed for organizing and training the engineer replacement drafts that would be called for in ever-increasing numbers for service on the western front in France. Washington Barracks in the District was simply too small to accommodate this requirement. During the summer and autumn of 1917, he repeatedly urged the establishment of such a camp on the Belvoir peninsula on the Potomac River, about 13 miles south of Alexandria. He was finally successful, and on December 23, 1917, the secretary of war approved the chief's memo for the construction of a cantonment at Belvoir for 16,000 engineer replacement troops, later expanded to 30,000. Authorization was extended for the acquisition of land, by condemnation if necessary, and $3.3 million was allocated for the construction of the camp. This cantonment was to be known as Camp Andrew A. Humphreys, and was to be under the direction of the chief of engineers.[1]

Maj. Gen. Andrew A. Humphreys (1810–1883), a brilliant engineer and administrator, rendered distinguished service during the Civil War as chief of staff of the Army of the Potomac, and commanding general of the II Army Corps. From 1866 until his retirement in 1879, he served as chief of engineers.[2]

The Belvoir tract was selected as the site for Camp Humphreys for several excellent reasons. It was especially suited for engineer training. It also contained a large amount of round timber, which was so essential in supplying engineer troops learning how to construct the various sapper devices used in trench or field warfare. The west shore of the peninsula on Gunston Cove provided an ideal site for pontoon and bridge training. The flat top of the peninsula, located about 180 feet above sea level, ensured the proper space for the wooden cantonment buildings, while the

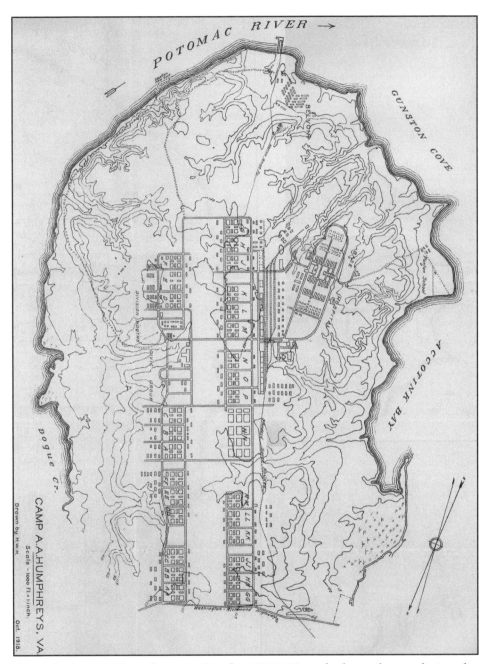

Camp Andrew A. Humphreys in October 1918. Note the barrack areas lining the central parade/drill grounds. (Courtesy Fort Belvoir historian)

lower slopes were ideal for the countless sites for trenches and obstacles. A few fields north of the peninsula were available for purchase, should the need for additional drill fields require. Deep water in the main river channel brushed close to the southern end of the peninsula, thus ensuring a proper site for a dock for river crafts of all sizes. The Richmond, Fredericksburg and Potomac Railroad (RF & P) was only four miles from the heart of the cantonment, providing rail communication by construction of a short spur. The main highway between Washington and Richmond skirted the northern limit of the camp, thus ensuring communication with the capital. The Washington-Virginia Electric Railway Terminal at Mount Vernon was only 4½ miles from the center of the camp, and by the construction of this short spur, Camp Humphreys would have access to Washington by electric line as well as steam railway. There was an abundance of water available in Accotink Creek, requiring only filtration and pumping up to the reservation.[3]

Beginnings of the Camp

Immediately after the camp was authorized, machinery was set in motion for the acquisition of additional land. During the last week of December 1917, a condemnation suit was instituted that eventually paid owner John West a total of $54,885 for 967 acres. By July, the Army had purchased an additional 3,800 acres for rifle ranges and tactical training areas. Finally, water rights and the right-of-way for the military railroad from Accotink Station to the reservation boundary had to be obtained.[4]

With the acquisition of suitable land, construction could begin immediately. Work was under the direction of a construction officer representing the War Department and assisted by a supervising engineer. A board of direction was formed, consisting of the construction officer (also known as the construction quartermaster), the supervising engineer, and the civilian contractor. P.F. Gormley of Washington, DC, was awarded the contract on January 19, 1918, to supply the civilian labor for the construction. No one who worked on the camp between the middle of December and mid-February could forget the deep snow and the intense cold of the winter of 1917–18. The temperature was almost always below freezing—often around zero—and went as low as –16 degrees. During much of this period, 12 inches of snow covered the ground. It was the most severe winter in Virginia in years. On February 11 came the thaw, with roads pounded to pieces, and endless trains of heavily laden trucks grinding their way through deep ruts over the various routes between Alexandria and Camp Humphreys. A contemporary observer commented on the miles and miles of mud that seemed almost bottomless.[5]

It was evident that the rural roads, the main highway to Alexandria, and the railroad to Accotink would go to pieces with the thaw, so the road system was supplemented by the use of water transportation. Cargo was transferred from river boats and barges to rail cars at the Belvoir dock, hauled by cable up a long incline to the camp base, and then distributed over a 20-mile network of 60.cm track, with

Military policemen apprehending civilians bringing liquor into camp. (Courtesy Fort Belvoir historian)

The light railway lines supplying the camp in May 1918. (Courtesy Fort Belvoir historian)

Working on the plank road. February 1918. (Courtesy Fort Belvoir historian)

Tents of the service battalion being aired out. Note the screens used to prevent influenza. October 1918. (Courtesy Fort Belvoir historian)

terminals at the various regimental training areas. This light railway system, on which work began March 1, 1918, was constructed and operated by soldier detachments, at a total cost of $352,231. By May, the camp had organized a light railway school from men who had constructed the railway system. This school was designed to train soldiers to construct and operate light railways in France. Concurrently, the standard-gauge railroad from Accotink Station into the camp was constructed largely by soldier labor.[6]

Perhaps the biggest job in terms of man-days was the clearing of land for the central parade and drill-ground, building sites, roads, and utilities. Nothing more than clearing for buildings and utilities was attempted until April, but with the arrival of large numbers of troops, work was undertaken on the various special school areas, besides cleanup in the regimental areas. It was not uncommon to see several thousand troops at work on the main parade, chopping trees, clearing away brush, driving mules hauling away the logs, burning brush, uprooting stumps with tractors or blasting out the more obstinate ones, filling in and then grading. One day, 10 acres of forest were converted into an equal number of acres of open level parade. During the height of construction, at least 6,000 civilian laborers were employed in the camp. These civilians normally arrived daily by truck from Alexandria. They posed a major problem for the camp military police, who were constantly engaged in countering alcohol-smuggling operations, loitering, and malingering.[7]

In late January, work was begun on a road from Richmond Highway (Route 1) into the interior of the camp and alongside the central parade ground. Originally a dirt road almost 1¼ miles long, it was constructed in five days. However, it was quickly realized that the heavy truck traffic would quickly destroy this thoroughfare. Therefore, log stringers were soon embedded in the frozen ground and covered by three-inch planks. This plank road was eventually double-tracked, at least 24 feet wide, and was the central roadway in the camp, especially during the February thaw. An extensive system of branch lines and unloading docks and turnarounds was constructed. By autumn, Richmond Highway from the camp up to Alexandria was paved with concrete. The extensive truck traffic had made this task imperative. This project was completed by the Cranford Paving Company. The construction quartermaster's office for this project was located at Gum Springs, at the junction of the road to Mount Vernon.[8]

Buildings and Troops

Once the central area was cleared, work was begun on the many buildings that would be clustered alongside the plank road and the central parade ground. All were fabricated of wood. These buildings included two-story barracks, mess halls, latrines, two-story officers' quarters, regimental administration buildings, two-story infirmaries, post exchanges, a stockade, and stables. All were heated by stoves or large furnaces.[9]

There was a small battalion cantonment down near the water's edge at the extreme south end of the Belvoir peninsula, and here were housed most of the troops who did the initial clearing, surveying, and road work during the bitter winter months. Some truck companies were housed in old shacks on the property. A battalion tent camp, called Camp Accotink, was established near Accotink Station, and another near the Belvoir cantonment to house the troops on railroad work. During the winter months, an average of 1,000 engineer troops was in garrison with the double duties of completing their organization and training, and playing a vital role in the construction program. The first drafts of replacement troops began to arrive in April. The average stay of the many units that began to arrive in strength prior to May 1 was only a few weeks. From Camp Humphreys they went overseas. Few of the soldiers of these early units found any harder work in France than they did during their brief tour of construction work at the camp. By the end of April, there were 200 officers and 6,200 soldiers in camp. From this time on, troops were available in sufficient numbers for construction work. Whenever a regimental area was roofed over so it could house troops, in they went. The work of the engineer troops, in connection with the construction of the camp, was excellent engineering training. Some of the units in the early months did this construction work at considerable sacrifice to the purely military phases of their training, but this could not be avoided. The officers received excellent experience in organizing troops for executing large engineering tasks.[10]

By May, large replacement drafts began to arrive and depart with some regularity. As of September 1, 1918, there were 1,385 officers and 21,400 enlisted men quartered in the camp. Between January and Armistice Day, more than 57,000 men received their training there, and were shipped overseas.[11]

Training Organization

The troops were organized into nine training regiments, all quartered around the long central parade ground. The original 2nd Regiment was formed in March at other installations, then consolidated at Camp Humphreys. The others organized there in monthly increments. The effective strength of a training regiment was 100 officers and 3,200 soldiers. Training regiments were designed to furnish trained soldiers as replacements. Various specialist schools were organized as companies in each regiment. Men were assigned based on their individual qualifications. These schools included forestry, light railway, bakery, pontoon and bridge, gas, and other specialties. The 2nd Regiment was a specialist "trade school unit"—training surveyors, blacksmiths, and mechanics. The 3rd Regiment trained general sapper replacements, and the 4th Regiment conducted basic training for all new arrivals. The 5th Regiment was organized largely as a receiving depot, which equipped, clothed, and conducted preliminary recruit training. The 6th Regiment was exclusively a non-commissioned officer (NCO) school. After basic training, selected soldiers were trained extensively for five weeks and then promoted. Notably, lots of recruits were illiterate, or immigrants who did not speak English well. Evening classes were organized in each regiment to address this problem.

Newly arriving commissioned or candidate officers underwent a 17-week course at the Engineer Officer Training School. This school was first organized at Camp Lee, outside Petersburg, Virginia, and later transferred to Camp Humphreys on August 10.[12]

On April 23, the camp organized 10 service battalions, composed exclusively of blacks, with white officers and senior NCOs. They were quartered at the southern end of the camp in tents under field conditions, and were employed in clearing, sewer and utilities construction, road and stevedore work, and a host of other construction tasks. Major Gillette, the commander of the service battalions, later noted, "The camp could not have been completed without them." Blacks, however, were not trained as combat troops at Camp Humphreys.[13]

By August 1918, the allied armies in France were pushing the German army back toward the frontiers, and Camp Humphreys was in full operation. On August 4, Brig. Gen. Charles Kutz replaced Col. Richard Park as camp commandant. Thereafter, Colonel Park served as the camp executive officer. An extensive rifle range network had been completed in Lorton, six miles from the camp, south of Richmond Highway, and was heavily used during this period. By summer, the Liberty Theater and the Hostess Service Club were constructed in the central camp. The YMCA was also active, as were the various regimental post exchanges. These, along with organized athletics, occupied the soldiers' spare time.[14]

In September and October, the camp, along with Europe and the Americas, was struck by the Spanish influenza pandemic. Brigadier General Kutz took immediate steps to head off the disease by preventive measures. For example, for two weeks in October all drills and close-order formations were suspended, and the soldiers were directed to spend as much time outdoors as possible. Lectures on the spread of this communicable disease were mandatory for all personnel. Hospital annexes were established in each regimental area to care for the many patients. During the five weeks of the epidemic, 4,237 cases were reported in the camp. It was noted that the blacks in camp had a lower incidence of the disease, no doubt because they were quartered in tents, rather than in enclosed, overcrowded barracks buildings. The mortality rate among all troops was reported at 35.2 percent.[15]

The war ended abruptly on Armistice Day in November. Although the camp did not close, all training was suspended, and the specialist schools began to turn in their equipment. A development battalion was formed in the 8th Training Regiment to handle turn-ins and preparation of the camp for peacetime operations. The camp also became a major demobilization station for troops returning from France. Camp Humphreys had proved its worth, and in 1919 was officially re-designated the U.S. Army Engineer School. Three years later, the name was changed to Fort Humphreys,

A section of one of the training regiment barracks areas. (Courtesy Fort Belvoir historian)

a reflection of the installation's permanent status in the Army's organization. That name remained in effect until 1935 when President Franklin D. Roosevelt changed the name to Fort Belvoir, in order to re-establish the installation's links to the colonial past. Fort Belvoir continues to serve the Army and the nation to this dae.[16]

Endnotes

1. Col. Richard Park, CE, compiler, "Historical and Technical Data, Camp A.A. Humphreys, Virginia," *The History of Camp Humphreys, 1917–18* (October 31, 1918), Chap. 1, 1–3. Van Noy Library, Fort Belvoir, Virginia. (Hereinafter cited as Camp Humphreys MSS.) We are indebted to Colonel Park, the first camp commandant, for the compilation of numerous reports and photographs that chronicled the organization and construction of Camp Humphreys. The manuscript collection eventually ran to 29 volumes contained in loose-leaf binders. *Fort Humphreys, Virginia* (NP, 1930), 15–19.

2. Ezra J. Warner, *Generals in Blue* (Baton Rouge, Louisiana: Louisiana State University Press, 1964), 240–42. During the 1850s, Humphreys and Lieutenant Henry Abbot were engaged in surveying the Mississippi River. Their report, later translated into many foreign languages, is still regarded as a model of hydrographical study.

3. Colonel Park, compiler, "Historical and Technical Data," Chap. I, 4.

4. Ibid., Chap. III, 1–4.

5. *Fort Humphreys,* 15–17; Maj. H.E. Kebbon, CE, "Brief Report of Construction Work, Camp A.A. Humphreys, Virginia," Camp Humphreys MSS, Vol. X, Appendix IX, 1–19.

6. Maj. W.A. Smethurst, "History and Report of Light Railways in Camp A.A. Humphreys, Virginia from February to 1 November 1918," Camp Humphreys MSS, Vol. IX, Chap. XI, 1–18, 23–24; Maj. W.J. Gough, "History of the Standard Gauge Railroad from Accotink Station on the RF & P RR to Camp Humphreys, Virginia," Camp Humphreys MSS, Vol. X, Appendix IX (b), 4–5.

7. *Fort Humphreys,* 19; "Historical and Technical Report of the Camp Humphreys Military Police. From January 20th to November 1st, 1918," Vol. VIII, Appendix VII, 1–7.

8. Maj. Guy Withers, CE, "Roads and Highways," Camp Humphreys MSS, Vol. I, Chap. VI, 27–29.

9. Maj. H.E. Kebbon, "Brief Report of Construction Work," Camp Humphreys MSS, Vol. X, 1–19.

10. *Fort Humphreys,* 17.

11. Ibid., 19; Maj. Fred H. Abbot, CE, "Camp Post Exchanges," Camp Humphreys MSS, Vol. XV, 1–14.

12. See Vols. XVI and XVII, Camp Humphreys MSS, for histories of the various training regiments and sapper units; also see Col. G.F. Lewis, CE, "Historical and Technical Report of the Engineer Officer's Training School at Camp Humphreys, Virginia, for November 1918," Vol. V, for a discussion of the school's role and curriculum.

13. Maj. D.H. Gillette, CE, "Historical Report of Service Battalions at Camp Humphreys, Virginia," Camp Humphreys MSS, Vol. XVII, 1–4.

14. Maj. Fred Abbot, "Camp Post Exchanges," Vol. XV, 1–14.

15. Lt. Col. Isaac W. Brewer, MC, "General Sanitary History, Camp Humphreys, Virginia," Camp Humphreys MSS, Vol. XIV, 1–17. Col. Brewer's report contains extensive information on all the preventive measures taken in the camp during this period.

16. Maj. Stefan Szumanski, CE, "Historical and Technical Report of the Development Battalion, for the Month of April 1919," Camp Humphreys MSS (May 1, 1919).

Herndon
Recalling Day-to-Day Life
By Charles V. Mauro, *Herndon, Virginia*

These stories were selected from interviews conducted from 1999 to 2001 when I researched the history of Herndon.

The Herndon Fortnightly Club

"It started about 110 years ago [in 1889], and it started with 11 women that lived here in the area that decided they would get together. Their mission was to improve their knowledge about world affairs.

"The people that got together and did this started collecting books so that they could study all these different things. They were very interested in what was going on all over the world, which was kind of unusual for that time. By the time they got all these books by 1900, I think they had close to 1,000 books.

"Anyway, then the library became their thing. They met every two weeks, that's why it was named the Fortnightly Club. I thought it was kind of interesting; all of the ladies brought a teacup from their home so they could have tea while they had their meetings.

"And then of course the new library—when that was built in 1995—we were very fortunate to have them name the library the Fortnightly Library after our club because it was not standard practice at that time. We really had to lobby the county a lot for that because they wanted to name it the Herndon Library. You've got Reston Regional and they did not want anything other than Herndon. But since we were the first library in the county, they did, they gave us that little of bit of glory, I guess."

—Lifelong Herndon resident Virginia Clarity, past president of the Fortnightly Club.

Early Dentistry

"The house that we lived in was built in about 1890 and one room was the dental office where my grandfather practiced, Ben Detwiler. He made his teeth in a little room off our kitchen, and in those days, people came and spent a lot of time when they went to the dentist. There were always extra people for a meal; they came and spent the day. Before that, he had his horse and buggy, and he spent part of his time out in the country doing teeth. A lot of patients. He also had a thing he ground teeth with that looked like an old treadle sewing machine. You can imagine the agony that the people must have gone through to have their tooth drilled. [It was] foot powered. Like an old treadle sewing machine, and that's how they got their teeth taken care of."

—Bobbie Keys, granddaughter of Dr. Ben Detwiler, who came to Herndon in 1887.

Detwiler Dentist House, circa 1890. (Courtesy J. Berkley Green Collection of the Herndon Historical Society)

Modern-day Detwiler house at 825 Elden Street. Note the roof has been changed to a raised-seam tin roof, the siding is different, and the porch has been extended on the right side to wrap around the house, although the railing style was not changed. (Courtesy Chuck Mauro)

Milking Cows

"We got up at 4:30 a.m. and milked the cows for two hours, did our work, and milked the cows again from 4 to 6 p.m. at night before dinner. The truck came for the milk to take it to Herndon around 7:30 a.m. The milk from the evening milking was put in the cooler until the next morning.

"A good, producing cow could well produce eight gallons of milk a day. But it took a good, powerful cow to do that. The average grade cow [could produce] five to seven gallons a day. A good cow could produce three gallons of milk a milking, and produce six gallons a day, if she was a good cow. With a milking machine, you could milk a cow in seven or eight minutes.

"They milked probably 20 or 25 cows in this place in the 1910s, and probably '20s. By the time I was a kid they got up to 30 cows. When I was a teenager we added 10 more cows to it, made it a 40-cow barn. They had an old milker system, a Delco Power Plant, that was run on batteries. But I don't know why they quit, but they discontinued the use of it. When I was a kid they milked by hand. I'd say just about the early part of the war [World War II], we got milking machines, in the early '40s, and they were used on through the duration of the dairy operation."

—Herndon dairy farmer Harry Middleton, Jr.

Early Telephones

Q. I see that in 1916 the Chesapeake and Potomac Telephone Company took over the local phones. When was the first time you had a telephone?

A. I don't know, we had it out on the farm, I'm not sure when. It was a party line, it was a man named Mr. [Guy] Church's company. It was not a part of the Bell Telephone system. I don't remember when we got it.

Q. You say it was a party line. Did you just pick up and dial?

A. Oh no, there wasn't a dial, you rang. The phone was a box on the wall with a receiver hanging on the side and a transmitter on the front. Two longs and short was our call. I guess there were about six or eight folks on our line. If there was someone else you wanted to call that wasn't on the party line, you had to go through the central office. One long ring and that got the office and you would tell her who you wanted and she would plug you in.

Q. So a number of different rings would get you to certain people?

A. On the party line. And our grandmother was two longs and two shorts.

—Interview with lifelong Herndon resident Elizabeth Ellmore, born in 1906.

Old Man Henry White

"Old man Henry White lived on that rural free delivery, a Herndon address, on Ashburton Avenue, just south of West Ox Road. I think he owned [land] north of West Ox Road, too, over in that general area. So blacks owned that [land] and [he] divided it to his children. He owned about 150 acres of land in that area, when he died in 1970 something. Because he had about 10 children, he willed each of them about 10 or 12 acres, to all of the children. And they acquired their wealth by bartering. Money wasn't the thing then. This is back, I would say, in the '20s. He acquired all of that land out there by bartering.

"He couldn't read nor write, [but] old man Henry White was a wheeler-dealer. He would take a cow, and trade it for a horse. He'd take that horse and trade it for two cows. Somewhere along the line he gonna take one of those horses and trade for an acre of land. So he built up an empire, as I call it, of all of that land through there by selling, trading, selling, trading, each time bettering himself. And because the land was not worth what it is today, he was land rich. So he built up around 200 or 300 acres of land which is now Ashburton. We didn't have that name back then."

—Herndon resident Frederick Washington, born in 1926.

On Vernon Cockerille, Herndon Town Sergeant from 1924 to 1952

"He couldn't drive a car. He didn't have a license, never had a car. And this Bob Church would pick him up and bring him into town in the morning. And Bob was going a little fast [one] morning evidently, and Vernon said when he got out of the car, 'Bob I'm sorry, but you were going too fast, I'll have to give you a ticket.'"

—Lifelong Herndon resident Ellen Kephart, born in 1916.

Floris Elementary School

"We walked to [Floris Elementary] school every day, where Frying Pan is now, walked up there [from Monroe Street]. My brother started teaching me how to drive when I was in seventh grade. I wasn't old enough to get a permit. I thought I knew enough, and so when we were coming home one day, Buddy didn't want me to drive, but I was determined. So I was driving and I met the car coming, and it was Mrs. Bradley and I was on the wrong side of the road and she just didn't bother, she just went on by.

"I do remember [Elizabeth Ellmore] being principal there, because her brother, Franklin, and I were in the same grade. And we were in the front row, and she was sitting in her desk, and this thing comes whizzing by my face and nobody looks up. But it was a rubber band with a spitball in it. And so when the class was over, Liz just got up and said 'Franklin, I will see you after school.' He didn't know she'd seen him throw the spitball. And I said 'Franklin, you missed me!'"

—Lifelong Herndon resident Ellen Kephart, born in 1916.

Dog Story

"I have to tell you we had a dog, a boxer, and it was our pet dog that everybody in Herndon loved. You never heard a story about a dog like this. His name was Kraut. He was Herndon's bum, if there ever was one. He knew everybody in Herndon. He used to get around.

"He went over to the barbershop because they had air conditioning at the time there. He met the Safeway truck every night when they came in; they gave him bones. It was down where Robert's Carpet is now. He went to every football game, sat in the bleachers. He visited all the classrooms, he'd scratch on the door, and they'd let him in. He got two write-in votes for town council.

"When the dogcatcher was coming, the town police had Kraut on the back seat of the car and would bring him home. He really was a wonderful animal. We got him about the time we put in the swimming pool, so it was 1953. He was probably about 10 when he died."

—*Lifelong Herndon resident Bobbie Keys.*

Integrated Schools

"[I went to] Douglass High School [a black high school in Leesburg], [from] seventh through 11th [grade]. In my senior year we chose to go to Loudoun County High School. I don't think Loudoun County wasn't desegregated until, it could have been 1966. You could go to the school but you had to provide your own transportation.

"There was a big difference in going to an all-black high school and an integrated school. The science equipment you saw in the science lab—much newer and more available. The athletic equipment was higher grade and they had more, and more modern and new equipment than we did. We usually turned around shoes from year to year. Helmets, we had some helmets, I remember in '67 when I played football we had some helmets that they had to screw birdcage facemasks on, and those kinds of things because the helmets didn't originally have a facemask. We had some really old stuff back in the old days.

"I was a little afraid when I first went to Loudoun County and thought that I would be treated a lot different. But, all the students were really friendly. The majority of all the teachers were real friendly and helpful. So that made it a lot easier."

—*Darryl C. Smith, Herndon's first black policeman and*
first black member of the Herndon Town Council.

Saving the Herndon Train Depot

"[In the early 1970s] one of the guys on the town council was just determined to tear the whole [train depot] down. Well, we knew that we wanted to put the road [Station Street] through [behind it] and we knew 20 feet had to go [off the end of the depot], so we let him take it down. The road was put in, in 1976. The town taking the building over to use as the Public Works Department is really what saved it. The remodeling was done with great respect for the original building.

"There was quite a lot involved in saving something like this. We had a lot of luck, too. At one point it was saved by one vote. Holden Harrison, who was on the town council, felt we needed parking spaces, but also, after listening to everybody, he abstained. He just didn't know what to do. It passed by one vote. But I'll give you an

Herndon Train Depot prior to 1912. (Courtesy J. Berkley Green Collection of the Herndon Historical Society)

Herndon Train Depot and Station Street. (Courtesy Chuck Mauro)

example of what kind of man he was. The building hadn't been painted in about 20 years. As soon as the decision was made to save the building, he said, 'Dick, we need to get that painted,' and he was down here, 70 years old, up with his ladder, scraping and painting to get the first coat of paint on the building, because the decision had been made to save it."

—Longtime Herndon resident and business owner Richard Downer.

Moving the Moffett Blacksmith Shop

From a newspaper article from Elma Mankin:

Henry Moffett, born April 26, 1897. Came to Herndon in 1904 when his father set up a blacksmith shop in Herndon. The original blacksmith burned down in the Pine Street fire in 1917. The shop was the last one burned and the first one rebuilt. It was the first building electrified in Herndon. Henry Moffett worked there until 1955 when he closed the Moffett Blacksmith Shop at the age of 68. In 1975, the building was disassembled and reassembled in Frying Pan Park.

"Moffett's Blacksmith Shop was located on Lynn Street beside the concrete block gas house started around 1900 by the Detwilers. When Fairfax County bought the blacksmith shop, my father said he wanted to be there when they took it apart and he supervised the disassembly and reassembly. He marked every board."

—Elma Mankin, daughter of Henry Moffett.

Changes

"One of the things I have noticed [since I've lived here] is the loss of our space. We're practically built out, and the biggest thing, I think they have done a good job of it. But the most amazing thing to me is the industrial part that goes around the [Herndon] Parkway. I'm just floored; I never thought that Herndon would have that type of thing. I'm amazed at the number of people that are in the town during the day because of their jobs being here. I have always—well, I never worked in Herndon, I never worked close to Herndon, I always had to go out of Herndon, so that's been a revelation to me that people actually live and work here."

—Lifelong Herndon resident Virginia Clarity.

Homeland Security, Cold War Style
Citizens Plan for Attack
By Mary Lipsey, *Springfield, Virginia*

To end the war with Japan, President Truman ordered atomic bombs dropped on Hiroshima and Nagasaki. The bomb dropped on Hiroshima on August 6, 1945, was equal to 12,500 tons of TNT. Each city suffered devastating loss of life and destruction.

World War II ended after Japan surrendered and soon a new age of warfare began—the Cold War. U.S. citizens' fear of communism and its aggression increased when the Soviets detonated their own nuclear weapon on August 29, 1949. The two superpowers became engaged in a prolonged war of ideology backed by the most destructive weapon known to man.[1]

Americans began focusing on self-preservation in the event of a Soviet nuclear attack. Also, new fears emerged as Americans worried about communists suspected of living within their midst. In 1938, the House of Representatives had established the House Un-American Activities Committee (HUAC) to investigate anyone thought to be communist. The committee was virtually inactive during World War II. However, in the late 1940s, HUAC became recharged.[2]

Starting in 1947, Hollywood's directors, screen writers, actors, and actresses came under HUAC's scrutiny. Membership in the American Civil Liberties Union could bring a person under investigation.[3] The FBI, under the leadership of J. Edgar Hoover, conducted surveillance of Americans and made lists of Americans thought to be security risks. On the Senate side of Congress, the Permanent Subcommittee on Investigations, led by Senator Joseph McCarthy of Wisconsin, conducted televised hearings where government employees and military personnel were accused of being communists. As a result of these investigations, many Americans' careers were ruined.[4]

In the 1950s, AWARE, Inc., a private organization established by script editor Vincent Hartnett, targeted radio and television personalities. Hartnett provided to the radio and television industry, for a fee, background checks of applicants. Also, Hartnett composed a suspicious persons list, which he published in his book *Red Channels*. Employers, using trivial reasons, fired workers whose names appeared on his list.[5] The "Red Scare" that began during the Cold War lasted well into the 1960s.

In April of 1963, the Fairfax County Public Library system was caught up in the citizens' fear of communism. The *Fairfax City Times* headline read "Protest Hit Film As 'Communistic.'" The film under attack was an animated cartoon called *The Brotherhood of Man,* whose message was that everyone is the same, regardless of race or religion. Prior to showing the film, librarian J.B. Runey had consulted with the FBI, the CIA, and other government agencies, because the two authors of the book associated with the cartoon had been listed by the HUAC for their "association with subversive groups." None of the agencies consulted indicated there was anything subversive in the cartoon. Fearing disturbances, Runey asked for Fairfax City police to be assigned to the showing of the cartoon. No disturbances occurred.[6]

Civil Defense Preparations

Citizens continued to worry about the threat of atomic warfare. In February of 1948, Secretary of Defense James Forrestal described plans for defense in case of Soviet attack. A government report advised "that an effective civil defense program should be largely under local civilian control . . . with the Federal Government confined to a supervisory role."[7] On January 12, 1951, President Truman signed the Civil Defense Bill and appointed Millard Caldwell as the administrator of the Federal Civil Defense Administration. Caldwell informed communities that the success of the U.S. surviving a nuclear attack depended upon the citizens' awareness of the dangers.[7] In an announcement six weeks later, Caldwell emphasized that the federal government would not be building community-sized bomb shelters. "It would require 300 billion dollars and all the labor and all the steel for the next several years—to the exclusion of the defense program and much else that is essential to life." He said federal funding would be used to strengthen and improve already existing structures to be used as bomb shelters.[8]

The Civil Defense Administration encouraged all families living within a 10-mile radius of the DC area to prepare bomb shelters. Booklets distributed by the government outlined plans for bomb shelters ranging from the simplest—a wooden lean-to in the basement—to the most elaborate—an underground shelter that included ventilation, water supply, and an aboveground, hidden entrance. All shelters would be stocked with food, medicine, and supplies to last the family for at least seven days.[9] Fairfax County's Operational Survival Plan, published in 1959, described the county as being part of the Washington metropolitan area, which could be targeted for attack.[10] Fairfax County families who were unable to afford construction of bomb shelters dutifully stocked their basements with emergency food and supplies and sealed their basement windows against radiation.[11]

The county's Operational Survival Plan described the "enemy:" "The potential enemies of the United States have the capability of attacking this country, its possessions, its overseas bases, and allies without warning, at a time of their choice, with thermonuclear, chemical, biological, conventional high explosive, incendiary, and psychological weapons. . . ."[12]

To school-age children in Fairfax County, air raid drills became commonplace. If an attack was imminent, an alarm sounded, prompting students to duck and cover under their desks. A different alarm sounded to announce a future attack and students exited to the hallways to crouch down and protect their heads from falling debris. Monthly, the big yellow horn on the school property would be tested as part of the civil defense warning system. Television and radio programs were interrupted for

Neil E. Jones of the Office of Civil Defense and Mobilization in an example of a residential fallout shelter. Note the concrete ceiling.

Temporary basement fallout shelter.

similar tests. Also, everyone quickly recognized the symbol used to designate a bomb shelter in a building.[13] Local civil defense coordinators spoke at firehouses and civic association meetings about home defense and the effects of the bomb.[14]

The Northern Virginia Regional Defense Council released evacuation plans that designated routes to move 650,000 residents out of the blast zone, "a 16-mile 'lethal area' surrounding the Ellipse." Each individual was warned about knowing which route he/she was to follow.[15] The Fairfax County Civil Defense Organization printed flyers advising families how to prepare themselves in case of enemy attack. The Operational Survival Plan outlined evacuation plans for the county residents, including public school students. The pamphlet explained that in the event of nuclear attack, students who walked to school would be sent home. Other students would be bused to the outer areas of Fairfax County where food and shelter would be available for a short time.[16]

The Buckingham Family's Plans

A Fairfax County family, the Buckinghams, received from the administration at Pine Spring Elementary School a letter that described the school's evacuation plan. The plan explained that children would be bused to Fairfax Circle, approximately five miles west on Arlington Boulevard. Staff would wait with the children for a half hour, then leave. The letter encouraged families to instruct their children what to do as they awaited their parents to pick them up. In the Buckingham family, both parents worked, so arranging for pickup would be complicated. The Buckingham children were instructed to find each other and wait. Once their mother arrived from her job in Clarendon, the family would wait one hour for dad, who worked in DC, to arrive. At the end of that hour, whether dad had made it or not, the family would drive to Indiana, where relatives lived. The children understood that in the event of nuclear attack there would be no reason to return home, so they committed the plan to memory.[17]

Communities conducted drills to prepare disaster teams and citizens in case of nuclear attack. On December 14, 1952, a drill was conducted in Fairfax County at the Falls Church Airpark (where Loehmann's Plaza on Arlington Boulevard is today). The *Washington Post* reported that an imaginary atomic bomb had been dropped, turning the area into "a nerve center of swarming activity." The Fairfax County Civil Air Patrol, Red Cross units, the Civil Defense Department, and the Falls Church Volunteer Fire Department participated in the simulation. During the drill, "blast victims" were evaluated and treated, a civil defense radiological team used Geiger counters to monitor the area for radiation, blood plasma was airlifted in, and planes departed with "injured" on litters and imaginary VIPs who were being evacuated out of danger.[18]

By 1954, the Army disclosed the construction of 16 missile sites to encircle and protect the Washington area. The *Washington Post* headline read: "First Underground

```
                    FAMILY CIVIL DEFENSE

        STEPS YOU SHOULD TAKE TO PREPARE YOUR HOME AND
                FAMILY AGAINST ENEMY ATTACK

        1.  LEARN THE CIVIL DEFENSE AIR RAID ALERT SIGNALS.

        2.  EQUIP THE MOST PROTECTED PLACE IN OR NEAR YOUR
HOME FOR AN AIR RAID SHELTER.

        3.  MAINTAIN A SEVEN DAY SUPPLY OF FOOD AND ADEQUATE
WATER FOR USE IN AN EMERGENCY.

        4.  PREPARE AN EMERGENCY FIRST AID KIT FOR YOUR HOME.

        5.  TAKE A REGULAR RED CROSS FIRST AID OR HOME
NURSING COURSE AS SOON AS YOU CAN.

        6.  PRACTICE FIREPROOF HOUSEKEEPING.  LEARN TO
FIGHT FIRES IN THE HOME.

        7.  LEARN THE EFFECTS OF AN ATOMIC EXPLOSION AND THE
SAFETY PRECAUTIONS YOU CAN TAKE AT HOME OR AT WORK TO MINIMIZE
DANGER AND INJURY.

        8.  GET OFFICIAL CIVIL DEFENSE IDENTIFICATION TAGS
FOR YOURSELF AND FAMILY.

        9.  REMEMBER CONELRAD - 640 and 1240 ON YOUR RADIO
DIAL.

                            FAIRFAX COUNTY CIVIL DEFENSE
                            FAIRFAX, VIRGINIA

                            Telephone:  Crescent 3 1540
                                and     Crescent 3 2000
                                            Ext.   256
(This flier originated and made
 here in the office.  Have put
 out several thousand.)
```

Nike Missile Unit to Guard Capital Started at Lorton." Two days later another article in the *Washington Post* announced the construction of another site on Popes Head Road, northwest of Fairfax Station. Each site was to cost approximately $500,000, excluding the radar equipment, missiles, and prefabricated housing. A third site was also constructed in Herndon.[19] The battery soldiers assigned to the Nike missile site at Fairfax Station appeared to be good neighbors. In the late 1950s, the *Fairfax Herald* reported on children's parties and plans for an open house to be hosted by the men at the missile site.[20]

Cuban Missiles Add to Fears

In 1962, the placement of these missile sites provided peace of mind for the residents of Fairfax County as they learned of Soviet-made missiles in Cuba aimed at the U.S. During the summer of 1962, Cuban refugees and CIA agents had provided information to the Kennedy Administration about the increase of Soviet shipping to Cuba and the buildup of Soviet troops and weapons there. On September 4, 1962, President Kennedy publicly announced the U.S. would only tolerate defensive weapons placed in Cuba, which is 90 miles from the southern tip of Florida. By September 26, Congress had passed a joint resolution giving the president permission to defend the U.S. from any military attack.[21]

On October 14, pictures taken of Cuba by U-2 pilots indicated the presence of three medium-range ballistic missiles, clearly offensive—not defensive—weapons. Subsequent flights captured pictures of more missile sites and long-range missiles. As the administration considered options, ultimate secrecy was stressed. Kennedy maintained his normal schedule as discussions continued. Soon newspapers got very close to printing the truth about what was causing all the tension and secrecy within the administration. President Kennedy personally called the publishers of the *New York Times* and the *Washington Post* to ask them to moderate their reporting on the crisis in Cuba.[22]

On Monday evening, October 22, 1962 at 7 p.m., President Kennedy addressed the nation in a televised, 17-minute speech:

> Good evening, my fellow citizens. This government, as promised, has maintained the closest surveillance of the Soviet military buildup on the island of Cuba. Within the past week, unmistakable evidence has established the fact that a series of offensive missile sites is now in preparation on the imprisoned island. The purpose of these bases can be none other than to provide a nuclear strike capability against the Western Hemisphere.

President Kennedy concluded his speech with his choices of action to end the crisis.[23]

In the wake of the president's speech, the federal government civil defense officials began mobilizing resources in public shelters.[24] Residents phoned their local civil defense offices asking about the location of nearby shelters and for advice on how to prepare their homes in the event of attack.[25]

As Fairfax County families watched the president's address to the nation, many of them discussed its meaning. Everyone understood this could mean war with Cuba and its ally, the Soviet Union. Although the black-and-white pictures of the Cuban missile sites were hard to interpret, even the younger children in the family understood the meaning of nuclear attack. The air raid drills in school were frequent reminders that Washington, DC, and the suburbs were likely target areas.

This lesson became even more a reality when the Buckingham children attended school the next day. Friends who lived down the street were absent. Their classmates soon learned the entire family had packed up the pets and belongings and left during the night to escape the possibility of nuclear attack. At home that night, the Buckingham children questioned their parents about whether their own family should leave. Their parents discussed the advisability of evacuation with nearby relatives. The Buckingham children were assured that the parents had faith in the government finding a peaceful solution. Other friends were experiencing fathers who did not come home at night, because they were involved in making emergency preparations for their government agencies in case of war. Stay-at-home moms fretted with worry while trying to maintain a calm atmosphere at home.[26] Headlines printed by the *Washington Post* such as "Battle Ready Troops Swarm Into Keys Area" and "Reds Could Fire Missiles In 15 Minutes, Bases Indicate" made life very stressful for the entire family.[27]

The United States and the world watched and waited as President Kennedy and his advisors dealt with the crisis. On October 28, the fear and tension eased when President Kennedy announced that Soviet Premier Khrushchev had accepted a peaceful solution and the missiles would be removed.[28]

After the crisis was over, families who had evacuated returned home, dads came home in the evenings again, and home life returned to normal. In the ensuing months families learned how close to the brink of war the U.S. had truly come during the Cuban crisis. As the crisis deepened, President Kennedy and Premier Khrushchev had negotiated the fate of the Western Hemisphere through messages communicated by emissaries. All over the U.S., military bases had been placed on red alert, our own ballistic missiles had been turned and aimed at Cuba, and a U-2 pilot had been shot down and killed by a Soviet missile located in Cuba.[29]

After the Cuban Missile Crisis, Fairfax County residents did not forego their awareness and preparedness. Emergency stockpiles and bomb shelters were still maintained and air raid drills and tests continued. Once the Cold War ended in 1989, however, many of their fears eased. Families no longer felt the necessity to be "prepared." Bomb shelters were closed. One family's backyard bomb shelter was put on display in the Smithsonian's American History Museum, and the secret underground facility for Congress, which was located under the Greenbrier Resort in West Virginia, was opened for tours. For more than 10 years, the U.S. citizens rested peacefully in their homes. However, new threats and enemies developed after the attacks on September 11, 2001, and the newly formed Department of Homeland Security provided "new" guidelines for preparedness for all Fairfax County residents.

Endnotes

1. Michael S. Lief and H. Mitchell Caldwell, *And the Walls Came Tumbling Down* (New York: Scribner, 2004), 111.

2. Ibid.

3. Ibid., 113–4.

4. Ibid., 114–5.

5. *Fairfax City Times,* April 11, 1963, 1.

6. *Washington Post,* February 15, 1948, M1.

7. Ibid., January 13, 1951, B4.

8. Ibid., February 24, 1951, 3.

9. Ibid., July 19, 1953, R11.

10. County of Fairfax Civil Defense Operational Survival Plan, August 1959.

11. Author's personal memory.

12. County of Fairfax Civil Defense Operational Survival Plan, August 1959, 2.

13. Author's personal memory.

14. *Fairfax City Times,* November 12, 1961, 1.

15. *Washington Post and Times Herald,* June 6, 1955, 1.

16. County of Fairfax Civil Defense Operational Survival Plan, August 1959.

17. Author's personal memory.

18. *Washington Post,* December 15, 1952, 3.

19. *Washington Post and Times Herald,* May 6, 1954, 1; May 8, 1954, 25; May 9, 1954, 4M.

20. *Fairfax Herald,* December 23, 1955, 4; November 18, 1957, 1.

21. Norman H. Finkelstein, *Thirteen Days/Ninety Miles: The Cuban Missile Crisis* (New York: Simon and Schuster, 1994), 28–32.

22. Ibid., 40–62.

23. Ibid., 66.

24. *Washington Post and Times Herald,* October 25, 1962, A13.

25. Ibid., October 24, 1962, A4.

26. Author's personal memory.

27. *Washington Post and Times Herald,* October 26, 1962, A11; October 28, 1962, A25.

28. Finkelstein, 131–2.

29. Author's personal memory.

Nike Missiles in Fairfax County
The County Played Its Role in Defense
By William O. Craig

The site where Fairfax County played a major role in the Cold War may someday be a museum that will serve as an educational facility, an archive of the era, and a memorial to those who served their country in those years. But, as of 2007, that is in the future. It is the significance of the site and its place in local, national, and world history that make it important today.

Because of its proximity to Washington, DC, Fairfax County has long played a role in the capital's defenses. During World War II, county residents participated in air-raid drills and other civil defense activities. During the Civil War, Washington was surrounded by a ring of 68 strategically placed forts; almost half of them in Fairfax County. A century later the county played a major role when a missile-age protective ring was established around the city.

The county's location made it vulnerable to possible attack by Soviet bombers as the Cold War was at its height in the 1950s. In 1954 and 1955, the U.S. Army began construction of a network of 20 anti-aircraft missile emplacements around Washington and Baltimore. Three Nike missile batteries were located in Fairfax County—one at Lorton near the District of Columbia prison, a second southwest of what is now Fairfax City, and the third north of Route 7 near Herndon.

"The Nike batteries were designed to fire at approaching Soviet bombers," explained Christopher Bright, who described the system in a 1996 magazine article. "They were different in size, design, and purpose from the much longer intercontinental attack missiles that were deployed in deep silos in the American Midwest in later years. The Nike batteries soon became an obvious and tangible manifestation of American defensive determination and capability to the residents of Fairfax County."

Bright explained the Nikes had many advantages over the anti-aircraft guns previously used by the army because of their long range, speed, and ability to be controlled in flight. The emplacements required two parcels of land for each battery. The radar and guidance electronics were housed on an eight-acre tract, together with support facilities. A second 15-acre tract, located less than a mile away, housed eight missiles in underground concrete storage areas.

The Army Corps of Engineers identified the locations for the three batteries in 1953. The first battery in Fairfax was built in 1954 in a cornfield near Lorton. It was one of the first two built in the nation. The early construction and the location near Washington made it a showpiece for a full-fledged public announcement of the Nike system in May 1955. Articles appeared in local newspapers, and over the ensuing years hundreds of senior military officers, congressional leaders, and foreign dignitaries toured the site. It was opened to the public for Armed Forces Day in 1956 and for later weekly open houses.

Another Nike site was located south of Popes Head Road between Route 123 and Clifton Road, where 30 separate property easements had to be obtained because of the topography. The land included five acres of an orchard belonging to M.F. Bowman and his wife. The third battery was located on two tracts of land between Georgetown Pike and Route 7, part of the 180-acre Turner dairy farm.

In 1958, a larger, more powerful version of the Nike with a nuclear warhead was developed. The Lorton battery was equipped with the new missile, but obsolescence and staffing problems led to the closure of the Herndon site in 1962 and the Fairfax site in 1963. The development of intercontinental missiles replacing bombers and military budget cuts led to the closing of all the missile sites in 1974. Control of the Lorton site reverted to the District of Columbia Department of Corrections. The Fairfax County school system and the Fairfax County Park Authority obtained ownership of the other parcels.

Aerial view, looking southeast, of the Nike Missile site at Lorton. Hooes Road crosses the photograph along the bottom edge. Army administrative buildings, which were still standing in 2007, are shown in the foreground, while the launching area for 24 missiles is in the background. Some missiles, raised from their underground storage area, are visible. Photo probably taken in 1955. (U.S. Army photograph courtesy of the U.S. Army Center of Military History)

U.S Army Warrant Officer George M. Vinson, originally from San Francisco, inspects a Nike antiaircraft guided missile in the underground storage area. Photo taken on December 9, 1954. (U.S. Army photograph courtesy of the U.S. Army Center of Military History)

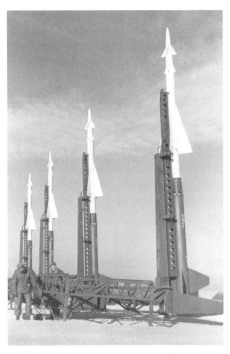

Four Nike missiles poised in firing vertical position. Photo taken on December 9, 1954. (U.S. Army photograph courtesy of the U.S. Army Center of Military History)

A Nike missile being raised on an elevator from an underground storage area. Photo taken on December 9, 1954. (U.S. Army photograph courtesy of the U.S. Army Center of Military History)

John Sidney (Sid) Holland, Sr.
Doing What He Felt Best for His Community
By Dorothy Mann, *Seattle, Washington*

John Sidney Holland, Sr. (1907–2000), was born in Palmyra, Virginia, one of 10 children of John and Mary "Odie" Holland. He came to Fairfax County in the mid-1930s to find work. He met and married Susie Crummy Holland and made Fairfax County his home until his death in 2000. Following the death of his wife, Susie, in 1982, he married Constance Lee Holland. She joined and supported him in his community-building efforts over the next 18 years.

Holland's contributions to the quality of life in Fairfax County are considerable. His activism focused on full participation of the African American community in the civic life of Northern Virginia. He became affiliated with the Mt. Pleasant Baptist Church shortly after his arrival in Northern Virginia. The church was his springboard for an activist career over a lifetime. His contributions are documented to a great extent in *Fairfax County—A History*, published by the Fairfax County Board of Supervisors in 1978. He had, by no means, curtailed his social and civic activities by that time. Through a myriad of organizations he worked to bring into being the Luther Jackson High School, as well as affordable housing throughout the county and in his own Mt. Pleasant neighborhood.

Holland was recognized over the years for his contributions and enjoyed looking over his many plaques and certificates while sharing his joy at being able to play a role in improving the lives of his neighbors and friends throughout Northern Virginia.

Over the years he was a member of, or held leadership positions in, the Mt. Pleasant/Lincolnia Civic Association, Harelco Land Development, Higher Horizon Day Care Center, Fairfax Countywide Black Citizens Association, Fairfax Human Rights Commission, the Fairfax County branch of the NAACP, and the Manassas Education Foundation. He served on a special commission of the Fairfax County Board of Supervisors charged with writing the county housing hygiene code and on a citizen's advisory committee to establish a housing authority. He was a past master of the King Tyree Lodge (Masons) and a charter member of the Fairfax County Democratic Party. His efforts to promote desegregation in Fairfax County are recognized in the recorded history of the county. While some may have seen him as a "yellow dog" Democrat, he won accolades from both political parties. He was not one to let partisan politics get in the way of doing what he felt best for his community.

Holland was proud to have been the longest-serving member of the Fairfax County Human Rights Commission, where he advocated for minority rights amid a growing and diverse minority population in the county. He urged his neighbors, church congregation, and civic colleagues to vote as the fullest expression of citizenship. He and his wife regularly provided transportation to the polls and served as poll watcher. He was fully engaged in the work of community building right up to the time of his death in July of 2000.

A Passion for Education

Holland was passionate about education as the pathway to opportunities in life. Both as a Sunday school superintendent for more that 30 years at Mt. Pleasant Baptist Church and through his efforts to establish the Luther Jackson High School, he challenged and urged African American children and youth to stay in school. He sometimes reflected on what more he could have done with a formal education. He exalted young African Americans to study hard and to take advantage of opportunities not available to him.

Thus, he was proud of the military accomplishments of his son, who became a paratrooper with the 82nd Airborne Division and retired from the army with the rank of master command sergeant major. His daughter earned a doctorate in philosophy and retired from the federal government as a senior executive with the U.S. Public Health Service. Their accomplishments, to him, stood as examples of having the next generation stand on the shoulders of their elders. As he saw his Sunday school students off to college, he told them to never forget where they came from. He was self made, in the truest American tradition. From working as a laborer with a construction company to operating complicated grading and bulldozer equipment, in the 1960s he went on to start his own business, J.S. Holland, Sand and Gravel Hauling. He retired—temporarily as it turned out—and soon thereafter purchased a limousine and leased it to Baker-Chinn Funeral Services in Arlington, Virginia, before retiring for the second and last time.

In 1997, Penelope Gross, Mason District Supervisor, Fairfax County Board of Supervisors, led the board to declare August 13 (Sid's 90th birthday) as J. Sidney Holland Day in Fairfax County, and a wonderful party was held in his honor.

At the time of his death in 2000, J. Sidney Holland, Sr., had devoted more than 60 years of his life to improving the condition of all people in Fairfax County but especially African Americans. He was a unique man for his era in that he never seemed to realize any limitation of education, race, or class. He was as comfortable with dignitaries, elected and appointed officials, people of letters as he was with his Sunday school students. He had the ability to focus on what could be accomplished if you put your mind and heart into it, undeterred by temporary setbacks. Those who did verbal battle with him in meeting halls throughout the county knew he always did his homework and was a force to be reckoned with.

One of his favorite Bible quotes was "He has told you, O man, what is good and what the Lord requires of you: only to do justice; and to love goodness, and to walk humble with your God. Then will your name achieve wisdom."

Photo of John Sidney (Sid) Holland, Sr., taken on his 90th birth-day, May 9, 2006.

Sources

Penelope Gross, "A Penny for Your Thoughts," *Falls Church News-Press,* July 13, 2000.

Arlington Journal, July 12, 2000 (Obituary).

"Remembering the Life of Deacon John Sidney (Sid) Holland," Congressional Record, July 27, 2000, submitted by the Hon. Thomas M. Davis of Virginia.

"Businessman J. Sidney Holland, Sr. Hauling Company Chief, Civic Activist," *Washington Post,* July 11, 2000.

Nan Netherton et al., *Fairfax County: A History* (Fairfax, Virginia: Fairfax County Board of Supervisors, 1978).

Desegregation in the 1960s
Judy Street Joins the March to Selma
By Linda Olson Peebles, *Alexandria, Virginia*

In Fairfax County, south of Old Town Alexandria, the Hollin Hills and Tauxemont communities were created in the post-World War II era. These wooded enclaves were settled in the 1940s and 1950s by immigrants from around the nation who then built the networks and institutions of their communities, including their churches.

In the mid-1950s, many of these newcomers started the Mount Vernon Unitarian Church. They were young families with children and with ideals. They lived in the civil rights era of the 1960s, and many of them made the commitment to lead the way for making changes, and in working for equal rights for blacks. The history books tell of famous institutions and people of that era. This is the story of the contribution of a small group, and the story of one woman in the Mount Vernon Unitarian Church.

Mount Vernon Unitarian Church Hosts CORE
In 1961, the Congress of Racial Equality (CORE) held a national interracial summer institute to train members in techniques of peaceful resistance, to be used when arrested or physically attacked while sitting at lunch counters in its campaign against segregation.

The Mount Vernon Unitarian Church (MVUC) offered a secluded site in the DC region. Located on an old estate, it was reachable only by a winding driveway through woodland. The church agreed to rent the property for the housing and feeding of about 30 participants for three weeks. On complaints from neighbors, the church board of trustees was summoned to appear before the Fairfax County zoning board, and directed to "cease and desist" these plans. They were told, informally, they could be held personally liable if there were any damages from violence that might occur because of the presence of these CORE trainees. Trudy Wright, MVUC trustee at that time, recalls the board "met, and when we realized we were under attack, no one flinched." Volunteers from the church protected the property from neighbors while the training took place. Luckily, other than some threatening vandalism—spreading nails and tacks on the long driveway—the visiting conferees were safely accommodated.

In recognition of the congregation's courage in hosting CORE, the continental Unitarian Holmes-Weatherly Award, the denomination's highest award for "commitment to faith-based social justice which is reflected in societal transformation" was given to MVUC and Rev. Ernest Sommerfeld. The award cites MVUC for "their courage and devotion to principle displayed . . . when the church was the subject of a campaign of intimidation and harassment for being host to an interracial training institute. . . . All stood their ground against great pressure, thereby gaining a significant victory for Human Brotherhood and Social Justice." The CORE efforts that followed succeeded in ending lunch counter segregation in Northern Virginia, and in many areas of the South.

In August 1963, MVUC chartered a bus to carry members to DC to join in the historic march and rally for civil rights on the National Mall, and to hear Rev. Martin Luther King, Jr., describe his dreams. MVUC followed up from that day to organize blacks and whites to go to Congress and support new civil rights legislation.

Fair Housing

The struggle for fair housing was a major campaign in the mid-1960s, to address a vitally important gap in the civil rights court rulings and legislation. While voting rights and integration in schools had been established, the question of where blacks could live was still a problem. Housing in Northern Virginia was virtually closed to blacks—even the most affluent and highly educated—because of fear and racial prejudice. A national fair-housing movement grew up in response, to help guarantee the right to live where one chose. A focused campaign was planned with churches from many faiths participating, leading up to the March 1965 "Fair Housing Sunday."

MVUC's social action committee, chaired by Elaine Bronez, went on to become a leader in the Northern Virginia fair-housing movement. The committee led a coalition that worked for fair housing, to ensure that homes could be sold and rented to blacks, and that white neighbors would be welcoming, avoiding a "white flight," fear-motivated response. They planned and carried out a concerted and intentional process of organization, door-to-door education of neighbors, and partnership with businesses, realtors, and elected leaders.

Maj. Gen. Robert F. Seedlock, then Ft. Belvoir's commanding officer, provided key leadership when he was enlisted to help in the cause of making sure apartment rentals could be successfully opened to integration. This was during the time the Vietnam War brought to the region a large number of families of service personnel deployed abroad. He worked to ensure that fair rental housing was made available so that all the families, including black families, could be housed in the Ft. Belvoir neighborhood.

Traveling to Selma

The story of one MVUC member, Judy Street, is worth telling. She was a volunteer and community activist. As a housewife and mother in fast-growing Fairfax County in the 1950s and 1960s, she was active in politics and later was instrumental in starting several human service agencies. Judy dressed beautifully, and was a shy and proper classy lady; she was an unlikely activist, protester, and marcher.

In March of 1965, a call came from John Wells, the minister of the Mount Vernon Unitarian Church. He had been asked by Rev. Martin Luther King, Jr., to send people to give support to the march for voting rights. Judy decided she was going, and that was that. Friends recall, "Her thunderstruck husband found his objections unavailing. To his astonishment, he found this gentle creature, who abhorred camping even under a tent, moving off down the train platform with nothing more than a rolled-up blanket, leaving Tom and the two teenage boys staring forlornly through the bars as all they held most dear in the world moved determinedly toward an unknown and possibly terminal fate."

Judy was joining in the third effort to march from Selma.

The first stage of the march had brought out all sorts of dangerous reactions from the local Alabama police and their dogs. So, the second time, John Wells went down with several hundred Unitarian ministers to join Reverend King. One of them was the young Unitarian minister James Reeb, known well to MVUC when he had been a new minister at All Souls Church in DC. James Reeb was beaten to death by a gang in Selma, and Reverend King spoke at his funeral. The press coverage of the events finally spurred the federal government to send in the National Guard to protect the marchers.

A third date was set, and the word went out for marchers. That was when Judy joined the 25,000 people who gathered there. Despite the danger, Judy got on a special train along with 130 people from the area to give support to the demonstration in Alabama.

Judy Street, who died in 1998, left us these recollections:

> We boarded the train at Union Station with our bed rolls and brown-bag supper. It was a special SCLC-commissioned train; SCLC being the Southern Christian Leadership Conference, headed by Martin Luther King. About 8 p.m. a meeting was called in the club car, which was the headquarters for the SCLC staff, led by Hosea Williams, who was the national program director. He told us what to do, what to expect: To remember to keep the blinds down as we moved through the South at night because of the antagonism that would be felt if they saw blacks and whites in the same car; and so forth. He also explained that when we got to Atlanta, we would change trains, but we couldn't leave the station because it would be too dangerous.
>
> The next morning we arrived at the station in Atlanta; standing around hungry—we'd run out of food we'd brought. We weren't allowed to leave; there was nothing there. We hung on and we found out that the engineers wouldn't take us any further. They refused to move the train.
>
> Finally Hosea Williams got through to Washington and someone with influence got the train going again. Then we got back on board, and we arrived in Montgomery, where we were taken to a classroom for lessons in non-violent behavior. They said, "Kneel down if you see you're going

to be attacked. Kneel down, cover your head, and don't talk, and hope for the best." Gosh, I thought, what have I gotten myself into!?

Then we were taken by bus after the train, off to Highway 80, the route between Selma and Montgomery. This was the last day of the five-day, 55-mile march. This was the point where they wanted everyone to join them. The marchers were coming at us, with Martin Luther King and his wife, Coretta, in the lead and his troops bravely followed with banners and flags. Then a long stream, as far as the eye could see, of walkers black and white, young and old, mostly poor. Along each side at intervals were the men of the National Guard in uniform and a few whites looking hostile and angry but impotent.

We joined the huge procession. The march ended for the night at a walled-in campus of St. Jude's College—walled in, chosen for obvious reasons. Food at last! We had a wonderful boxed supper—standing though, because it had rained that afternoon and it was terribly wet and there was mud up to here—so we stood around and ate our supper. Then they had marvelous entertainment for us that evening. They had people from New York and Hollywood; from radio and TV and theater and music. I remember Bill Cosby particularly being terribly funny and fun. And the other one I remember is Leonard Bernstein who got up and said, "I just feel terrible, there's nothing I can do for you! I don't have my orchestra!"

After the entertainment, we were taken to a small, poor, black, little church, where we spread out our bedrolls under the wooden benches. The next morning, only scraps of food were available. We couldn't leave that church to go buy anything, and they had very little to offer.

The march came down past our church, and we joined in with our bedrolls, and marched on down to the capitol. The whole purpose of this march was to ask Governor Wallace to implement measures to permit registration to vote. This was the whole Selma objective—voting rights. At the capitol, Martin Luther King made a wonderful speech. There was a great feeling of exhilaration and pride and solidarity all over this huge gathering.

Then suddenly, it was all over. A public announcement was made over the loudspeaker: "The National Guard is disbanding. There are no local police. Go back to the railroad station immediately, walk on the main streets, don't take side streets. Don't stop to buy anything [we were still hungry] and do stick together."

So we picked up our bedrolls and we made it to the station, but that was probably the most anxious and lonely moments we had. Finally, the train pulled out of the station and what a relief to leave that hostile

The Mount Vernon Unitarian Church in Mount Vernon, Virginia.

Judy Street, member of the Mount Vernon Unitarian Church, political activist, and founder of human services agencies, joined other church members in the march on Selma in 1965.

ground. We got back; John Wells and many church members greeted us at Union Station with a tumultuous welcome. And then I slept for 24 hours.

That same trip Judy was on, in another part of that march as it disbanded, Mrs. Viola Liuzzo, a Unitarian housewife from Detroit, was killed. So Judy, a local Fairfax County woman with a commitment to justice, had placed herself in a situation that had included a death just before her visit and another just after. Her friends remember her courage.

The Legacy
Carrying on the work of the 1960s, the Mount Vernon congregation continued to help its area of Fairfax County be socially responsible.

As schools in the MVUC neighborhoods began to be integrated, MVUC members tutored black students, to support their achievement.

With a number of neighboring congregations, MVUC helped start a new coalition that became United Community Ministries. MVUC has worked for and supported this agency that has grown over the almost four decades of its life, to become a major human services agency with an annual budget of close to $4 million, and serving hundreds of families through its programs, which include social-service counseling, food and clothing, emergency relief, transitional housing, employment training, health and parenting counseling, affordable childcare, and much more.

The story of the Mount Vernon Unitarian Church and some of its members is integral to the larger story of Fairfax County's journey of becoming a place where human rights, compassion, and justice could thrive in a diverse community.

The Honorable Martha V. Pennino
They Called Her "Mother Fairfax"
By Sally B. Ormsby, *Fairfax, Virginia*

Many people drive by, or even attend meetings at, the Pennino Building, an office building in the Fairfax County complex on Government Center Parkway in Fairfax, but they don't know the Pennino behind the sign on the building. Who was this person?

The Pennino Building houses the human services functions of the Fairfax County government. It was aptly named in honor of Martha Pennino, who used her elected position as a member of the Fairfax County Board of Supervisors over a period of 24 years (1968–1992) and as vice chair for 17 years to advocate for less fortunate people in the community.

Pennino's entry into politics began in the Town of Vienna, where she was elected to three terms on the Vienna Town Council (1962–1968), serving as vice mayor during one of those terms. During that period, according to Maude Robinson, "Martha was the Vienna Town Council's liaison to the Fairfax Board of Supervisors, so she attended the county board meetings. She was fully engaged with both governing bodies and was fully supportive of many county initiatives. She was bigger than life—a presence, even—on the town council."[1]

In 1966, during her third term on the Vienna Town Council, Pennino felt the council should pass an open housing ordinance. She pushed through such an ordinance, the first of its kind in the country.[2]

Elected to the Fairfax County Board of Supervisors in November 1968 to represent the new Centreville District (now the Hunter Mill District), Pennino was sworn into office in January 1969.[3] In that same election, Fred Babson was elected as the first board chairman-at-large, the chairman having previously been elected by and from among the board members.

The author interviewed a number of Pennino's associates and friends who knew her well during her long, active political life. Pennino's daughter, Bonita, also provided some insights about her mother. Here are their remembrances of her.

A Politically Independent Board Member

Robert Wilson was the deputy county executive and county executive during Pennino's first term on the board. His most vivid memory of her was her political independence. "She was more conservative in some ways than some other board members, and she was very constituent oriented. Her primary endeavor was to protect her district. She was very close to Reston's development and took pride in that part of the county."[4]

One of Jean Packard's many memories is Pennino's continually advocating for Northern Virginia to secede from Virginia because we did not get a fair share in return for our monies sent to Richmond. She was quite vehement about this.[5]

Longtime friend and associate Kohann Whitney said a government center was very important to Pennino because she felt Fairfax County needed to develop first-class public facilities like those in Washington, DC, and Richmond that would last hundreds of years. This was her brainchild and vision.[6]

The Centreville District during Pennino's tenure included the area that was to become the planned community of Reston. Pennino was extremely interested in this new concept of a self-contained community and played a strong personal leadership role in its development and continual growth. She loved Reston, its people, its diversity, and its potential. In 1985, Pennino tried to establish the Town of Wiehle.[7] Obviously, she was unsuccessful, since the Reston area still does not have town status.

Longtime friend Priscilla Ames said that Pennino had a vision of how the county-owned land should be used for governmental purposes. She felt that homeless adults and children sleeping outside and in the woods was "not right;" they needed a warm, safe place to sleep and eat. Until a shelter could be built, Pennino allowed them to use a room in her offices. She later got the North County Shelter in Reston, opened in 1987, renamed for Priscilla's husband, Embry Rucker, a longtime human services advocate.[8] Pennino's daughter, Bonita, recalls that her mother was proudest of having received the IMBY (In My Back Yard) Award given by the Fairfax County Human Services Commission for her efforts on behalf of the homeless.

Jim Cleveland, president of the Reston Land Corporation, worked closely with Pennino during many planning meetings for the town center and other Reston parcels. According to Cleveland, "Pennino respected the corporation as being responsible and honest with Bob Simon's vision for Reston. (Robert E. Simon, Jr., began development of Reston as a self-contained community, an original concept in the early 1960s.) She was a unique and wonderful lady; she could be tough at times but also collegial. She could drive a hard bargain!"[9]

Cleveland recited an event to illustrate the last point. Around 1987, Cleveland received a call that Pennino wanted to see him *immediately.* When he arrived at her office, Pennino told him the county would lose a federal grant to provide affordable housing if a site could not be found, and she wanted Reston Land to give three undeveloped acres next to her office to the county for this purpose—*right now!* Since Reston Land did not yet have its rezoning for the town center, Cleveland acceded to her request—and nearly lost his job. The 15 brick, affordable townhouses were so attractive that, during construction, doctors asked if they were building offices.

Standing Firm in the Face of Political Opposition
Pennino appointed John Thillman to the planning commission and the Environmental Quality Advisory Council in 1979, telling him to use his judgment on issues. John says they "never disagreed on an issue. Pennino believed in common sense and would ask me and others, 'Does it make sense?' If it did, she'd go with it, even in the face of political opposition."

From left to right, Supervisor Joe Alexander, Redskins coach Joe Gibbs, Supervisor Martha Pennino, and Jack Herrity at a celebration of the Super Bowl win in January 1983.

From left to right, Chairman of the Board of Supervisors Jean Packard, Fairfax County Park Authority board member Fred Crabtree, and Martha Pennino. Photo taken between 1972 and 1975.

Thillman added, "She was the heart and soul of Fairfax County. When the county needed a homeless shelter, she put it in Reston. Affordable housing was needed in the county and again she put it in Reston when other board members were fleeing the issue. She was a great supporter of libraries and we in Reston got one of the best in the county at a great location. A community center was needed in the Reston area and she set up a special tax district to establish one—it was the first in the county. To my knowledge, a special tax district had never before been done. She was a true environmentalist and strongly supported cluster development, reduction in parking to cut back on driving, tighter environmental pollution limits on the Potomac River and upgrades to the lower Potomac sewer treatment plant.

"She was also a deal broker. When Gulf Reston (before its purchase by Mobil) had financial problems, Pennino had the county buy 50 acres near the town center that now contain the North County Government Center, library, homeless shelter, and Cameron Glen Nursing Home. She was visionary."[10]

David Bobzien, Centreville District planning commissioner from 1987 to 1992, feels Pennino worked well with communities and the developers during all the growth taking place in the Centreville District at that time. Bobzien said she was able to assert herself and get benefits and needed facilities for communities, such as parkland, a transportation grid, and a good design for the town center in Reston. According to Bobzien, "Many have said Reston was Robert Simon's dream and its achievement was Pennino's political leadership in making it happen.'

"Martha had strength of character and convictions; she was a role model for hundreds of women. And she did it two decades before other women—wife, mother, community leader, and successful political operative who could get things done. Many women saw her as a mentor in growing, contributing, and providing leadership opportunities."[11]

According to Michael Horwatt, Pennino and Jack Herrity had a multifaceted relationship the 12 years Herrity was chairman of the Board of Supervisors and Pennino was the vice chair. They cooperated, competed, and fought on the political level but they actually liked each other. While Pennino had a vision for a new government center, Herrity opposed it. Sometimes their visions overlapped and that is where they connected. They learned to trust each other and to stand their ground when positions differed. They shared the view that Fairfax County, sitting as a gateway to Washington and the home of educated people, had to have a high quality of life with outstanding schools, police, libraries, and other services. They may have varied on strategies but they had a common vision.[12]

Working for the Welfare of the Citizenry

Kate Hanley served with Pennino on the Board of Supervisors from 1986 to 1992. "Martha had exceptional instincts. When discussing an issue she could always be counted on to have great instincts regarding the best things to do for the welfare of citizens, especially those not as affluent. She was always cognizant that some in the community needed extra support. An example of that is opening her office to the homeless and spearheading the effort to get the Reston shelter built. She had great capacity to accept change; she was not afraid of the future."[13]

Soon after Jack Herrity was sworn in as the new chairman of the Board of Supervisors in January 1976, he suffered his first heart attack. The board had just elected Pennino the vice chairman, so she had the immediate challenge of assuming the chairmanship role for a few months while Herrity recovered.

Jay Lambert, acting county executive from 1978 to 1980, had a close working relationship with Pennino for 16 years, accompanying her to regional, state, and other meetings. He said Pennino played a large role in maintaining the county's regional relationships through her activities in the Metropolitan Washington Council of Governments (COG) and shepherding through a large number of long-term regional agreements, including the regional water supply agreement and purchasing agreements. She mastered the art of the cooperative working relationship. During Herrity's terms as chairman (1976–1988), she was our senior elected voice in Richmond. Pennino (Democrat) and Nancy Falck (Republican) were a great team in Richmond, working on the Dulles Toll Road, funding for widening Route 28, and later for the Route 28 tax district. Pennino and Kohann Whitney, her school board appointee, helped obtain increased funding for county schools and George Mason University.[14]

"Martha was one of the most remarkable public servants I have ever had known or had the pleasure of serving with," commented supervisor Gerald Hyland. "She had an uncanny ability to look at, not only specific problems in her district, but global issues that affected all the citizens, not only of Fairfax County, but of Virginia.

"She was truly a people's representative. People felt comfortable with her understanding and her insight on what was best to do for folks. Of all the public officials that I have met over the years, she was one of my favorites.

"Martha was ahead of her time. She felt that we should be emphasizing arts in Fairfax County, should have in a central location a center for the arts and should start planning for it. The county is now starting an arts niche in Laurel Hill with the Lorton Arts Foundation and is looking at a location near the government center."[15]

Pennino was instrumental in working with the Environmental Protection Agency at the federal level in Washington and Philadelphia, trying to clean up the Potomac River through expansion of the Fairfax County Water Authority plant on the Potomac. Pennino defined her role as "regionalistic" and got everyone to work together. According to Lambert, "She was a catalyst for many things that happened at Washington regional and state levels; that was her vision of government."[16]

Pennino served as the president and first vice president of the Virginia Association of Counties. She also served as president of the Virginia Municipal League. At the Washington COG, she held the posts of president and chairman, as well as being a member of the board of directors for 17 years.

Citations for Service

Others also recognized her extraordinary service to our community. In 1985, Pennino won the Tom Bradley Regional Leadership Award. In giving her this honor, the National Association of Regional Councils cited her efforts in developing the first energy policy for a metropolitan area, the region's car pool program and a fair-share housing program. In 1986, *Washingtonian* magazine named her "Washingtonian of the Year."

Martha and Walter Pennino were the parents of three girls and a boy. Youngest daughter, Bonita, and her husband live in the Pennino family home. She can't say enough about Pennino as a mom. Pennino was athletic and loved swimming, golf, and tennis. She taught Bonita how to swim before she could walk and everything else important about life, such as, "be gracious under fire, be charming, and take the high road." Bonita recalls her mother as very warm, very strong, intelligent, her role model, and heroine—and fun. Pennino sometimes took the children out of school for "daycations."

Pennino died from Parkinson's disease on September 17, 2004. On January 20, 2005, the U.S. Congress passed a House resolution co-sponsored by congressmen Jim Moran and Tom Davis to name the post office on Sunset Hills Road in Reston the Martha V. Pennino Post Office Building.[17] At its renaming ceremony, daughter Bonita referred to a vision of her mother looking down and chuckling because she went to the post office not just to buy stamps but to talk with everyone she met there.

Bonita also cited in her speech the one act by her mother of which she was proudest; something she did not know about until years after it happened. She referred to the 1980s when plans for the Reston shelter were being considered but the homeless had no place to sleep, so her mother opened her office to them at night, providing a makeshift shelter for more than a year. In accepting the IMBY award, her mother commented, "We are the richest county in the richest country in the world. When Mary and Joseph were turned away, an innkeeper found them shelter in a manger. We should all look in our hearts and follow the innkeeper's example."

After Pennino's death, Walter Scheiber, Washington COG executive director in the 1970s, wrote the following to Bonita Pennino: "I remember her courage, her willingness to step out in front on tough issues which others ducked. I remember her taking the lead in 1973 in putting the Washington COG board on record in support of DC home rule as it was being debated in Congress; to do so as a suburban official took guts, but she succeeded, and I've always thought that she was responsible for changing the lives of thousands of people with that one act, an act which she regarded as a matter of principle."

John Thillman summarized Pennino's qualities very well, saying, "Martha was always a glass-half-full, never a glass-half-empty person! She overcame polio as a child and never asked for a crutch. Her lust for life on its terms was evidenced at her funeral when she made sure that there would be a jazz band for the mourners because she wanted people to be happy at a life well lived."[18]

Endnotes

1. Maude Robinson, January 11, 2007, interview (longtime Vienna resident, Vienna Town Council member).

2. Bonita Pennino, January 13, 2007, interview.

3. Nan Netherton et al., *Fairfax County, Virginia: A History* (Fairfax County, Virginia: Fairfax County Board of Supervisors, 1978), 647.

4. Robert Wilson, January 10, 2007, interview (Fairfax County executive, 1972–1975).

5. Jean Packard, January 13, 2007, interview (Board of Supervisors chairman, 1972–1975).

6. Kohann Whitney, January 11, 2007, interview (Centreville District School Board member, 1985–1993).

7. Mason Archival and Reference Service, item 1920/1850.

8. Priscilla Ames, January 16, 2007, interview.

9. James Cleveland, January 12, 2007, interview.

10. John Thillman, January 15, 2007, interview (Fairfax County and Reston planner, 1972–1979; USEPA, EQAC appointee, 1979; Planning Commission appointee, 1979–1987).

11. David Bobzien, January, 2007, interview (Fairfax County attorney, 1992–present).

12. Michael Howatt, January 14, 2007, interview (Government Relocation Committee chairman, Government Center Site Selection Committee chairman, Government Center Master Plan Committee chairman, 50–66 Planning Committee chairman, Pennino appointee to Fairfax County Economic Development Authority).

13. Kate Hanley, January 11, 2007, interview (Providence District supervisor, 1986–1995; Board of Supervisors chairman, 1996–2003).

14. J. Hamilton Lambert, January 16, 2007, interview (acting Fairfax County executive, 1978–1980; Fairfax County executive, 1980–1990).

15. Gerald Hyland, January 19, 2007, interview (Mount Vernon District supervisor, 1988–present).

16. J. Hamilton Lambert, interview.

17. Library of Congress.

18. John Thillman, interview.

The Mayor of Fairfax County
John Francis "Jack" Herrity
By Matthew McGuire, *Chesterfield, Virginia*

Jack Herrity was the most important political leader in 20th-century America's most prosperous jurisdiction. In the second half of the 20th century, no jurisdiction in the United States changed more than Fairfax County. Many individuals helped transform Fairfax from a rural agricultural community into an economic juggernaut. But John Francis "Jack" Herrity became the public face of Fairfax during the days of the county's most tumultuous growth. He was the first person to serve a full elected term as Board of Supervisors chairman, and he remains the only person to serve three full terms. Between 1976 and 1988 he redefined the job of board chairman and more than any other elected official he successfully promoted the economic development of the county. Herrity was a coarse man but he was also a visionary. He had working-class roots and led Fairfax in a style that would have made Ed Koch or William Donald Schaeffer proud. Herrity was a bold agent of change in a county that confronted problems radically different from those faced by the big-city politicians he resembled.

Herrity's style was unique in Virginia. He was demoted in the Coast Guard for brawling and his physical appearance called to mind an ex-prizefighter campaigning to run a tough union local more than it did a polished contemporary politician.[1] Herrity distinguished himself as a media impresario. To make a point on sewage, he had a portable toilet hauled into the board room. He brandished a crossbow that a student made in shop class to decry threats to school safety.[2] Annoyed at colleagues during a vote, he substituted "baloney" for the customary yea or nay. When his colleagues proposed forming a county human-rights committee, Herrity accused them of trying to form a "vigilante committee" that would lead to "snoopism" in the tradition of totalitarian states.[3] He practically invented the Lorton Reformatory as a political issue. The District of Columbia's prison was located in Herrity's district. Whenever there was an escape, which was frequently, Herrity would be on the scene at Lorton faster than you can say "News at 11."[4] Some county residents perceived Herrity as a straight-talking protector of the suburbs eager to do battle against bureaucrats. Others regarded Herrity as a shameless self-promoter and demagogue, but there is no denying that his colorful persona and media antics increased his profile and helped set the stage for much of his political success.

Herrity was elected board chairman with only 51.5 percent of the vote over incumbent Jean Packard in 1975. The outcome was an upset.[5] Packard had led the only board to make important efforts to limit residential development in Fairfax County. Herrity was part of that board as Springfield supervisor, but enjoyed little success in getting his motions passed as the lone Republican who had a poor relationship with most of the Democrats in the board's slow-growth majority, many of

Herrity relished any chance to meet voters or to promote the county's economy. Here he does both as he cuts the ribbon at the 1978 opening of the Vienna McDonald's restaurant.

whom regarded Herrity as an obnoxious publicity hound.[6] The election hinged on the popularity of that board's aggressive measures to halt development.

The previous board had slowed development in Fairfax through moratoria on sewer construction and new zonings. In addition, members of the board, including Herrity on occasion, removed many roads from the county's master plan. To say that area real estate developers were not amused is an understatement. Many had purchased large tracts of land slated for future development along proposed roads. The board's actions jeopardized their investment.[7] Herrity was sympathetic to the developers' plight and genuinely thought the board's actions were counterproductive. Nostalgia for a less urbanized Fairfax didn't impress Herrity. From his point of view, the county's rapid growth presented opportunities for Fairfax County to offer its residents the kinds of job and social options that previously could only be found in the District or Arlington.[8]

Initially the board's slow-growth measures attracted favorable national attention and should have put Packard in a good position to win reelection. But several factors came together to give Herrity the edge. Unfortunately for board Democrats, the area's premier developer, John T. "Til" Hazel, was also Virginia's finest land-use attorney. The county suffered an embarrassing string of defeats in the courtroom at the hands of Hazel and other developers.[9] The courts allowed the board 18 months to devise a planning and land use system (PLUS) program. But the PLUS task force lacked adequate resources and was not able to complete a plan that could draw widespread community support.[10] Promoting slow growth had been a good campaign tactic in 1971 but the political value of that position was more ambiguous in 1975. Finally, and perhaps most importantly, Herrity out-hustled Packard on the campaign trail. Packard, more the policy wonk than the pol, spent too much of her time in her Massey Building office, convinced voters wouldn't choose the flamboyant Herrity.[11]

Herrity Takes Office

Board members advocating the most stringent measures to halt development had miscalculated politically. In January of 1976, their miscalculation equaled Jack Herrity as board chairman. Now it was Herrity who had a working majority on the issues that were most important to him. The 1975 election signaled a shift in the county's political geography away from slow-growth forces.

With a new policy agenda and a board more sympathetic to him and his policies, Herrity took charge as chairman in 1976. Herrity's first year as chairman was the most successful of his political career. "His first big move," recalls Annandale Supervisor Audrey Moore, "Was on 66."[12] Within days of taking office, Herrity got the board to reverse its position on roads and to pass a resolution on a 6–3 vote supporting the construction of I-66 inside the Beltway.[13] Herrity worked overtime lobbying Gov. Mills Godwin and U.S. Secretary of Transportation William T. Coleman to approve the project. Coleman reversed the U.S. government's initial decision not to build the road.[14]

While the board was changing its position to support I-66, Herrity was also busy planning to keep the county's financial house in order. His efforts to trim the budget, however, were put on hold when he suffered two life-threatening heart attacks in January and February of 1976. But he quickly recovered and received favorable publicity for his tenacious return to county politics in March. Upon returning as chairman, Herrity entered into tough negotiations to raise taxes and bridge a budget shortfall. The shortfall was resolved and the county's AAA bond rating was kept intact. Even Alan Magazine, with whom Herrity frequently sparred politically, acknowledged that "Jack overall did a good job on the budget, and there won't be a more pressing problem."[15]

Budget problems only reinforced Herrity's determination to promote the development of the county's commercial and industrial base. Residential growth doesn't pay for itself. The cost of services that new residents impose on counties, particularly new residents with school-age children, inevitably forces an upward pressure on property taxes.[16] For Herrity, economic development was the rising tide that would lift all boats in Fairfax County. Only 14 percent of county revenue came from commercial establishments in 1976. The rate was declining and the threat of Fairfax becoming an overtaxed bedroom community was real.

A commission supported by Herrity and headed by Noman Cole was formed to investigate ways to increase the commercial development of the county. The commission presented its findings to the board in November of 1976. The report was highly critical of the PLUS program and of the preceding board's actions to limit growth. The solution, according to the commission, was to enhance the county's efforts to attract businesses from around the country.[17]

Ceaseless Advocacy for County Economic Growth

Herrity was the report's most enthusiastic supporter. His ceaseless advocacy for the basic economic vision outlined in the report became his greatest policy contribution to the county. He arranged massive increases in support for the cash-starved Fairfax County Economic Development Authority (EDA). Within a few years, the EDA experienced a 10-fold budget increase, conducted an aggressive nationwide advertising campaign, and became a major research center on the county's economy and demographics.[18] The investment paid off. By 1981, the EDA was receiving 12,000 inquiries a year from businesses interested in Fairfax County. Mobil Corporation moved its headquarters to Gallows Road and numerous businesses relocated major operations to Fairfax. The Economic Development Authority's goal was to increase the commercial tax base to 25 percent by the year 2000.[19] Moore complained that the goal was "mathematically impossible." She felt too much of the county had been zoned for residential use to even allow for the possibility of such a big jump in commercial activity. In 1987, the last year of Herrity's chairmanship, the county's commercial tax base topped 25 percent.[20]

Beefing up EDA wasn't the only contribution Herrity and his board colleagues made to the county's economy. By 1985, they had built sewers and arranged for adequate sewer treatment facilities to serve a county of one million residents.[21] Herrity also became the most persistent advocate of additional road construction of any elected official in the region during the 1970s and 1980s. While there were disagreements about its precise location, Herrity labored mightily to ensure the successful construction of the Fairfax County Parkway that now bears his name. He worked with developers to make sure the right-of-way was secure and he also lobbied hard to have the Dulles Toll Road open to non-airport commuters.[22]

Despite carrying Fairfax County, Herrity lost a close race for Congress to incumbent Herb Harris in 1978.[23] Consequently, Herrity remained "Chairman Jack" to voters and, notwithstanding his loss to Harris, he entered the height of his popularity in Fairfax County. He scored decisive re-election victories over Vivian Watts in 1979 and Patricia Watt in 1983.[24] He was the most recognizable personality in Northern Virginia and was named Washingtonian of the Year by *Washingtonian* magazine in 1980.[25] An internal Democratic Party poll in 1979 showed that Herrity's name recognition was higher than 90 percent, and he enjoyed a 7–2 favorability rating. Interestingly, some of Herrity's strongest support came from blue-collar workers, a strong demographic group for Democrats at the time.[26] Herrity exuded an anti-establishment persona and message that resonated with ordinary people.

Herrity's support collapsed in his third term. Fairfax voters were beginning to suffer from Herrity fatigue. His colorful personality had always been a double-edged sword politically. It allowed him to redefine the role of chairman from parliamentarian to county spokesman and leader. But in important respects it hurt him and the county. Herrity told the Senate Education Committee that the people of the commonwealth would be better off if the committee never met again.[27] He off-handedly referred to teachers as being highly paid "part-time employees" during a classroom visit.[28] His propensity for shooting from the hip verbally began to take its toll.

Two additional problems damaged his reputation in his third term. Herrity received four speeding tickets in rapid succession. The tickets prompted widespread rumors that he had a drinking problem. Herrity didn't, he was just a bad driver, but it was a political minus.[29] Worse, he was successfully prosecuted on a minor conflict-of-interest charge for participating in a vote involving a developer with whom he had a financial relationship. He actually voted against the developer's request, but in the public mind it only reinforced Herrity's ties with developers.[30]

Bad Traffic Foments Voter Fury

Most significantly, traffic had become terrible on Herrity's watch. The economy was booming and voters were more worried about the worsening traffic than they were about increasing the county's commercial tax base.[31] Perhaps ironic given his policy priorities, but voters were starting to direct their fury over bad traffic at Herrity. Increasingly, Herrity was perceived by the electorate as an arrogant, out-of-control chairman, leading an overpopulated, out-of-control county. He also faced his toughest opponent in 1987. Fellow maverick Audrey Moore, his popular Annandale colleague, was the most prominent foe of development in the county. She was the perfect person to capitalize on a political tsunami of anti-development and anti-Jack sentiment.[32] The election results weren't pretty for Herrity. He lost by 21 percentage points to Moore in an election that featured a massive 50-percent increase in voter turnout compared to 1983.[33]

Did Jack Herrity make Fairfax County a better place? The case against Herrity deserves serious consideration. He was not a man of refinement. Short-sleeved dress shirts and canary yellow sport coats were Herrity's idea of high fashion.[34] He would respond with incredulity at being served the most Americanized of Chinese food.[35] His crudeness and inability to censor himself turned off some of the key people he had to work with.[36] Had Herrity developed a better working relationship with the General Assembly and regional officials, it is possible that additional progress could have been made on a variety of issues, including transportation. His energetic efforts to assist constituents wound up alienating some board colleagues who thought he was muscling in on their territory.[37]

Herrity's policy stands are not above criticism either. There were understandable reasons the Packard board was concerned about the county's rapid growth. Herrity wanted to reduce red tape for developers so they could produce an affordable product for consumers.[38] It could be argued that his efforts translated into looser regulations allowing substandard buildings to be constructed, hurting some consumers.[39] Herrity's continuous criticism of Metro did not serve the county well. He was right that subway construction was stupendously expensive. Herrity was also ahead of his time in anticipating that Metro's value had been overstated because the job market, and traffic patterns, would shift from the District to Fairfax County.[40] However, Metro was too far along to stop or change dramatically by the time Herrity became chairman. His criticisms never promised to do more than slow down the subway's expansion, increase its cost, and alienate regional partners.[41]

But in hindsight, Herrity's virtues as a leader outweigh his vices. He was right on most of the big public policy questions the county encountered. No 21st-century politician in Fairfax County would be regarded seriously if they asserted that building I-66 or the Fairfax County Parkway were mistakes. Anyone perturbed by their property taxes in Fairfax County today would not want to see what their bill would look like if the county had not engaged in such a massive commercial expansion. And Herrity's influence was not limited to the development of the county. In his last year as chairman, he worked to obtain private funding to start the Medical Care

Herrity redefined the role of board chairman and helped put Fairfax County on the national map.

for Children Partnership. Since its inception, the program has served 85,000 low-income children in the county.[42]

None of these achievements was inevitable. Herrity was just one vote on the board, but he saw a potential in the office others missed. "He was the mayor of Fairfax County," recalls Delegate Vincent Callahan, who sponsored the legislation naming the Fairfax County Parkway after Herrity.[43] He lived and breathed politics. He was ubiquitous. No event was too small and no person was too unimportant not to merit an appearance or a phone call from Chairman Jack. Anyone who loves politics misses Herrity's sense of showmanship. Many liked and admired Herrity and, it must be said, a respectable number detested him. His bombastic style seemed altogether from another time and place. Yet he commanded the attention of one of America's most cosmopolitan communities as no local official has before or since.

Herrity wanted to be remembered. Somewhat embarrassingly, he shared with friends late in life his disappointment that his name was not more prominently displayed on signs for the parkway.[44] No doubt he dreaded sharing the fate of so many Virginia politicians and second-tier Confederate generals; a meaningless name on a nondescript building or a crowded road that leave passersby wondering why anyone bothered to name it at all. Even now there are motorists driving on the parkway who don't know and probably don't care who John F. "Jack" Herrity was.

But Herrity's importance isn't contingent on his future name recognition. His personality was so big and his achievements so consequential that his place in Fairfax County's history is assured.

Endnotes

1. "Herrity Keeps Tight Grip on Fairfax," *Washington Post,* June 2, 1986.
2. "Herrity Runs Hard on the 'Gut Issues'," *Washington Post,* October 31, 1986; Moore interview; Alexander interview.
3. "Herrity Keeps Tight Grip on Fairfax," *Washington Post,* June 2, 1986.
4. Magazine interview.
5. "Conservative Look Seen for County Board," *Fairfax Journal,* November 6, 1975; Packard interview.
6. "Panel Forms to Check Herrity," *Northern Virginia Sun,* October 20, 1977.
7. Hazel interview, Moore interview, Packard interview.
8. Moore interview.
9. Hazel interview, Moore interview, Packard interview.
10. Packard interview, Phillips interview.
11. Magazine interview.
12. Moore interview.
13. "Fairfax Shifts, Votes 4-Lane I-66," *Washington Post,* January 6, 1976.
14. "Herrity Urges I-66 Compromise," *Washington Post,* January 1, 1976; Lambert interview; Moore interview.
15. "Board Chairmanship Sweetens Herrity's Style," *Washington Post,* May 17, 1976.

16. "Study Says Services Suffer as Fairfax Grows," *Washington Post,* April 9, 1981; Frey interview; Gordon interview; Moore interview.

17. "Fairfax Supervisors Laud Industrial Report," *Washington Post,* November 11, 1976; Cole Commission report; Williams interview.

18. "The Selling of Counties and Cities: Business is the Buyer," *Washington Post,* January 1, 1982.

19. "Fairfax Intensifies Campaign to Attract Business to County," *Washington Post,* June 1, 1978.

20. Gordon interview, Williams interview.

21. "Fairfax Set to Lead Area in Developing," *Washington Post,* November 14, 1976.

22. Falck interview, McConnell interview.

23. Frey interview, Harris interview.

24. Official returns from 1979 and 1983, Fairfax County Electoral Board.

25. "Washingtonians of the Year," *Washingtonian,* January 1981, 82.

26. 1979 Democratic Party Poll courtesy of Vivian Watts.

27. Alexander interview, Lambert interview.

28. "Students Find Herrity Unbending on Teacher Pay," *Washington Post,* May 2, 1979; Watts interview.

29. "In Wake of 4th Ticket, Herrity to Use Chauffeur," *Washington Post,* July 7, 1987; Falck interview; Moore interview.

30. "The Many Faces of Jack Herrity," *Connection,* August 20, 1986; P. Herrity interview; Spevacek-Herrity interview.

31. "Eyes on Fairfax in Va. Races," *Washington Post,* September 6, 1987; Cikins interview; Frey interview; Moore interview.

32. Frey interview; Moore interview.

33. Official 1987 election returns, Fairfax County Electoral Board.

34. "Herrity Keeps Tight Grip on Fairfax," *Washington Post,* June 2, 1986. Williams interview.

35. Watts interview.

36. Lambert interview; magazine interview; Packard interview.

37. "Herrity, Travesky Trade Verbal Sniper Fire in Fairfax Feud," *Washington Post,* February 27, 1983; Moore interview; Ragan interview.

38. "Building Houses in Fairfax: Years of Paperwork," *Washington Post,* October 20, 1977.

39. "Defective Sewer Pipes Plague Fairfax Homeowners," *Washington Post,* January 4, 1976; Moore interview.

40. Cikins interview, Hazel interview.

41. Alexander interview, Harris interview.

42. Lowe interview.

43. Callahan interview.

44. Callahan interview, Hazel interview.

Oral History Interviews

Joseph Alexander, former Lee District supervisor (1964–96), July 7, 2006.
Vincent Callahan, Virginia House of Delegates (1968–present), August 15, 2006.

Warren Cikens, former Mount Vernon District supervisor (1974–80), July 25, 2006.

Nancy Falck, former Dranesville District supervisor (1980–88), July 25, 2006.

Michael Frey, former Herrity aide, Sully District supervisor (1992–present), July 5, 2006.

Gerald Gordon, Fairfax County Economic Development Authority, July 26, 2006.

Herbert Harris, former Mount Vernon District supervisor (1968–1974), August 18, 2006.

John T. Hazel, real estate developer and attorney, July 25, 2006.

Justine Herrity, Jack Herrity's first wife, July 28, 2006.

Patrick Herrity, Jack Herrity's son, August 5, 2006.

George W. Johnson, former George Mason University president (1978–96), July 6, 2006.

J. Hamilton Lambert, former Fairfax County executive (1980–90), August 14, 2006.

Sandra Lowe, founder of the Medical Care for Children Partnership, August 11, 2006.

William Madden, Herrity campaign manager (1971 and 1975), August 13, 2006.

Alan Magazine, former Mason District supervisor (1972–80), July 6, 2006.

Elaine McConnell, Springfield District supervisor (1984–2008), July 7, 2006.

Virginia McEnearney, Herrity's 1971 Democratic opponent, July 26, 2006.

Audrey Moore, former Board of Supervisors chairman (1988–92), August 5 and 9, 2006.

Jean Packard, former Board of Supervisors chairman (1972–76), July 29, 2006.

Rufus Phillips, former Dranesville District Supervisor (1972–76), July 3, 2006.

Joseph Ragan, former Fairfax County GOP chairman (1976–79), August 18, 2006.

JoAnn Spevacek-Herrity, Jack Herrity's widow, July 15, 2006.

Marie Travesky, Springfield District supervisor (1976–84), July 24, 2006.

Patricia Watt, Herrity's 1983 Democratic opponent, August 13, 2006.

Vivian Watts, Herrity's 1979 Democratic opponent, July 19, 2006.

Earle C. Williams, former EDA commissioner, July 22, 2006.

The Ghost of Keene Mill School
The Miller Finally Gets Recognition
By Irene Martinko (age 8, with Eva Martinko), *Springfield, Virginia*

Ms. Morris, the school librarian, looked up in surprise as a big stack of books dropped noisily on the desk in front of her. She smiled when she saw that it was Hillary, a fourth-grader from Mrs. McCarthy's class. She piled up the books, and started scanning them one by one, so the library computer could keep track of which books were checked out.

"Thanks, Ms. Morris," Hillary said, as she struggled to get the huge pile of books out the door.

Ms. Morris glanced at the clock and realized the school day was almost over, and it was time for her to close the library and leave for home. She walked through the room, putting stray books on shelves, picking up trash, pushing in chairs, and collecting pencils and other things kids had left behind. She picked up her jacket, turned off the lights, and headed toward the door that led from the library into the school parking lot.

Nobody noticed something—or someone—sneak into the room before Ms. Morris shut the door.

The Stamp Incident
Springfield, Virginia, is a small corner of Fairfax County, in the vast Washington, DC, area. The main street that runs through Springfield is Old Keene Mill Road. Right off that street is a small neighborhood school called Keene Mill Elementary School.

The library at Keene Mill School is not the biggest library around, but it has a great variety of books for kids from kindergarten all the way up to sixth grade. On one side of the room are the picture books, on shelves decorated with colorful signs and stuffed animals. In another section of the library is an area with carpeted steps that are big enough for kids to sit on and listen to stories or watch a video. Other parts of the room are filled with shelves of all kinds of books, and there are round tables with chairs, and three computers for looking up information. The main desk is near the front of the room and has an office behind it.

Ms. Morris had been the librarian at Keene Mill School for five years. She secretly felt she had the best job in the school. She did not have to worry about giving children grades or report cards, she did not have to plan tests or quizzes, and she did not have to schedule parent conferences about their children's progress in school. The best part of the job was that she got to spend her whole day in the library, which she considered to be a peaceful, comfortable, happy place to be. When children were excited about books, she felt excited, too.

It was an early morning in October and Ms. Morris had just entered her office in the library. Her first job of the day was to stamp "Keene Mill Elementary School" on the inside cover of all the new books. She picked up the rubber stamp and started to stamp each book. As she worked, she realized she had forgotten to stop at the office that morning to pick up her mail. She put down the rubber stamp and walked down to the office.

When she returned about 15 minutes later and sat down at her desk, she was in for a shock! There, right in front of her, covering her desk, were the words "Keene Mill Elementary School" stamped everywhere. Never, in all her years in the library, had she seen such vandalism to school property.

"What student would do such a thing?" Ms. Morris thought. "Such a mess!"

She picked up the phone and dialed the number for the principal, Mr. Burke. When he heard what had happened, he hurried to the library to see for himself. He, too, was shocked by what he saw!

"How long were you out of the room when this happened?" he asked.

"Only a couple of minutes," she answered, still very upset.

"Was anybody else in here?" Mr. Burke asked.

"Nobody but me," replied Ms. Morris.

"I'll ask Mr. Carranza, the custodian, to come right away to help clean this up," he told her. "Meanwhile, let's try to figure out who is responsible for this mess."

Ms. Morris was very worried, but did not have much time to think about this, because the first class of the day was filing in.

The Trash Surprise

The next morning was a sunny Friday. Ms. Morris arrived at the library, happy to see that her desk was spotless. She decided to tackle the stack of overdue book notices. These were pieces of paper that let students know their Keene Mill School Library book was overdue. She noticed some of the books had been returned, so she threw the notices for those books into the wastebasket. The rest of the morning went by without any trouble, and she went to the teacher's lounge for lunch at noon.

When she returned from lunch, she headed to her desk. Soon the second-graders would be coming in to select books, and to listen to stories being read aloud. However, when Ms. Morris saw what was on her desk, she got very surprised once again! All of the overdue book notices that she had thrown in the trash were back on her desk, in a big messy pile. Someone had cut out the words, "Keene Mill," from each notice, and had neatly made a separate pile for just those words, at the center of the desk.

"I could have sworn I threw those out!" exclaimed Ms. Morris, in confusion. "And I know I did not cut any words out of those papers! What is going on here?"

She did not have time to call Mr. Burke about this, because the second-graders had just walked into the room. She had to be calm and relaxed to read to the class.

She read several Halloween stories to the children, but her mind kept wandering, wondering who had been disturbing her office.

Later in the day, four students from Mrs. McCarthy's fourth-grade class came into the library during their Friday Free Time. Sophia and Helina walked over to the library desk to ask whether the latest Harry Potter book was in yet. Patrick and David went over to the shelves to find some scary stories. They each picked out a book and sat down to read at one of the round tables. Sophia and Helina took their Harry Potter books over to the same table, and settled down to read. It was hard for the girls to concentrate, because the boys were so excited about the creepy stories in the ghost books they were reading.

"This is so cool!" said Patrick.

"Look at that awesome picture," said David, "It looks like a real ghost!"

Ms. Morris came over to see what was so interesting to the boys.

When she saw what they were reading, she joked, "It's getting close to Halloween. With all the strange things going on around here, maybe I have a ghost in the library!"

"What strange things are going on?" Helina asked, full of curiosity.

The librarian decided to tell the four students about the rubber stamp incident, and about the trash ending up cut apart on her desk.

"It sounds like trick-or-treat without the treat!" joked Patrick.

"It's a mystery!" exclaimed Sophia.

"And I can tell you the first clue," said David. "Whoever is doing this is very interested in the words 'Keene Mill.'"

Scary Happenings

The following Monday, in Mrs. McCarthy's fourth grade, Sophia, Helina, David, and Patrick were very restless. All they could think about was the mystery in the library. They had decided to keep it a secret, and to try to help find out who was at the bottom of it.

Meanwhile, Ms. Morris was getting used to unexpected things happening every day. None of these things really hurt anybody, they were just little pranks. Even though they were just mischievous pranks, they were still very annoying, especially this week. This week, she was preparing for the Keene Mill School book fair, which would take place on Friday after school. The whole room was being rearranged so kids and their families could select books to buy. She would have to work overtime every day this week to get it all done, and she did not have time for extra worries.

That afternoon she started to set up for the book fair. As she was opening big boxes of books, suddenly the room became dark, and all the noises stopped. The hum of the computer ended, and the room became very cold. She stood still for a moment, then realized the power must have gone off, so she picked up the phone to call the janitor.

"That's strange!" he said. "The rest of the building has electricity."

At these words, the phone went dead!

"What can be happening?" thought Ms. Morris. "This is getting more and more spooky!"

She decided to continue her work in the dark, thinking the custodian would fix the problem. Sure enough, the lights, computer, phone, and heater all came back on. Ms. Morris dialed Mr. Carranza's number to thank him.

"Don't thank me yet," the custodian told her in a surprised voice. "I haven't done anything to fix it."

"That's odd," she said. "The power is back on!"

When she hung up the phone and got back to work, she suddenly jumped in fright! She heard someone working at the computer, but nobody was there!

"Maybe when the power came back on it did something to the computer," the librarian thought. "I guess I should turn it off."

As she made her way closer to the computer, she could see the whole screen was covered with jumbled letters that made no sense. At the bottom of the page were two words that did make sense. In all small letters, someone had typed the words "keene mill."

The Mill

The next morning, Ms. Morris was a little bit nervous as she sat at her desk. She was still frightened by what had happened the previous afternoon. She was thinking of telling Mr. Burke about the latest strange happenings in the library, but he would probably think she was crazy!

"I'll worry about this after the book fair is over," she told herself. "I am sure I'll be able to catch the culprit in the act soon."

She went over to the section of the library labeled "History" and picked out a book about George Washington to read to the first-graders later in the day. She placed the book on her desk, and began to work on putting up book fair posters. After lunch, the first-graders arrived, and Ms. Morris went to her desk to get the George Washington book. She was surprised to find the book was open, and she couldn't help but notice what page was showing. It was a picture of George Washington's old grist mill.

Miss Morris had visited the old grist mill, a historic site in Fairfax County. She knew an old-fashioned grist mill was a building with equipment to grind grain into flour. Usually, Ms. Morris would not have paid much attention to this picture, but the word "mill" caught her eye right away. All of the eerie things that had happened lately had involved that word!

After the first-graders went back to class, in came Patrick and Helina. They had been sent by Mrs. McCarthy to pick up some books about water cycles for their science lesson.

"Has anything else strange happened in the library this week?" Helina asked.

"As a matter of fact, yes!" said Ms. Morris. "You're just in time to help me figure out the latest mystery."

She told them about the power going out, the words mysteriously appearing on the computer, and the book being left open to the picture of the mill.

"Wow! Every single thing that has happened is somehow connected with a mill," said Patrick.

"I was thinking the same thing," said Ms. Morris. "But I don't know what it means."

"Excuse me, Ms. Morris," said Helina. "I was just wondering, where did Keene Mill School get its name? Is there a real mill called Keene's Mill?"

The librarian thought this was a good question, but she really did not know the answer.

"Well, we know the busiest road around this area is Old Keene Mill Road. So, I suppose the road was named after the mill, which must have been around here, too." she guessed. "I think it is time for us to do some research."

She took Patrick and Helina over to the library computer, and typed in the words "Keene Mill." All the Web sites that came up were about Keene Mill Elementary School. So she tried again, adding the word "history." One of the Web sites listed was for the Fairfax County Historical Society. She went to that Web site, and scrolled through the articles until she saw one that mentioned Old Keene Mill Road.

Patrick read aloud: "The main road in the area used to be Rolling Road. Another road, called Rolling Road Number Two was built. It became confusing to have two roads with the same name, so the county changed the name of the second road to Old Keene Mill Road, because the road passed by the location that used to be Keene's Mill, one of the largest and best grist mills in Fairfax County."

"So there was a real Keene's Mill!" said Helina.

"There doesn't seem to be any more about it on the computer, "complained Ms. Morris. "We need to look somewhere else."

The Book Fair

During Friday Free Time, Helina, Sophia, Patrick, and David went quickly to the library. The librarian was busily setting up displays for the book fair, and didn't notice them until Helina tapped her on the shoulder.

Startled, Ms. Morris said, "You scared me! I've been a little jumpy lately."

"We were thinking," said Sophia, "we could be lookouts tonight at the book fair."

"We could watch for anything suspicious," said David.

"I am wondering why anybody at our school would be so interested in old Keene's Mill," said Patrick.

Sophia added, "I am wondering how words got on the computer screen with nobody in the room."

Helina said, "Maybe tonight we'll catch the person who has been doing all this."

"Thanks for helping," said Ms. Morris. "I will be too busy to watch for clues."

That night at 5:00 the library started filling up with people. The shelves were covered with blue cloth, and displayed lots of brand-new books for sale. There were also computer games, magazines, and other school supplies and toys. The room was full of excited sounds, as children begged their parents to buy them books and other great things they found at the book fair. The four fourth-grade helpers were stationed in the corners of the room, keeping an eye out for trouble.

"This is getting boring," Patrick told David. "Nobody's doing anything, and I want to look at books."

At that moment, the lights went out! Everyone screamed, and young children called out for their parents. Then, the door to the parking lot flew open, and a gust of wind blew through the room.

"Remember Keene's Mill," a low, whispery voice said in the darkness.

The lights came back on, and everybody breathed a sigh of relief. Mr. Burke, who had seen what happened, announced to everyone, "I think our librarian has played a clever Halloween trick on all of us! Thank you, Ms. Morris, for helping us get into the Halloween spirit at our fall book fair. Now, get back to buying those books!"

Ms. Morris was bewildered. Of course, she would never play a Halloween prank like that. But then . . . who did? The four fourth-grader helpers ran over to her, knowing she had nothing to do with what happened.

"I didn't see anybody turn out the lights," said Helina, who had been closest to the light switch.

"I was near the door, and I did not see anyone open it," said Patrick.

"Did you hear that voice? It was creepy!" added Sophia.

Ms. Morris, who was still very shaken up, said in a soft voice, "Children, I know this might sound crazy, but I think we really do have a ghost in this library."

Looking into the Past

The weekend was a good time to do more investigating about the mystery. David and Patrick had the perfect opportunity to do that on Saturday night. David's parents were taking them to a special Halloween presentation at the local nature center, Hidden Pond. The title of the presentation was "Legends and Ghosts of Fairfax County." The boys sat down with a group around a campfire, listening to the stories. Clara, who worked at the nature center, was an expert on local history. She told about ghosts that were said to haunt some of the famous estates in the Fairfax County, such as Mount Vernon, George Washington's mansion. Other stories she told were about murders and mysteries that had taken place in the area long ago. Her final story of the evening really got the attention of Patrick and David.

"As you may know," she said, "Keene's Mill was a very successful grist mill located in Fairfax County. James Keene built it in the late 1700s, and later his son, William Keene, ran it. A man named Mr. Hall came to the mill one night in October of 1855, and got into an argument with William Keene. Nobody knows exactly what happened, but Mr. Hall was injured that night, and died two days later. William Keene was accused of the crime, and was sent to prison, and that was the last anyone ever heard of him. Some members of the Keene family were buried in the small family cemetery right down the road from here, but William Keene was not one of them. The whole episode of the murder at the mill is one of the most gruesome legends of our county."

On the way home, Patrick and David discussed the story they had heard. They had both been thinking the same thing: The story of William Keene was definitely an important clue to the mystery in the library.

Meanwhile, Helina had called Sophia excitedly, to tell her about something she had noticed in her own neighborhood. Sophia came right over, and she and Helina walked past the rows of houses to the corner where Helina's street crossed Old Keene Mill Road. Helina pointed to a small sign on the side of the road. It was a highway historical marker that said: "KEENE'S MILL."

"You mean the real Keene's Mill was right here near your house?" asked Sophia.

"I guess so," said Helina. "My mom and I drive past this sign every day, but I never noticed what it said until now."

The two girls went closer to the sign to read the small print on it: "A saw and grist mill built by James Keene between 1796 and 1800 . . . just to the east of this marker. The mill served the surrounding farm community for approximately sixty years. . . ."

The girls walked for a while in the direction of the place where the mill had been located, but there was nothing remaining of the old building.

Sophia said, "Isn't it strange to imagine that more than 200 years ago none of these houses were here, and there was a saw mill where we are walking right now?"

Helina wondered, "What could this mill have to do with our school library?"

Ms. Morris was also doing some research of her own. Since school was closed over the weekend, she went to the big public library, located right off Old Keene Mill Road. She went straight to the section with books about ghosts. Many of the ghosts she read about were said to have caused mischief, such as making lights go out, or moving objects around a room. One thing all the books had in common was that the authors believed the reason for a ghost to haunt a particular place was to complete some kind of unfinished business, or to ask for help or understanding.

"If the Keene Mill School Library is really being haunted, maybe the ghost will go away if it can finish the unfinished business that brought it here in the first place," thought Ms. Morris. "Maybe it needs our help."

Ghost Hunters

The four fourth-graders rushed to the school library after school on Monday. Eager to share what they had learned, they all started talking at once.

"One at a time!" said the librarian.

The girls told about finding the location of the mill, and the boys told the story of William Keene. Ms. Morris, who had never before believed in ghosts, was reaching an uncomfortable conclusion about the trouble in the library. Before she could say it, the four students reached the same conclusion.

"I think there is a ghost in this library," said Patrick.

"I think the ghost wants something," said Sophia.

"I think the ghost has something to do with the murder at the mill," said David.

"I think we should help the ghost," said Helina.

"I agree," said Ms. Morris. "We'd better get started."

She shut the library door and they all sat down at a table.

David was impatient to find the ghost and he called out loudly, "Okay, ghost! Show yourself!"

"Wait a minute! That's no way to talk to a ghost!" exclaimed Helina. "Let's figure out how to make the ghost *want* to show himself."

"I know," said Sophia. "We have to let him know it's safe to come out."

Patrick said, "I think the ghost is Mr. Hall, coming back to get revenge for his death."

Then he said loudly, "Mr. Hall! It's all right for you to come out now!"

It was silent in the room for a moment, and they were beginning to think nothing would happen. The silence was broken by a sudden crash, as a big shelf of books fell to the floor. Everyone jumped!

"I guess it isn't Mr. Hall!" said Helina. "I think you made the ghost mad!"

"I've had enough scares for today," said Ms. Morris. "Can you all come back tomorrow after school?"

"Okay, but I sure was hoping to see that ghost today," said David.

They all helped pick up the fallen shelf and put the books away. Then they all left for the day, wondering what the next day would have in store for them.

The next day, school went slowly for the four children, as they waited for the school day to end. When it was time to go, they rushed to the library, and found Ms. Morris reading a children's book called *Ghosts and Poltergeists.*

"I found this book in our school library," she told the kids. "It says here there is no need to be afraid of the ghost. I have a feeling our mischief-maker is the ghost of William Keene himself. Maybe if we let him know we aren't afraid, and we want to help him, he will show himself."

"I'd like to give it a try," said Helina, bravely. Then, in a loud, calm voice, she called out, "Mr. William Keene! Are you there? We are here to help you!"

They all looked around the room, and there at the table next to them a faded figure slowly began to appear. He was there, but not quite there; the librarian and the students could see right through him! They gasped, but tried hard to hold back their fear, so the ghost would stay. The image they saw was clear enough to make out the shape of a middle-aged man, with longish brown hair, and a short beard. He was wearing the clothing an old-fashioned farmer might have worn—a dirty white shirt, brown pants, and short boots.

When he spoke, it was the same whispery voice they had all heard at the book fair: "This table is made of nice strong wood, like the kind I made at my mill."

"So you are William Keene!" David blurted out.

The man answered, "Yes, I am William Keene. I ran the best sawmill and grist mill Fairfax County ever had."

Ms. Morris, who had been too shocked to speak, now asked in a shaky voice, "Why have you come to our school?"

"Well," said William Keene, "I have some business to settle, so I came back to look for my mill, but it was gone. I don't have much education, but I do know how to recognize the words 'Keene Mill,' because I had to be able to read my name, and my mill had a sign that said 'Keene Mill' on it. So, I saw those words on this building, and came in."

"Excuse me, Mr. Keene," said Sophia, politely (she didn't really know how one was supposed to address a ghost). "What is the business you have to take care of? Can we help?"

"More than 200 years ago, I was a successful, happy business owner right down the road. Then, one night I lost everything—my mill, my home, and my friends and family. I haven't been back here since then, and I wanted to see if anyone remembered me."

"What really happened that night?" asked Patrick.

"To tell you the truth, it was so long ago, I really don't remember the details," said Keene. "I remember arguing with that scoundrel, Hall, but I don't remember killing him. I am not a dangerous person. Whatever happened to him, he deserved it. He and his whole family were a bunch of mean characters, and everyone knew it."

"What is it you want now?" asked Ms. Morris, quietly.

"I had no children of my own, so nobody carried on my name. I see even in a school named after my mill there is not even one word about me anywhere. I bet nobody here has even heard of me before."

The kids had to admit he was right. Except for them, nobody else in the school had ever heard of William Keene, or the Keene family.

"I just want to be remembered as the owner of Keene's Mill. If I know people remember me, then I can be at peace at last," he said.

The Class Project

"I feel sorry for Mr. Keene," Helina told Sophia the next morning. "There must be something we can do to help him."

"What if we tell Mr. Burke about him, and see if he can do something?" suggested Sophia.

"We'd better not tell anybody there is a ghost here. They might get very scared, and might scare the ghost, too," said Helina. "Maybe we could make something to put up on the school wall that tells about Mr. Keene. After all, our school has his name."

"Great idea!" said Sophia. "We can do it as a class project, and everyone can help."

They told Patrick and David their idea, and all of them went to talk to their teacher, Mrs. McCarthy. They explained they had discovered where Keene Mill School had gotten its name, and they thought it would be nice if the whole school knew about it. Mrs. McCarthy agreed, and let them tell their idea to the class. They told the class about Keene's Mill and its owner, William Keene. They told about how important and successful the mill was in Fairfax County. They did not say too much about the dark incident that occurred there and, of course, they did not mention they had met Mr. Keene themselves!

Mrs. McCarthy divided the class into groups of four people, to design a poster that would let people know the story. The whole class would vote on two posters each, and the poster with the most votes would go up on the wall of the school.

The class got busy working on their posters, and soon had completed their projects. All the posters were very well done, but only one could be chosen. The class chose the poster made by the team of Sara, Rachel, Amanda, and Aneeka. Sophia mentioned to Mrs. McCarthy that Ms. Morris had helped them a lot with learning about Keene's Mill. So, Mrs. McCarthy invited Ms. Morris to come to the room to see the final poster. Mr. Burke came, too, and was very impressed with what the class had done.

"I think this is great!" he said. "I am going to have this poster framed and put up in the school lobby where everyone can see it."

The class cheered and Ms. Morris smiled.

Finished Business

The day the framed poster was hung up in the lobby, Ms. Morris waited until everyone had gone home. Then, she and the four children took William Keene to see it.

"It's wonderful!" he said. "Now there is one place where people will remember William Keene was here. Now I can go and rest. There is just one problem—I have no place to go."

"I know where you can go," said David. He told them about the Keene family cemetery he had learned about from Clara, at Hidden Pond.

Ms. Morris made a quick phone call to Hidden Pond to ask Clara the exact location of the cemetery. All the children had to go home because it was getting late, so Ms. Morris was alone in the library with the ghost.

"Have you ever ridden in a car?" she asked him.

"I don't even know what a car is," he replied.

"Well, come with me. I think you are going to like this," she said, laughing to herself.

She closed the door to the library and led the ghost to her car in the parking lot. When he was sitting in the car, looking a little out of place, she started the car. William Keene was amazed at how fast they were going.

"This is a lot faster than a horse!" he said.

"A car has a lot of horse power!" Ms. Morris told him.

She drove down Old Keene Mill Road and turned left near the place where Keene's Mill used to be. She drove into a neighborhood of townhouses, around winding streets, and came to a stop in front of a small, fenced-in area. Ms. Morris unlatched the short, iron gate and went in. Inside was a small grove of trees and several old gravestones that were falling down. The names on the stones were so old it was hard to make out the letters, but Ms. Morris was able to read one name out loud: "Addison Keen."

The ghost slowly smiled, "This is the resting place of the Keene family, so this is where I belong. Thank you."

Ms. Morris looked down at the old gravestone, almost wishing the ghost would stay longer so she could learn more about the old days. When she looked up again, William Keene was gone.

Epilogue

Everything was back to normal at the library. Ms. Morris began to scan the first-graders' books. One of the children had a lot of Halloween books.

"I see you are getting ready for trick-or-treating," she told him. "What is your costume going to be?"

"I'm going to be a ghost!" he told her, happily. "Really scary, huh?"

Ms. Morris smiled. "Maybe not so scary after all," she thought. "Maybe not."

Author's Note

All the historical information in this story is based on what we know today about the Keene family and their mill. The Keene family cemetery is located off Field Master Drive in the Greentree Village neighborhood. During the 1700s and 1800s, the Keene family name was spelled "Keen," and that is how it appears on the gravestone of Addison Keene. The Keene's Mill historical marker is near the corner of Huntsman Boulevard and Old Keene Mill Road in Springfield.

Headstone of Addison Keene in the small family cemetery in the Greentree Village neighborhood in Burke, Virginia. (Photograph by Kathy Marinucci)

Appendix: Legacy Book Project Description

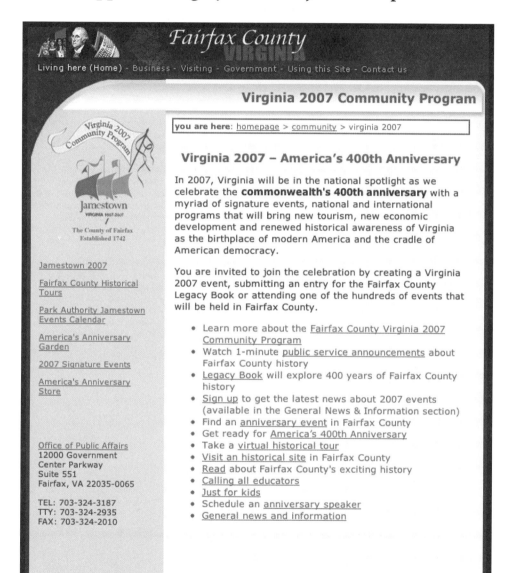

Fairfax County
VIRGINIA

Living here (Home) - Business - Visiting - Government - Using this Site - Contact us

Virginia 2007 Community Program

Virginia 2007
Community Program

Jamestown
VIRGINIA 1607-2007
/
The County of Fairfax
Established 1742

Jamestown 2007

Fairfax County Historical
Tours

Park Authority Jamestown
Events Calendar

America's Anniversary
Garden

2007 Signature Events

America's Anniversary
Store

Office of Public Affairs
12000 Government
Center Parkway
Suite 551
Fairfax, VA 22035-0065

TEL: 703-324-3187
TTY: 703-324-2935
FAX: 703-324-2010

you are here: homepage > community > virginia 2007

Virginia 2007 – America's 400th Anniversary

In 2007, Virginia will be in the national spotlight as we celebrate the **commonwealth's 400th anniversary** with a myriad of signature events, national and international programs that will bring new tourism, new economic development and renewed historical awareness of Virginia as the birthplace of modern America and the cradle of American democracy.

You are invited to join the celebration by creating a Virginia 2007 event, submitting an entry for the Fairfax County Legacy Book or attending one of the hundreds of events that will be held in Fairfax County.

- Learn more about the Fairfax County Virginia 2007 Community Program
- Watch 1-minute public service announcements about Fairfax County history
- Legacy Book will explore 400 years of Fairfax County history
- Sign up to get the latest news about 2007 events (available in the General News & Information section)
- Find an anniversary event in Fairfax County
- Get ready for America's 400th Anniversary
- Take a virtual historical tour
- Visit an historical site in Fairfax County
- Read about Fairfax County's exciting history
- Calling all educators
- Just for kids
- Schedule an anniversary speaker
- General news and information

you are here: homepage > community > virginia 2007 > fairfax county legacy book

Fairfax County Legacy Book

The Fairfax County 2007 Community Citizen Planning Committee has announced plans to publish a book as a legacy project for county residents. The book will feature vignettes, anecdotes, essays and anecdotes that highlight the history of Fairfax County through the last 400 years, since the founding of Jamestown in 1607. The committee is soliciting original, non-published, history-related items for publication in the book.

A committee of historians from the county, area educational facilities and the Fairfax County Public Library will evaluate the work submitted. The selected articles will be published in a softbound volume to be distributed to libraries, historical sites and schools within the county. The publication also will be available for sale at sites throughout the county. Articles or photographs not included in the volume will be filed in the unpublished manuscript file at the Virginia Room of the Fairfax City Regional Library. It is anticipated that the volume will be available in the spring of 2007. Watch for more information on this Web site and in the local media.

Jamestown 2007

Fairfax County Historical Tours

Park Authority
Jamestown Events Calendar

America's Anniversary Garden

2007 Signature Events

America's Anniversary Store

Office of Public Affairs
12000 Government
Center Parkway
Suite 551
Fairfax, VA 22035-0065

TEL: 703-324-3187
TTY: 703-324-2935
FAX: 703-324-2010

Living here (Home) - Business - Visiting - Government - Using this Site - Contact us

Search: [ ] Go
Advanced

2007 Legacy Book

you are here: homepage > today in fairfax > general county news releases > 2007 legacy book

Fairfax County Office of Public Affairs
12000 Government Center Parkway, Suite 551
Fairfax, VA 22035-0065
703-324-3187, TTY 711, FAX 703-324-2010

July 14, 2006

Make Your Mark on History: Submit an Entry for the 2007 Legacy Book Sept. 1 Deadline for Entries

Do you have a great story, photograph or anecdote about Fairfax County's history? The Fairfax County 2007 Community Citizen Planning Committee is accepting entries for its legacy book celebrating 400 years of Fairfax County history. The deadline is Sept. 1.

The historical anthology is part of the larger Virginia 2007 Community Program to commemorate 400 years of Virginia history. The book will feature vignettes, anecdotal articles, photographs and essays that highlight the history of Fairfax County through the last 400 years, since the founding of Jamestown in 1607.

The committee is soliciting original, non-published, history-related items for publication in the book. Each contribution — written, photographic or other — must be the sole property of the person submitting it, or it must be shown that the owner has given permission for its use. This is a volunteer project with no compensation for any submission. The authors will have the satisfaction of being a part of this great project and having their work reflect the pride Fairfax County feels about its rich and diverse history.

The publication will contain a minimum of four vignettes, anecdotal articles or essays from each of the last four centuries, from 1607 to 2007, for a total of at least 16 selections. Writers may submit articles or photographs about events, personalities, geographical features, localities or any subject that has historical significance within the geographical boundaries of Fairfax County today.

A committee of historians from the county, area educational facilities and the Fairfax County Public Library will evaluate the submissions. The selected articles will be published in a softbound volume to be distributed to county libraries, historical sites and schools. The publication also will be available for sale at sites throughout the county. Articles or photographs not included in the volume will be filed in the unpublished manuscript file at the Virginia Room of the Fairfax City Regional Library.

Procedure for submitting material for the history book

Written submissions should contain no more than 2,500 words, not including footnotes, be double-spaced in 12-point type with one-inch margins on white 8.5-inches-by-11-inches bond paper.

When submitting photographs, place a label on the back of the photograph with a description of the photograph, your name, address, telephone number and e-mail address. Do not write on the back of the photograph. Do not submit original photographs since they will not be returned.

All entries must be accompanied by a completed submission form. The form is available to download at www.fairfaxcounty.gov/opa/va2007. To request a form by mail or fax, please call the Fairfax County Office of Public Affairs at 703-324-3187, TTY 711. Entries must be submitted by Sept. 1. Material can be submitted via e-mail to wwwopa@fairfaxcounty.gov or by mail on a disk along with the hard copy to the following address:

Virginia 2007 History Book Project
Fairfax County Office of Public Affairs
12000 Government Center Parkway, Suite 551
Fairfax, VA 22036-0065

Fairfax County's 2007 Commemoration

Fairfax County's Virginia 2007 Community Citizen Planning Committee promotes and publicizes events taking place in the county that commemorate Jamestown's 400th anniversary. Appointed by the Fairfax County Board of Supervisors, the committee represents the diversity of communities and resources in the county, including the African-American, Hispanic and American Indian communities and representatives from Fort Belvoir, Wolf Trap, George Washington's Mount Vernon and the Fairfax County Convention and Visitors Corporation.

As an official Virginia 2007 Community, Fairfax County is participating in next year's statewide celebrations commemorating the founding of Jamestown. Settled in 1607, Jamestown was America's first permanent English settlement and is, in essence, our nation's birthplace.

To celebrate the county's role in the birth of our nation, the committee will publish an anthology of county history during the past 400 years. To learn more about this project or submit an entry, visit www.fairfaxcounty.gov/opa/va2007.

For more information about the committee, contact the Fairfax County Office of Public Affairs at 703-324-3187, TTY 711, or visit www.fairfaxcounty.gov/opa/va2007. For more information about Jamestown 2007 and the Virginia 2007 program, visit www.americas400thanniversary.org or www.jamestown2007.org

To request this information in an alternate format, call the Office of Public Affairs at 703-324-3187, TTY 711.

Virginia 2007 History Book Entry Form

*This form must be completed and sent with your submission via e-mail to
wwwopa@fairfaxcounty.gov or by mail to: Virginia 2007 History Book Project, Fairfax
County Office of Public Affairs, 12000 Government Center Parkway, Suite 551, Fairfax, VA
22035. Submission sent by mail must include a copy of the entry on a disk as well as a
hard copy. All entries are due by June 1, 2006*

Name _____

Address_____

_____

Daytime Telephone Number _____

E-mail Address _____

I am submitting the following items for consideration;

Original text _____   Original photograph _____

Non-original text that is not copyrighted _____

Non-original photograph that is not copyrighted _____

Copyrighted text with written permission from copyright owner _____
(Written permission must be attached to this form.)

Copyrighted photo with written permission from copyright owner _____
(Written permission must be attached to this form.)

I hereby certify that:

> the material I am submitting is my original work and that I am the sole
> copyright owner or
> I am not the sole copyright owner, but I have written permission from the
> copyright owner(s) allowing the material to be used in the Virginia 2007
> History Book.
> the material is not original, but is not copyrighted

I understand that it may be published and displayed publicly and that I am liable for any
copyright infringements that may result if this material is printed in the Virginia 2007 History
Book.

_____

Signature

If you have any questions about the Virginia 2007 History Book Project or the Fairfax County
Virginia 2007 program, call the Fairfax County Office of Public Affairs at 703-324-3187, TTY
711.

Acknowledgements

Producing a book is no easy task. One might think that writing it would be the hardest part, but that is not necessarily the case. When the Fairfax County 2007 Community Citizen Planning Committee decided to produce a book about Fairfax County history over the period of 1607 to 2007, I thought that shouldn't be too difficult. Well, I'm older, wiser and yes, grayer because of this naive assumption. Dozens of authors submitted interesting and colorful stories and a task force assembled for the purpose selected more than 30 stories for the book.

For their many hours of reading and critiquing every story I am grateful to historian Susan Hellman, Department of Planning and Zoning; librarian Suzanne Levy, Virginia Room, Fairfax County Public Library; Legacy Book Subcommittee member Sally Ormsby; and volunteer Kathy Marinucci, proofreader/copyeditor for the *Chronicle Newspapers*.

On the subject of volunteers, putting this book together was the result of countless hours of volunteer effort. In the fall of 2006, when I approached Kathy Marinucci about doing the copyediting for the project, there was not a moment's hesitation, although she realized there would be no compensation other than the self-satisfaction of knowing she had contributed to a worthwhile project. Words will never be able to express the appreciation and the debt I owe Kathy for her many tireless hours spent burning the midnight oil and giving short shrift to her family so this book could come out close to schedule. My computer is weighed down with e-mail messages from Kathy reminding me of things I need to do to keep to the schedule. Armed with her copy of *The Chicago Manual of Style*, nothing gets past her eagle eye. She's as close to perfect as they get.

Getting the stories selected and together, then getting them edited and illustrations captioned is only half of the story; next came the layout and print preparation. For that phase we were lucky to have experienced project manager Paula Elsey come forward and offer to help. Tutored by the late county historian Donald Senese, Fairfax County History Commission Publications Committee Chair Paula dug right in like the professional she is. Her experience in handling other publishing projects for the History Commission made her an invaluable member of the team. Simple thanks will never be enough for all she has done to get this book into the hands of the reader. Her can-do attitude buoyed us all during the low points when we thought the project would never be completed. Her relentless drive kept us and the project moving and on track, even in the face of daunting deadlines. Kathy and I often chuckled, thinking about Paula's favorite comment: "We don't have to worry about that now." She added much to her car's mileage ferrying copy and cover samples back and forth between the compositor and the rest of the team. Paula, powerhouse perfectionist that she is, never let up until the book was finally printed.

Of all the talented and professional people who helped with this book, none stands out more than Joe Marinucci. When the project team determined, late in the game, that a map may help orient readers to sites in the stories, Joe jumped in with both feet and, in record time, produced the great map that became part of this book. To Joe goes a very special thanks.

There are numerous others who contributed time and expertise to this project and, if I failed to mention you, it's not because I don't appreciate what you contributed. To Matthew Graham, Brian Worthy, Carrie Brill, Catherine Chianese, and Michael Gatti, your help in navigating the county bureaucracy made life a lot easier. To Corazon Foley, who was not an appointed member of the Legacy Book Subcommittee but attended every meeting and added her special insights, thank you. Brian Conley of the Virginia Room, Fairfax County Public Library, could always track down a needed photo. Every time a panicked e-mail was sent or a desperate phone call was made to any of our contacts employed by the county, we got instant, accurate results.

Thanks also to the Legacy Book Subcommittee, whose members included Irma Clifton, Chair; Shirley Fegan; Henry Mackall; Bud Mayo; Esther McCullough; Sally Ormsby; and Mayo Stuntz.

This book is truly the product of people who have a love and respect for Fairfax County history and who want that love and respect to be reflected into the next 100 years. To those who read these words in 2107, I hope you will be inspired to pass the legacy even further into the future.

Irma A. Clifton, Chair
Legacy Book Subcommittee

Fairfax County 2007 Community Citizen Planning Committee

Stephanie Brown
Traci Claar
Irma A. Clifton
Shirley Fegan
Esther Ferington
Chris Guerre
Olga Hernandez
Carole Herrick
Ben Hiatt

Connie Hutchinson
Margaret Koplitz
Kimberli Lile
George E. Lovelace
Henry C. Mackall
Esther McCullough
Frank McNally
Hung Q. Nguyen
Sally Ormsby

Luis Parada
Gustav Person
C. Arnie Quirion
Ann Rodriguez
Timothy J. Sargeant
Paul D. Snodgrass
Mayo S. Stuntz
Britt Weaver

Index

bomb shelters, 190-191, 195, 196
Booth: Paulina, 95, 96; Sally, 96; William, 95
Bowman, M.F., 198
Boyce, W.W., 47
Bradby, Joyce, 134
Braddock Road, 16, 24, 55, 57
Bren Mar, 53
Brent: George, 5; Robert, 7
bridges, 9, 24, 40, 59, 72, 149, 157
Brighton Mall, 55, 57
Brighton Square, 57
Briscoe, Elizabeth, 39
Bristow, Robert, 7
Bristow subdivision, 16
Broders: John H., 47; Joseph, 43
Bronez, Elaine, 206
Brooke: Benjamin, 93, 94, 99n7; Margaret Adams, 93, 94, 97, 99n7; Walter, 47
Brosius: Anna Mary Wilkinson, 109; Samuel, 105, 109
Bryant, Samuel G., 62
Buckingham family, 192, 195
Buckman Road, 35
Bull Run, 71
Burbage, Thomas, 6
Burgundy Plantation, 46, 47, 49
burial and burying grounds. See cemeteries
Burke, G.H., 118
Burke, 147
Burns, Lucy, 167
Burritt, Mary F., 119
Burtons, The, 133
Bush Hill, 45, 47
Bush Hill Drive, 45
Butler: Barbara, 98; Henry, 95

C

Callahan, Vincent, 226
Cameron Glen Nursing Home, 214
Cameron Methodist Church, 46
Cameron Station, 157
Camp Accotink, 176
Camp Alger, 141, 143, 156
Camp Andrew A. Humphreys. See Camp Humphreys
Camp Howard, 49
Camp Humphreys, 46, 109, 110, 153, 171-179. See also Fort Belvoir
Camp Knox, 46
Camp Michigan, 46
Camp Russell A. Alger. See Camp Alger

Cannon Lane, 46
Capital Beltway, 16, 221
Capital Traction, 133
Carey, Lillian, 126, 131
Carpenter, B.D., 94
Carroll: George Washington, 45; Jane, 45
Carrolltown, 45
cars. See automobiles
Carter: Bladen, 71; Ella Crump, 54; Ethel, 56; John B., 54; Landon, 71; Robert (King), 7, 9, 71; Tasco, 71; Wesley, 54, 56
Cassedy: Berta, 55; Bill, 55; Lenna, 55
Catt, Carrie Chapman, 167, 168
cemeteries, 46, 47, 51, 53, 54, 55, 60, 72, 83, 84, 98, 111n21, 164, 240
Centerville. See Centreville
Centreville, 23, 24, 25
Chain Bridge Road, 98
Charles, 94
Cherokee Avenue, 57
Cherokee Business Center, 57
Chichester: Daniel McCarty, 113; George, 113; Mary Dent, 113
Church, Bob, 184;
Church of England, 19. See also religion and religious freedom
churches, 44, 45, 51, 53, 55, 57, 83, 98, 99, 126, 127, 130, 131, 144, 205-206, 209
civil defense, 190-196
Civil Defense Administration, 190
Civil War, 25, 39, 45, 46, 47, 49, 51, 53, 60, 61, 66, 72, 78-80, 81, 83, 87-90, 96, 98, 156, 171, 197
Clarity, Virginia, 181, 187
Clark, Minnie Howdershell, 55
Clark House, 55
Clay, Henry, 28, 29, 30, 32, 33
clergyman's reduced rate permit, 129
Clermont, 46, 47
Cleveland, Jim, 212
Clifton, 113, 117, 159-165
Cockerille, Vernon, 184
COG (Metropolitan Washington), 215, 216, 217
Cohen family, 47
Colchester, 23, 24
Cold War, 189-196, 197-198
Cole: Margaret, 125; Norman, 222
Collingwood, 111n17
Colonial settlements, 3-10
colonies, English, 3, 4, 5
colonies, Spanish, 3, 4

T

U

V

W

X, Y, Z

[no entries]

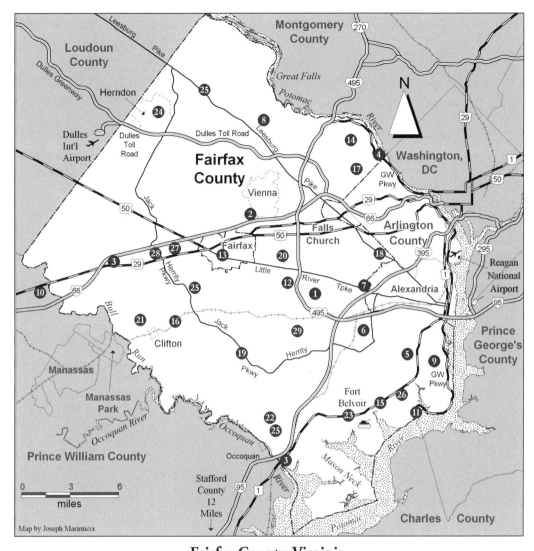

Fairfax County, Virginia
Locations of Places, Events, and People from the Text

1. In the Shadow of Ravensworth
2. Jeremiah Moore's Lasting Legacy
3. Fairfax County's First Two Post Offices (2)
4. Fairfax County's Most Famous Duel
5. The History of Mount Zephyr
6. A History of Franconia
7. A History of Lincolnia
8. The Olivers of Fairfax County
9. Historic Huntley
10. Gentleman Jim Robinson
11. The Formation of the Mount Vernon Ladies' Association
12. Elhanan Winchester Wakefield
13. Was She or Wasn't She? (Antonia Ford)
14. Robert Gunnell of Langley
15. My Dear Son (Gray's Hill near Woodlawn)
16. Fairfax County's Poor House
17. The Metropolitan Western Railroad
18. The Family History of John Bell and Clarence Raymond Summers, Jr.
19. It Began with the 1898 Spanish-American War
20. The Neck
21. Ivakota Farm, 1915 to 1962
22. Suffragists at the Occoquan Workhouse in Lorton
23. Camp Andrew A. Humphreys, 1917 to 1919
24. Herndon
25. Nike Missiles in Fairfax County (3)
26. Desegregation in the 1960s
27. The Honorable Martha V. Pennino
28. The Mayor of Fairfax County, Jack Herrity
29. The Ghost of Keene Mill School

Composed in 11-point Garamond with 12- and 14-point heads. Editorial style according to *The Chicago Manual of Style (15th Edition)*.